Building from the Rubble

Building from the Rubble

The Labour Movement in Zimbabwe since 2000

Lloyd Sachikonye

Brian Raftopoulos

and

Godfrey Kanyenze

WEAVER

W

—PRESS—

FRIEDRICH
EBERT
STIFTUNG

Published by Friedrich-Ebert-Stiftung,
6 Ross Ave., Belgravia, Harare, Zimbabwe

and

Weaver Press, Box A1922, Avondale, Harare. 2018
<www.weaverpresszimbabwe.com>

Typeset by Weaver Press
Cover Design: Danes Design
Printed by Directory Publishers, Bulawayo

The editors would like to express their gratitude to the
Friedrich-Ebert-Stiftung, Zimbabwe for their assistance with the
development of this text.

ISBN: 978-1-77922-341-8 (p/b) Weaver Press
ISBN: 978-1-77922-342-5 (e-pub) Weaver Press
ISBN: 978-07974-9494-7 Friedrich-Ebert-Stiftung

Table of Contents

Foreword by Peter Gift Mutasa, ZCTU President   ix

Preface by Ulrich Golaszinski, Director, Friedrich-Ebert-Stiftung, Zimbabwe   xi

Chapter 1

Introduction: *Godfrey Kanyenze, Brian Raftopoulos and Lloyd Sachikonye*   1

Chapter 2

The Labour Movement and the Working Class in post-2000 Zimbabwe: a literature
review – *Lloyd Sachikonye and Brian Raftopoulos*   12

Chapter 3

State Politics, Constructions of Labour and Labour Struggles 1980-2000
   – *Brian Raftopoulos*   46

Chapter 4

Economic Crisis, Structural Change and the Devaluation of Labour
   – *Godfrey Kanyenze*   75

Chapter 5

Labour, State and Crises in the post-2000 era – *Lloyd Sachikonye*   124

Chapter 6

Changes in Trade Unions and Trade Union Influences. – *Brian Raftopoulos,*
   Godfrey Kanyenze and Lloyd Sachikonye   145

Chapter 7

New Forms of Work Organization and Employment Patterns
   – *Lloyd Sachikonye, Godfrey Kanyenze and Brian Raftopoulos*   163

Chapter 8

Gender, Youths and Disability in the Changing Industrial Landscape
   – *Naome Chakanya*   185

Chapter 9

Political, Judicial and Legislative Responses to Labour and the
   Changing Regime of Industrial Relations – *Zakeyo Mtimtema*   215

Chapter 10

Conclusion: *Brian Raftopoulos, Lloyd Sachikonye and Godfrey Kanyenze*   245

Bibliography   249

Contributors

Lloyd Sachikonye is based at the Centre for Applied Social Sciences (CASS) at the University of Zimbabwe. He has published widely on Zimbabwean politics, social movements and labour issues.

Brian Raftopoulos is the Director of Research and Planning for Solidarity Peace Trust/Ukuthula Trust and Research Fellow in the International Studies Group, University of the Free State. He has published widely on Zimbabwean history, politics and labour issues.

Godfrey Kanyenze is the Director of the Labour and Economic Development Research Institute of Zimbabwe (LEDRIZ). He has published widely on economic policies and labour market issues in Zimbabwe.

Naome Chakanya is a Development Economist and Senior Researcher at the Labour and Economic Development Research Institute of Zimbabwe (LEDRIZ). Her areas of expertise include Gender, Socio-economic rights, Decent Work Agenda, Climate Change and Green Jobs.

Zakeyo Mtimtema is the Legal Advisor of the Zimbabwe Congress of Trade Unions (ZCTU). He is a member of the Labour Advisory Council, the Retrenchment Board and the Midlands State University Council.

Foreword

In the words of Marcus Garvey: 'A people without the knowledge of their past history, origin and culture is like a tree without roots'. The history of the labour movement in Zimbabwe has been documented in two path-breaking books, *Keep on Knocking* (1890-1980) and *Striking Back* (1980-2000). Cognisant of the wrenching structural changes, and the political, social and economic crises the country has undergone, the general council of the Zimbabwe Congress of Trade Unions made the decision to update this historiography for the period since 2000.

The 1990s had witnessed a resurgent labour movement mobilising beyond the traditional bread and butter issues. The movement took up wider struggles for democratisation and inclusive governance on the back of a vicious structural adjustment programme that had resulted in deindustrialisation, job losses and the informalisation of the economy on an unprecedented scale. Riled by the emergence of an oppositional civil society movement and a strong opposition party that for the first time threatened its very existence, the ZANU(PF) regime responded with ruthless repression and the implementation of populist policies. This was designed to peg back the emerging social movement under the leadership of strong trade unions.

If the 1990s were challenging, higher levels of state repression and economic mismanagement marked the new millennium. Unsurprisingly, the labour movement and its allies became the prime targets of state-sponsored violence, intimidation and repression. International condemnation of the flagrant abuse of human and trade union rights and tenets of good governance resulted in the country being isolated. Undeterred, the state continued on its warpath, driven by imperatives of self-preservation and retained hegemony.

The update of the history of the labour movement contained in this book is therefore of particular significance to all those interested in unravelling the complex forces at play and the rapidly unfolding developments in Zimbabwe in the new millennium. The book captures the political, economic and social upheavals that created paralysis at all levels of the polity and society. The period under review coincides with the rapidly changing economic structure, and the emergence of new forms and patterns of employment characterised by vulnerability and precarity. It not only documents what has happened since 2000, but also painstakingly analyses the impact of the various forces at play that resulted in a state of stasis and paralysis, as well as polarisation. No country outside of a war situation has ever experienced such levels of political, social and economic crises, structural regression and persistent devaluation of labour.

This publication is a collaboration between the ZCTU and the Friedrich-Ebert-Stiftung, supported by long-time friends of labour, Lloyd Sachikonye, Brian Raftopoulos and Godfrey Kanyenze, our long-standing publishers, Weaver Press, and our research institute, LEDRIZ.

We hope this book will help interested parties unravel developments during a dark period of our post-independence history, revealing the underlying logic of state capture and repression that left labour in a parlous state. It is the very contradictions of the repressive system that eventually led to successionist faction fights that would culminate in a military intervention that deposed the long-serving President Robert Mugabe in November 2017.

Peter Gift Mutasa

ZCTU President

Preface

This book, *Building from the Rubble: The Labour Movement in Zimbabwe since 2000*, is the third in a trilogy about the history of the labour movement in Zimbabwe. The series started in 1997 with *Keep on Knocking*, which covered the period between 1900 and 1997. It was followed by *Striking Back*, which provided an overview of the labour movement in Zimbabwe after independence until 2000.

Building from the Rubble continues the history of the labour movement from 2000. The new millennium saw a deepening economic crisis in Zimbabwe, exacerbated by political authoritarianism and neoliberalism. As a result, the labour movement had to fight on three fronts: politically against the authoritarian regime of Robert Mugabe; economically against the outflows and consequences of a declining, and pulverised economy which brought factory and business closures, unemployment and a massive growth in the informal sector; and against the use of informal work practices which increased the burden on the workers. Whilst these challenges stretched the organisational and political capacity of the labour movement, they simultaneously showed its resilience, and its ability to stick to its values and defend the rights of the working people.

This book describes the struggle of the labour movement, its grit and determination in the face of extreme adversity. FES is proud to be part of the journey of the unions and the labour movement in Zimbabwe. It is with great pride that FES presents this product of the longstanding cooperation between ZCTU and FES. We would also like to thank the authors who have contributed to this book for devoting their time and efforts and for sharing their knowledge.

To all who want to have a better understanding of the last 18 years in Zimbabwe, I highly recommend this book, *Building from the Rubble*.

Ulrich Golaszinski

Director

Friedrich-Ebert-Stiftung

Harare

Chapter 1

Introduction

Godfrey Kanyenze, Brian Raftopoulos and Lloyd Sachikonye

'Until the lion learns how to write, every story will glorify the hunter' – African proverb.

Background and Objectives

Desirous to record its history, in an effort to shape its future, the labour movement in Zimbabwe commissioned studies on its evolution since 1900. Its history has therefore been researched and documented in two seminal books: *Keep on Knocking: A History of the Labour Movement in Zimbabwe 1900-1997* (1997)[1]; and *Striking Back: The Labour Movement and the Post-Colonial State in Zimbabwe, 1980-2000* (2001)[2]. The period covered by the first book was the century from the second decade of colonialism to the second decade of independence. In greater detail, the second volume covered the momentous years between 1980 and 2000.

Cognisant of the far-reaching structural changes the economy had undergone since 2001, the Zimbabwe Congress of Trade Unions (ZCTU) commissioned a third book covering the period since 2000. This period (2000-2017) was probably the most tumultuous since Zimbabwe's independence in 1980, as it coincided with the emergence of a strong oppositional political party, the Movement for Democratic Change (MDC), the descent into political and economic crisis that culminated in hyperinflation in 2007-08, the signing of the Global Political Agreement (GPA) in September 2008 and the formation of the Government of National Unity (GNU) in 2009. With the downfall of Robert Mugabe in November

---

1 Raftopoulos and Phimister, 1997.
2 Raftopoulos and Sachikonye, 2001.

2017, it was decided to end in 2017.

The fallout resulting from the implementation of the Economic Structural Adjustment Programme (ESAP) during the period 1991-96 spawned an unprecedented oppositional social movement under the leadership of the ZCTU during the second half of the 1990s. As the recalcitrant regime failed to seize on the opportunity for dialogue offered by the emerging movement, the alternative was the creation of a broad-based movement for change borne out of the Working People's Convention of 26-28 February 1999 which culminated in the formation of the MDC in September 1999. Meanwhile, pressure was mounting from the National Constitutional Assembly (NCA) for the drafting of a new constitution through popular participation, as well as the resurrection of the land question.

The 'no' vote in the referendum of February 2000 triggered a return to a radical liberation narrative ('patriotic history'), and hence a departure from the neoliberal policies of the 1990s on the part of the ruling party ZANU(PF), combining authoritarianism with populism (authoritarian populism) in order to shore up its waning support and address the incipient threat to its hegemony. Critically, the emergence of a militant civil society movement made it difficult for the government to continue implementing neoliberal policies as they became politically unsustainable, resulting in the adoption of ad hoc knee-jerk policies (short-termism). This presented oppositional forces with a much more complex set of contextual factors to deal with, namely a combination of nationalist rhetoric and authoritarianism. The involvement of the military to prop up the political edifice since 2000 had created a complex maze that civil society and oppositional forces had to contend with, brewing a politico-socio-economic crisis that was unprecedented since independence in terms of its scale, depth and longevity.

Even though the period of the GNU provided some respite, with an economic rebound, this was short-lived and also served to sever the relationship between the MDC and its social base in civil society. The end of the GNU following the national elections of 2013 resulted in the re-emergence of a dominant party system, with the predictable return to fiscal indiscipline, unsustainable deficits, rising domestic debt which had been eroded by hyperinflation, a debilitating liquidity crisis and fratricidal succession battles that culminated in the ouster of the long-serving President, Robert Mugabe in a 'palace coup' in 2017.

As this book explains in considerable detail, throughout the the 2000s, as the Zimbabwe economy entered a period of profound decline, the loss of formal sector employment and the radical reconfiguration of the political economy had a far-reaching impact on the labour movement. This reconfiguration took the form of massive changes in employment patterns in the country, characterised by the cumulative informalisation of employment in the manufacturing, mining and other sectors coupled with the move away from large-scale commercial farms to the predominance of small-scale farms resulting from the fast-track land resettlement process. A combination of these changes with the incessant authoritarian assault on the labour movement and civil society more generally resulted in the increased weakening of trade unionism in Zimbabwe. Consequently, there was a drastic reduction in membership numbers and influence, in contradistinction to the massive trade union presence in the country's polity throughout the 1990s.

It was against this background that the ZCTU commissioned an update study with the following objectives:

- Update the state of the labour movement in Zimbabwe since the year 2000;

- Highlight the emerging issues in the labour movement, such as new forms of employment, non-payment of wages, new emerging social base, sustainability of trade unions and the role of women in the labour market.

Hence the ZCTU intended to decipher the structural changes that emerged, their impact on new forms and patterns of employment and their implications on labour and the social movement. Key questions to be unravelled included documenting and tracking the structural shifts in the economy, and assessing what these changes imply for the labour movement in terms of:

- Formal / informal sector dichotomy;

- New forms of work and organising;

- New social base and movements;

- Reactive role: defending workers against retrenchments and casualisation of labour;

- Trade union densities, weakened bargaining power of trade unions and sustainability of unions;

- Weakened political influence of trade unions;
- Weakening participation of women, youth and persons living with disabilities in the labour market.

As highlighted in the literature review, there is a lacuna of comprehensive literature that documents in a systematic and analytical way the history of the labour movement since 2000. Yet this period witnessed the most dramatic structural shifts in the economy, as reflected in the fast-track land redistribution programme that started in March 2000, the persistent deindustrialisation and informalisation of the economy, the economic crisis that reached its nadir with the hyperinflation of 2007-08, the cumulative loss of 52 per cent of GDP between 1999 and 2008, the introduction of the multi-currency regime since January 2009, the liquidity crisis since 2013, and the internecine succession struggles in the ruling party that led to the removal of Robert Mugabe in November 2017. With these wrenching structural changes, the economy of 2000 is barely recognisable as it lost its former structural diversity. In order to begin to confront the challenges facing it the ZCTU will therefore first have to take stock of the current state of the labour movement, which this update study provides.

Study Methodology

The update study was divided into two phases. The first phase, which focused on an overview of the developments since 2000 and a review of the literature was presented at the ZCTU Congress that was held from 29 September to 1 October 2016 in Harare. Some useful feedback was received following the presentation of the overview.

The second phase involved the detailed study which was pitched at both the macro and sectoral levels focussing on (i) agricultural and extractive sectors; (ii) manufacturing, and the informal economy; (iii) services; (iv) the public sector; and women, youth and people with disabilities as the cross-cutting issues. Beyond these thematic areas, the lead researchers decided to also include a chapter specifically tracking and analysing the judicial rulings that have redefined the conduct of industrial relations in Zimbabwe since the inception of labour law reform in the early 1990s to deal with the perceived over-regulation of the labour market.

To benefit from lived experiences, the study included voices and stories of the key actors in industrial relations: employers, government officials, trade unionists, working people and informal economy players. These ethnographic life histories were included in order to present qualitative information on changes in the lives of working men and women. Most of the chapters therefore draw on them to enrich the discussion.

Critically, a comprehensive study of this nature had to employ a triangulation of research methods, a multi-method strategy involving both qualitative and quantitative approaches, to enhance the credibility and persuasiveness of the research account. As the early proponents of this approach, Webb et al. suggested that, 'Once a proposition has been confirmed by two or more independent measurement processes, the uncertainty of its interpretation is greatly reduced. The most persuasive evidence comes through a triangulation of measurement processes.'[3]

The qualitative approaches employed during the study included desk reviews; questionnaires targeting trade union leaders, unionists, workers, informal economy players and other key informants; face-to-face interviews with key informants; and direct observation and focussed group discussions. Quantitative approaches used included, for instance, extrapolating or estimating from historical trends to assess what could have happened to employment levels in the absence of the crisis (the counterfactual).

At the planning meeting of the ZCTU leadership, the research team and Friedrich-Ebert-Stiftung staff on 13 April 2016, the second phase of study was organised into four thematic areas:

- Agriculture and Extractive sectors, under Lloyd Sachikonye;

- Manufacturing, Employer Organisations and the Informal Economy, under LEDRIZ;

- Services and non-ZCTU organisations, under Brian Raftopoulos; and

- Public Sector, Women and Youth, under the leadership of LEDRIZ.

Four Research Assistants were identified to work with each cluster:

- Manufacturing, Employer Organisations and Informal Economy – Clinton Musonza;

- Services and non-ZCTU organisations – Innocent Dande; and

- Public Sector, Women and Youth – Lynette Nyathi-Ndlovu.

---

3   Webb et al., 1966, p. 3.

The research assistants had to go through the specific literature review pertaining to their allocated sector(s) and issues, and interview trade union leaders, relevant employer organisations, union and non-union members and other key informants. They assessed the changes and trends at sectoral level and their implications for workers in terms of:

- Changing employment levels and patterns;
- Wage trends and other employment benefits;
- Trade union membership and organising strategies;
- Collection of union subscriptions;
- Workplace organisation and other challenges;
- Workplace organisation and the multiplicity of trade unions;
- Relationship between workers' committees and trade unions;
- Collective bargaining processes and outcomes;
- New forms of worker organisations and other non-labour organisations dealing with labour issues;
- Evolution of trade union networks and emerging networks based on new social movements (e.g. residents' associations);
- Impact of any changes in legislation at national or sectoral level on industrial relations in the sector, employees and trade unions;
- Key developments in industrial relations during the period, including strikes, lock-outs, lock-ins, disputes, etc., and their outcomes;
- How the sector was impacted by hyperinflation and how workers, trade unions and employer organisations adapted to the hyperinflationary environment;
- The specific impacts of the GNU and the adoption of the multi-currency regime on the sector and working people and how workers and trade unions and employers' organisations responded to this development;
- How the emergence of oppositional parties and their fragmentation impacted on the working people and trade unions;
- Whether unions have been able to sustain themselves through membership fees, subscriptions and other sources of income (donor support, investments, etc); and the relative weighting of each;

- Analysis of the relevant stories and articles on the labour movement from the *Financial Gazette, The Herald, The Worker* and other newspapers.

The input from the research assistants provided the basis for the final analysis in chapters by the lead researchers as summarised below.

Problems of Data

A comprehensive study of this nature requires reliable time-series data. However, the study encountered challenges with respect to data consistency and reliability. For instance, formal sector employment in agriculture has gaps between 2003 and 2008, but is available for the period 2009-14. The levels of formal sector employment for the period 2009-14 for agriculture at 204,000 in 2009, 395,000 in 2010, 346,000 in 2011, 304,000 in 2012, 267,000 in 2013 and 328,000 in 2014[4] compares favourably to the levels before and in the early years of the fast-track land redistribution programme at 337,700 in 1999, 324,700 in 2000, 290,200 in 2001 and 220,900 in 2002. This raises serious questions in terms of the quality of the recent data (2009-14) given the massive decimation of formal employment in agriculture following the land redistribution programme.

Secondly, ZCTU were able to provide membership data for the period 2006-17 by affiliate, and only aggregated data for the period 2000-04. Such membership levels differed from the figures provided by affiliates as the ZCTU data simply referred to those for whom subscriptions were being remitted by the affiliates, yet the affiliates included members on their register who may not be paying subscriptions for various reasons. Trade union federations such as the Zimbabwe Federation of Trade Unions (ZFTU), which indicated that its current membership stands at 700,000, failed to provide the data by affiliate. Furthermore, such data were not broken down by gender, age and disability, yet the study had to assess the extent of marginalisation. Labour market statistics on retrenchments, mass actions such as stayaways, strikes and demonstrations, were generally unavailable. Retrenchment data provided by the Retrenchment Board did not reflect the reality on the ground given the decentralisation of retrenchments to the sector and company level, and hence could not be relied on.

Thirdly, a study of structural changes in the economy and labour market would require disaggregated data on employment by tenure to allow for an

---

4   ZimStat, 2015.

7

evaluation of trends in formalisation and informalisation of labour. Formal sector data are not available by tenure of employment. However, the study had to piece together the detailed information on formality/informality from the 2004, 2011 and 2014 labour force surveys when such a distinction was systematically made. This proved quite helpful in assessing the emerging employment patterns and trends. The challenge however related to the lack of consistency in the levels of aggregation, and the concepts employed in the various labour force surveys. Painstakingly, the team pieced together the data to provide time-series analysis of employment patterns and trends.

Much of the information used in Chapter 3 draws on reports from the Ministry of Labour archives accessed by Brian Raftopoulos in the mid-1980s. The regional and national reports provide detailed information on a number of areas. These include the extent and causes of the strikes in the early 1980s; the challenges and limitations of state capacity in the institutionalisation of a new industrial relations regime; the narratives of the state on labour questions; state attempts at political control of the labour movement; ruling party narratives of the labour movement; and divisions in the labour movement.

Structure of the Book.

When the first draft of the chapters was ready, a half-day validation workshop was held with the ZCTU elected leadership and all heads of departments with the authors on 16 May 2018. This workshop was critical to ensure that the terms of reference given to the researchers by the elected ZCTU leadership on the 13 April 2016 were adequately addressed.

The chapters are organised as follows. Chapter 2 provides the overview and literature review, highlighting the glaring lacuna of research into the context of social, economic and political changes in the country; the associated structural changes to the economy as well as a comprehensive overview of developments in the labour movement since 2000; and the current state of the ZCTU, thus following up on the last major study, *Striking Back*. Chapter 3 assesses relations between the state and unions in the 1980s and 1990s, and then examines the emergence of an independent social movement in Zimbabwe, initially against attempts to impose a one-party state in the late 1980s, and later against the impact of ESAP in the 1990s. Foreclosure of social dialogue led to the formation of the broad-based movement for change in February 1999 which culminated in the formation of the MDC in September 1999.

The descent into crisis, which started in earnest in 1997, intensified at the turn of the new millennium, spawning a long-drawn-out crisis characterised by persistent deindustrialisation and informalisation of the economy. These profound structural changes, as well as the emerging new patterns of employment and devaluation of labour, are captured in Chapter 4. The labour responses to the crisis are the subject of Chapter 5, while Chapter 6 focusses on the changes in trade unions, and in particular the precipitous decline in membership, and diminishing trade union influence.

Chapter 7 traces the new forms of work organisation, and especially the precariousness of work related to informalisation, including the emergence of 'labour brokering' whereby employees have contracts with third party agents. Issues of gender, youth and disability and their marginalisation, are dealt with in Chapter 8. Instead of abating, the marginalisation and vulnerability of these groups was accentuated during the period under review. Chapter 9 tracks the political, judicial and legislative responses that have reshaped the course of industrial relations in Zimbabwe since the liberalisation of labour laws in the 1990s. Whilst some positive outcomes emerged from the judicial and legislative interventions, the lasting impacts have been negative for the working people and have taken them back in time. Lastly, Chapter 10 provides the concluding remarks and way forward.

Acknowledgements

A study of this magnitude, covering such a turbulent and complex political, social and economic terrain, involved much discussion, disputation, reflection and engagement. As such, many debts of gratitude have been incurred.

In this regard, we would like to put on record our indebtedness to the ZCTU leadership that made the bold decision to update the earlier historical accounts recorded in *Keep on Knocking* and *Striking Back*. The planning meeting of the elected leadership of the ZCTU of 13 April 2016 provided the roadmap and terms of reference for the study, as well as mapping its contours. It was at that meeting that it was agreed to proceed in two phases, with the first involving an overview and literature review, the outcome of which was presented and discussed at the pre-ZCTU Congress workshop held on 28 September 2016.

Thereafter, the second phase began in October 2016. We would like to thank the new leadership that was elected at the ZCTU Congress in October 2016 for continuing with the project and providing it with new impetus. Our appreciation also goes to the leadership of the ZCTU affiliates and ZCTU staff for putting up with our relentless search for information that they so generously shared with us. We owe you a huge debt of gratitude.

The Permanent Secretary at the Ministry of Labour and Social Services, Ngoni Masoka, gave us access to his colleagues who assisted us with data. We would like to thank in particular the Principal Director at the Ministry, Simon Masanga, for his relentless efforts to make sure we were assisted. We thank the Director of Labour Administration, Clement Vusani, for granting us an elaborate interview, and the research unit at the Ministry as well the Registrar of Trade Unions for sharing their publications and providing the requested information. We can never thank you enough for your assistance.

The Executive Director of the Employers' Confederation of Zimbabwe, John Mufukare, the Secretary General of the Zimbabwe Chamber of Informal Economy Associations (ZCIEA), Wisborn Malaya, the Secretary General of the Zimbabwe Federation of Trade Unions (ZFTU), Kenias Shamuyarira, acceded to our request for interviews and shared their insights on the industrial relations scene since 2000, for which we are forever grateful.

This study would have been difficult to accomplish without the support of the research assistants who not only gave of their time, but exhibited a dedication that went beyond the call of duty and worked so tirelessly to unearth information, and to gather voices and stories from ordinary workers and informal economy actors. In this respect, our sincere appreciation goes to Lynette Nyathi-Ndlovu, Tarisai Mike Nyamucherera, Innocent Dande and Clinton Musonza.

We would especially like to thank the ZCTU leadership and staff for taking time to validate the draft chapters at the half-day session on 16 May 2018. LEDRIZ staff also provided logistical support throughout the course of the study, for which we are grateful.

Special thanks go to the Friedrich-Ebert-Stiftung for funding this third edition of the history of the labour movement, as they did the earlier two editions. We thank you for your unwavering support and for giving true meaning to solidarity. In addition, the ILO-ACTRAV provided supplementary financial support to the project, which we gratefully acknowledge.

Lastly, our publishers, Weaver Press, deserve special mention for their dedication to excellence. You were most patient with us and so rigorously and meticulously edited the final version of the book, for which we are eternally grateful. You are indeed worthy partners to this cause.

While it is such a pleasure to place on record our appreciation for all the support provided, we remain solely responsible for any errors of omission or commission, and for the analyses and positions reflected in this book.

Chapter 2

The Labour Movement and the Working Class in post-2000 Zimbabwe: A literature review

Lloyd Sachikonye and Brian Raftopoulos

Introduction: theoretical questions

There exists a wealth of literature on the labour movement and the working class in post-Independence Zimbabwe. The purpose and motivation of this literature varies from academic pursuit of research and knowledge, to policy oriented literature that seeks to strengthen the negotiating capacity of unions, and writings to mobilise workers around specific issues. The variety of the literature testifies to the significant economic, social and political roles of organised labour and the working class.

This review provides a synopsis of the major contributions to that body of literature. It highlights the importance and relevance of the literature, and underlines its strengths and limitations, besides identifying gaps in it. Equally importantly, the review identifies areas and issues that require sharper focus as the labour movement and working class move into the fourth decade after Independence.

Before moving on to the different themes of the review it is useful firstly to track the more general changes in labour studies that have occurred since the 1990s. In an important critique of the volume *Striking Back: The Labour Movement and the Post-Colonial State in Zimbabwe'* Teresa Barnes made some acute comments on the book. Barnes critiqued the linearity in the conception of the labour movement that dealt insufficiently with the contesting forces in the movement and the different conceptions of democratic change; she noted the absence of a more general sensitivity to the unstable categories and the different discursive formations of labour; and, through the work of Michel Foucault, insufficient attention to the more decentred forms of disciplinary power away from the state that affected a variegated workforce.[1]

Barnes was also correct in relating these weaknesses to the political project of *Striking Back*. As she observed:

> There is a sense in which *Striking Back* was in itself meant to be a political statement; collecting opinions and debates between academic/activist colleagues directed eventually at dialogue with ZANU-PF government. Again this is not an illegitimate activity, but it means that the book should be read, not as a carefully harmonized scholarly collection but as an attempt to keep labour's discourses going.[2]

Much of the work on the labour movement in Zimbabwe that had been done up to 2001 was influenced by the broader radical scholarship around labour questions that emerged in the 1970s, influenced by Marxist theory. As Bill Freund describes it, these scholars

> discovered an African working class and armed with more flexible means of considering application of class consciousness, they began to change the way labour in Africa was being written about.[3]

As Barchiesi and Belluci observe, this generation of scholars had, in the processes and concepts they emphasised, studied areas such as strikes, unions and self-conscious class identities 'emphasizing labour's progressive, transformative and modernizing capacities.'[4] These studies were in accordance with the international labour movement's long-term attachment to the hopes and aspirations of the eighteenth-century Enlightenment.[5] However, the major structural dislocations resulting from the global neoliberal policies from the 1980s inaugurated a new period of crisis for labour politics. This crisis pushed labour scholars into new areas of study that examined 'cultural practices and discursive formations surrounding work and labour'.[6] Working classes, we are reminded, are always a complex mix of communities and occupations divided by type

---

1 Barnes, 2002.
2 Ibid., p. 470.
3 Freund, 1988, p. 22.
4 Barchiesi and Belluci, 2014, p. 5.
5 Hobsbawm, 1984, p. 314.
6 Barchiesi and Belluci, 2014, p. 6.

of work, ethnicity and national origin, language, residence, region and many other distinctions. Moreover, as Eley observes, workers 'become a collective for political purposes only via creative and continuous efforts'.[7]

This new focus moved away from reductionist ideas of class consciousness along a teleological path of transformation, towards an understanding of the entanglement of 'different employment relations with diverse social agencies and cultural expressions' within the context of growing informalisation and the precariousness of work.[8] As Mike Davis writes, this growing number of informal workers fall outside the trajectory of industrialisation and urbanisation envisaged by the classical social theory of Weber and Marx. These workers are the 'novelty of a true global residuum lacking the strategic economic power of socialised labour, but massively concentrated in a shanty town world encircling the fortified enclaves of the urban rich'.[9] In the face of such massive changes in the social structure and relations of production it will be essential to understand the impact of such reconfigurations on the forms of struggle, adaptation, protest and politics emerging in Zimbabwe's informal sector, in ways both similar to but also different from other parts of the African continent.[10]

In studying the new complexities of this transformed social structure it will be essential to track changing gender relations. More particularly there is a need to understand the gendered constructions of these changes not simply through the social and economic roles of men and women, but also through the 'articulation in specific contexts of social understandings of sexual difference'.[11] How, for example, have the increasing numbers of women in informal labour impacted on gendered ideas of respectability in the household, and in turn how have such changes affected workplace solidarities?

In addition, labour studies have increasingly moved towards African labour questions beyond the confines of the national framework and within the broader context of globalisation. By locating labour studies within the complex engagement with globalisation, such studies question the idea

---

7   Eley, 2002, p. 397
8   Ibid., p. 7.
9   Davis, 2004, p. 27.
10 Chaturverdi, 2016.
11 Scott, 1987, p. 3.

that 'free wage labour' can any longer be considered the capitalist norm, [12] or that issues of identity, solidarity or opportunity can be constructed with a predictable end point.[13]

Closer to Zimbabwe a similar trend has occurred in South African labour studies where scholarship has moved from production-based studies, the political traditions of resistance of black workers and the analysis of cultural and working life to a more recent focus on the precarity of work and the changes it has produced in understanding the future of labour and social citizenship.[14]

Finally, to encapsulate many of the above issues the work of Mike Davis reminds us that the wage relation is more than just the sale of labour power. There are several processes which need to be understood and kept within a theoretical frame. Firstly, the ways in which labour has been dispossessed of the means of production and subsistence. This is the process that Harvey calls 'accumulation by dispossession' and refers to the ways in which peasants and workers have been deprived of their means of livelihoods and forced into market exchange.[15] Secondly, the different forms in which the labour market is organised. Thirdly, the historically variegated forms in which the wage relation is constituted. Fourthly, that wage relations are determined by the 'actual forms of the reproduction of labour-power', namely 'waged and unwaged, capitalist and pre-capitalist ... private-familial or collective consumption'.[16]

In moving forward in our study of the Zimbabwean labour movement it will be important to learn from these recent conceptual advances in. This will enrich our understanding of both the changes in the structures and identities of labour more generally, and the more specific challenges of the formal labour movement. Such an analytical framework will therefore need to combine an understanding of both the legacies of the radical political economy studies of labour and class and the insights of the more recent work.

Organisation of the Review

The review is organised into six sections. The first surveys the literature

---

12 Mazzadara, 2011; Munck, 2004; Bonner, Hyslop and van der Walt, 2007; McIlroy and Croucher, 2013.
13 Schler, Bethlehem and Sabar, 2011, p. 6.
14 Webster, 2004; Barchiesi, 2011.
15 Harvey, 2011.
16 Davis, 1986, p. 105.

on the making of the post-colonial regime of industrial relations, looking at both the continuities and changes in this structure. The second surveys literature on the labour movement defined as the collective of individual unions and the national centre, namely the Zimbabwe Congress of Trade Unions (ZCTU). There is, however, a need to avoid conflating the organised labour movement with the broad working class: some segments of the working class may not belong to unions, and their interests may lie outside the ambit of the labour movement. The third section focuses on the growth followed by contraction of the size of the working class during the post-2000 period.

In the fourth section, we highlight the significance of outmigration of workers during the economic crisis from 2000 to 2008, and the consequences for skills formation and retention as well as for union membership. Most literature on the working class and organised labour has not adequately factored in the consequences of the flight of scarce working class and professional skills for the economy and union organisation. The fifth and sixth sections of the review deal with literature on trends, structures and processes in working conditions and union organisation in specific sectors, namely agriculture and mining.

In a schematic form, the structure of this review is thus as follows:

• The Post-Colonial Regime of Industrial Relations

• Growth, Consolidation and Stagnation of the Labour Movement

• Growth and Contraction of the Working Class

• External Migration Impact on Working and Professional Classes

• Post-2000 Trends, Structures and Processes in Agriculture

• Post-2000 Trends, Structures and Processes in Mining.

The post-colonial regime of industrial relations

As with colonial regimes in the past, post-colonial states, particularly in their optimistic, developmentalist aspirations immediately after achieving independence, 'went to some lengths to articulate the knowledge upon which their power claims lay'.[17] Commissions of Inquiry were set up, as Cooper points out, to 'try to delineate the problem and bound the problem area and reveal the state's command of the techniques and resources to set

---

17 Cooper, 1996, p. 16.

things right'.[18] In the case of Zimbabwe the new ZANU(PF) government set up the Riddell Commission in 1981, whose central objective was

> ... to inquire into and make recommendations in relation to the conditions of employment and service and the remuneration and other benefits for all categories of workers in Zimbabwe. [19]

Similarly, the government produced a study of the state of trade unions and industrial relations in Zimbabwe, a study conceived within the context of the government's purported aim of achieving 'scientific socialism'.[20]

After the nationwide strikes that marked the industrial relations terrain in the early 1980s,[21] the state moved quickly to produce an industrial relations structure that would produce a more disciplined worker. Officials in the labour department, as with the rest of the public service still going through the process of Africanisation of staff, complained about,

> ... the new generation of workers which was far more vociferous and far less reasonable than the relative moderation in this sphere hitherto.[22]

Reports from the labour ministry also complained about the inexperience and lack of training of the new labour officers. As one such report noted:

> The major problem is precisely that there is no formal training programme to equip labour relations officers on how they should interpret and implement the labour regulations. Ultimately it has been noted that officials interpret specifically the Labour Relations Act differently and as they see fit.[23]

Faced with such challenges the new state developed two major strategies. Firstly, it introduced new legislation to improve the conditions and establish the rights and responsibilities of workers. These included the Minimum Wages Act and Employment Act of 1980 that aimed to provide some legal protection of incomes and employment security. This was followed by the repeal of the colonial Industrial Conciliation Act through

---

18 Ibid. p. 16.
19 Government of Zimbabwe 1981, p. 1.
20 Government of Zimbabwe, 1984, p. 1.
21 Sachikonye, 1986.
22 Monthly Reports of the Acting Regional Hearing Officer, Manicaland Region, for the month ending 31 August 1986.
23 Monthly Report of the Acting Provincial Labour Relations Officer, Mashonaland, for the month ending 30 April 1986.

the introduction of the 1985 Industrial Relations Act. Amongst other changes this Act covered all workers except public sector employees, entrenched the rights of workers to belong to unions through the principle of 'one industry one union', protected centralised collective bargaining and the right to strike, and extended the reach of the state in employment matters.[24]

A central feature of these developments was the 'marked continuity in industrial relations policy' since the colonial period with an extension of the institutionalised structures of employment regulation, wage setting and dispute settlement that had begun in the colonial period.[25] However, the particular ways in which the post-colonial state adapted this structure produced a 'paternalistic state corporatism' that tempered 'authoritarianism with benevolence'.[26] Thus this governmental regime combined sovereign state power with key areas of worker protection and the welfarist protection of significant social expenditure in the first decade of independence.

The second strategy was to establish a new labour centre under the control of the ruling party that would 'participate actively in the maintenance of stable industrial relations'.[27] In ZANU(PF)'s conception of the national democratic revolution, labour organisations had to be subordinate to the nationalist movement's constructions of unity and development. The subservience of the ZCTU to the ZANU(PF) government was made clear in its first press statement:

> On the whole it was the unanimous opinion by the meeting that we trade unionists, being the vanguard of our party Zanu PF, fighting many different battles from different fronts in order to preserve, uphold and promote our political ideology, so that we can in the long term analysis rescue the working class masses from exploitation by the various types of bourgeoisie and capitalists, multinational and transnational monopolies.[28]

The period of the structural adjustment programme in the 1990s saw a deregulation of the labour market through the 1992 Labour Relations Amendment Act and the Export Processing Zones (EPZ) Act 1995. The

24 Madhuku, 2015; Gwisai, 2006.
25 Schiphorst, 2001, p. 181.
26 Shadur, 1994, p. 230.
27 Sachikonye, 1986, pp. 256-7.
28 ZCTU Press Statement, 12 December 1980.

first set aside the principle of 'one industry one union', while the second enabled immunity from the main labour legislation, easy retrenchment and dismissal laws and severe restrictions on trade unionism. The most recent work in this field by Madhuku[29] tracks the changes in labour law from the 1980s until the enactment of the new constitution in 2013 in formal legal terms. More theoretical work needs to be done to understand the changing uses of law and politics in the post-colonial period, looking beyond the narrow legal framework of existing work in the field. In this respect the historical work of George Karekwaivanane could be instructive. Karekwaivanane sets out his theoretical framework as follows:

> In trying to understand the role of law in the constitution of state power in Zimbabwe ... I attend to the ways in which that law was used in constituting and legitimizing ... political order... I argue... that the operation of the law... exemplified the ways in which that power was simultaneously productive, coercive and constitutive. However, the degree to which it was either, and the level of success achieved, varied over time. Examining the shifting balance between repression and legitimation allows for the complexity of the role of law ... to be more clearly grasped. In addition, it reveals important changes in the nature of ... rule.[30]

Other work in the area of industrial relations has tracked the failure to develop a sustainable social dialogue process. One study, by Booker Mugure, points to the persistent breakdown in this process between 1996 and 2007, as a result of what he identifies as the government and the employers' confederation, EMCOZ, 'negotiating in bad faith'.[31] Mugure's article provides a good account of the various ways in which this 'bad faith' manifested itself and brings out the intense contradictions in the process.

Growth, consolidation and stagnation of the labour movement

Most of the literature on the Zimbabwean labour movement has been developed and presented in a framework of its resilient rise from the mid-1980s to its flowering in the 1990s. The narrative is cast in terms of its 'rise' through its assertion of autonomy from the state and ZANU(PF)

---

29 Madhuku, 2015.
30 Karekwaivanane, 2012, p. 7.
31 Mugure, 2008, p. 45.

following a period of subordination. Notable contributors to this narrative include Norbert Tengende[32], Freek Schiphorst[33] and Paris Yeros.[34] This narrative of the ascendancy of the ZCTU built on earlier contributions that linked the historical growth of unions to its consolidation under effective and charismatic leadership in the 1990s.[35]

Significantly, the key contributions to the literature consist of several doctoral theses that were eventually developed into journal articles and books. The 'ZCTU Rising' narrative is aptly captured in the title of a well-researched study which observed that:

> The arrival of Morgan Tsvangirai at the helm of the ZCTU was a tide marking the adolescence of a young trade union movement. What was once a rudderless boat, floating aimlessly around with too many mediocre seamen claiming to be captain, was now put slowly, yet steadily, on a firm course. The national trade union centre was given a sense of purpose, its office re-energised and enlarged to cater for a growing number services to be delivered to its member unions. At the same time, the labour centre was set to regain a place in Zimbabwean society as a voice of labour.[36]

The star of the ZCTU continued to rise in the 1990s despite the effects of ESAP and state repression. One analyst observed that the nationalism of the labour centre in those early years was also anti-imperialist, expressly rejecting the authority of the World Bank and the International Monetary Fund, and the 'developmental' pretensions of ESAP.[37]

Other notable developments that accompanied the ZCTU's rise included: strengthening shop-floor structures and the membership base, and carrying out a comprehensive education and mobilisation campaign to raise unionisation levels; raising gender awareness; reaching out to employed and unemployed youth; building solidarity with informal sector and unemployed workers; and promoting of unification of workers across private and public sector workers.

The culmination of the rise of the labour movement was its growth into a wide social movement that spanned economic, social, constitutional

32 Tengende, 1994.
33 Schiphorst, 2001.
34 Yeros, 2001, 2013a and 2013b.
35 Raftopoulos and Phimister, 1997; Sachikonye, 1993.
36 Schiphorst, 2001, p. 2.
37 Yeros, 2013a, p. 222.

and political issues and spheres in the 1990s. For instance, there were massive national stayaways in 1997 and 1998 around economic and social issues that spanned various social groups apart from labour.[38] It was not accidental that a debate had grown within the movement about participating directly in national politics, including constitutional reform. The ZCTU leadership was at the forefront of the National Constitutional Assembly, and in 1999 the formation of the Movement for Democratic Change (MDC) was largely an initiative of the labour movement.

These social and political developments occurred in a broader global and regional context,[39] including the collapse of socialism with the break-up of the Soviet Union; the shift to neoliberalism in a unipolar world dominated by the United States; and uneven democratic transitions in many African states, as well as the end of apartheid in South Africa. This global and regional juncture witnessed the centrality of labour movements to transition such as in Zambia in 1991, Malawi in 1992 and South Africa in 1994. Zimbabwe's labour movement could not remain detached from these momentous developments. However, the Zimbabwean state was not ready or willing to bend to these winds of change blowing across the continent, hence the stage was set for an epic confrontation at the end of the 1990s.

The period 1999-2000 was destined to be a turning point in the fortunes of the labour movement, and in the response of the state to the rising democratic movement. The organisational limits of the ZCTU became much more obvious than before. What were those limits, according to the literature? They included:

> The severe dependence of the labour centre on US and European funding to carry out capacity-building programmes ... and the almost exclusive focus of the labour centre on formal sector workers, at a time of increasing unemployment, at the expense of mobilization outside formal employment sectors, imprisoned the labour centre in a logic of action which was not congruent with the semi-proletarianised nature of peripheral capitalism.[40]

Yeros developed a trenchant critique of the ZCTU, pointing out that by the end of the 1990s, the 'oppositional voice' of the labour centre was no longer targeted on production, while its notion of 'democratisation'

---

38 Bond, 2001; Bond and Manyanya, 2002; Saunders, 2001; Tandon, 2001.
39 Raftopoulos and Sachikonye, 2001; Beckman and Sachikonye, 2001.
40 Yeros, 2013a, p. 231.

became stuck in what he termed the rut of 'regime change'.[41] In his view, new social forces had emerged to reclaim a 'radical national liberation project' which the ZCTU proved incapable of evaluating and adjusting to. Yeros further claims that this juncture represented polarisation between 'radical nationalism' and neoliberalism; and in the process, the labour centre was demobilised. In sum, by its active engagement in politics, especially by sponsoring the formation of the MDC, the labour centre had sown the seeds of its own decline in power and influence.

The critique concludes by stating that it is necessary to acknowledge the organisational and ideological developments that the ZCTU underwent in the 1990s in positive and negative terms. For instance, it claims that the labour centre absorbed and accepted what he termed the 'regime change' agenda of the West.[42] Finally, no trade unionism was 'worth its name' if it did not take seriously the social structure, especially the new agrarian structure of the post-land reform period.

This line of thinking had earlier been flagged by Yash Tandon, who took a gloomy view of the position of the ZCTU over the land question, and particularly its alleged unwillingness to build a worker-peasant political alliance on this issue. He argued:

> Once the ZCTU took on the leadership of opposing the government on its failed policies, it was quickly surrounded by urban-based, dissident middle class forces, including human rights activists, white neoliberals, and eventually white farmers themselves.... On the land issue specifically, the MDC was ambiguous, its leadership making contradictory statements.... It failed to create a rural base between the deprived peasantry and farm workers.[43]

The critiques by Yeros and Tandon have their shortcomings. The situation in 1999 and 2000 was perhaps more complicated than they make out. For instance, once the state had begun to implement its authoritarian response laced with violence, open politics and mobilisation by unions and MDC in rural areas were blocked. A 2009 ILO report noted the

> systematic targeting of ZCTU officials and members, particularly in the rural areas, involving significant violence and anti-union

---

41 Yeros, 2013b.
42 Yeros, 2013b, p. 408.
43 Tandon, 2001, p. 249.

discrimination in employment, in what appeared to be a calculated attempt to intimidate and threaten ZCTU members.[44]

Whether there should have existed a ZCTU position and strategy on the land question and a possible alliance with rural-based social forces is a legitimate question which remains germane even in the period after 2013. On the whole, however, Yeros's critique of the ZCTU's political line of opposition to the authoritarian state is exaggerated and even unfair since there is nothing undemocratic in seeking a change of government. For Yeros to assume that the labour movement's call for greater democratisation was merely an echo of the Western 'regime change' agenda on Zimbabwe, was to lose sight of the ways in which labour movements on the continent have long drawn on particular universal discourses precisely, as Cooper observes, because they 'provide a reference point outside particular power structures',[45] especially when such structures are of an authoritarian nature. Finally, the rhetoric about a 'radical nationalist project' and even an alleged 'interrupted revolution' in Zimbabwe based around agrarian reform rings hollow in our view in the context of the post-2000 developments.[46]

Other perspectives on the effects of ZCTU engagement in politics appear elsewhere.[47] These are more nuanced accounts. The possibility of tensions between the ZCTU and MDC was forecast by Dansereau. She observed that labour warned the MDC to avoid developing a 'chef' syndrome, and not to forget labour's role in the movement's formation. She noted that:

> the ZCTU warns that forgetting it will lead to the movement's demise. At its Congress in 2001, it tabled resolutions as to the best strategy to employ in its collaboration with the MDC; some advocated a formal link with the movement, others a less direct link.[48]

The risk of complete identification with the MDC was that some members of the labour movement would reject a partisan identity, thereby causing a split or at least an alienation of some unions. This was an opportunity that the state exploited through its support of the breakaway

44 ILO, 2009, p. vii.
45 Cooper, 1996, p. 467.
46 Moyo and Yeros, 2007.
47 Alexander, 2000; Dansereau, 2001a; Bond and Saunders, 2005; Sachikonye and Matombo, 2010.
48 Dansereau, 2001a, p. 412.

Zimbabwe Federation of Trade Unions (ZFTU). In a broader sense, the issue of political affiliation by the ZCTU does not appear to have been satisfactorily resolved during the post-2000 decade.

In concluding this part of the review, the issues of leadership in the post-2000 period, the wider impact of the economic and political crises on that leadership should not be overlooked. First, most of the experienced and visionary leadership of the ZCTU was drawn into national and local government leadership under the MDC auspices. The most notable examples included Morgan Tsvangirai, Gibson Sibanda, Gift Chimanikire, Isaac Matongo, Thokozani Khupe and Pauline Mpariwa. Thus there was almost a wholesale transfer of a key leadership layer into the MDC that would have significantly weakened the strength and confidence of the ZCTU as an organisation. This was soon demonstrated in the decline of mass worker mobilisation through stayaways that had been effective in the 1990s. The frequency, size and potency of strikes declined after 2000.

However, the decline in use of the strike weapon should not be solely attributed to the quality of leadership at union and national centre levels. New structures of repression had been enacted with the deepening of authoritarianism. Post-2000 laws such as the Public Order and Security Act and the Access to Information and Protection of Privacy Act made freedoms of assembly and expression precarious. Frequent use of police brutality and torture was applied to protesters, including union leaders, most notably in 2006. At the same time, the worsening economic crises between 2000 and 2008 had a direct impact on employment levels and living standards. Not only did unemployment levels worsen but the informal sector expanded exponentially during the post-2000 period. Some of the most draconian assaults on the informal sector were carried out during the decade, most notably Operation Murambatsvina in 2005. The combination of severe contraction of the economy – GDP declined by about 40 per cent – and deep retrenchments, together with hyperinflation that made wage incomes too little to live on, had a painful impact on companies, unions and workers.

These multiple crises would have taxed the leadership resources of any labour movement. In such circumstances, it was challenging for the ZCTU and its constituent unions to develop workable strategies about how to navigate through the crises. Fragmentation within the movement, informalisation, heightened state repression, and tension in relations with the MDC made the decade the most difficult for the ZCTU since its creation.[49] It was observed, for instance, that:

> ... the ZCTU lost much of its impetus after 2000 owing to state harassment, employment shrinkage and declining union membership (down from 16 per cent in 1990 to 12 per cent in 2000). The ZFTU established by Zanu PF also weakened the ZCTU by creating splinter unions in nine sectors of the economy: furniture and timber, engineering, catering, leather, clothing, commerce, agriculture, sugar plantations and construction. The general informalisation of the economy made it extremely difficult for the labour movement to organize as informal sector workers turned to various methods in the 'kukiya-kiya economy'....[50]

The wider impact of all these developments on the working class would be far-reaching, as we observe in the next section.

In sum, there have been few analytical studies of the fortunes of the organised labour movement since 2001. Yet this post-2000 period represents a watershed in its history: the decline of the economy, of the size of the formal workforce and of membership in unions. Outstanding questions relate to the movement's strategic relationship with parties and civil society groups, rural social forces, the burgeoning informal sector and the emerging youth-based protest movement. The implicit crosscutting issue is therefore how the labour movement should regenerate itself in a context of economic stagnation, if not contraction, and of widening political polarisation.

Growth and contraction of the working class

In the reviews referred to above, Theresa Barnes raised pertinent questions about the composition of the working class and union membership in Zimbabwe.[51] These related to the class basis of individual unions, and more generally about the membership of the ZCTU itself: did the ZCTU increasingly represent the lower middle classes rather than working class unions in the 1990s? The same questions could be raised in relation to the changes in composition of the working class, and the class basis of the ZCTU in the post-2000 period.

While the literature on developments in the working class in the 1980s

---

49 ILO, 2009.
50 Raftopoulos, 2009, p. 225.
51 Barnes, 2003.

and 1990s is extensive, there is very little covering the post-2000 period. However, some of the literature in the 1990s was prescient about possible trends in deindustrialisation and its impact on the composition of the working class and the capacity of unions. One such study observed deindustrialisation in the textile and metal industries due to ESAP and incoherent industrial policy in the 1990s.[52] This took the form of liquidation of companies, and significant retrenchments. Hyperinflation, price controls and poor investment cut the capacity utilisation in most firms to as low as 35 per cent, with attendant consequences for employment and wage levels.

Perhaps one of the few studies on the relationship between de-industrialisation, informalisation and contraction of the working class is that by Tapiwa Chagonda.[53] Chagonda observed that the ZCTU was adversely affected by the deindustrialisation and economic crisis that then contributed to the 'partial disintegration' of the working class in a number of ways:

> First, the depletion in the numbers of formal sector employment, resulted in a drop in the rate of unionization and subscriptions, thus undermining the capacity of unions to carry out various organizational and educational activities of their working class members. Secondly, as a result of the shrinkage of the working class ... the labour movement was debilitated in terms of its organizational and mobilization activities. Thus the ZCTU was less able and willing to lead broad civic alliances as it did from the late 1980s to 2000, even in the face of unprecedented hyper-inflation and a political crisis..[54]

Thirdly, the informalisation of the labour force moved workers away from formalised labour practices and protest actions in the public sphere into more individualised and (into what were termed) criminalised modes of 'survivalism'. Consequently, at the ideological level, a sense of working class consciousness that could have encouraged members of this class to unite in protest against hyperinflation, retrenchments, falling incomes and the political crisis was missing during the peak of the Zimbabwean crisis.[55]

Specific examples of the contraction of the working class include the

---

52 Sachikonye, 1999.
53 Chagonda ,2011 and 2016.
54 Chagonda 2011, p. 139.
55 Ibid.

diminished size of the agricultural workforce by almost two-thirds after 2000; and the decline in the number of teachers from about 100,000 to around 55,000 until the resumption of recruitment in 2009. Indeed, the period from 2000 witnessed almost every sector downscaling levels of employment with the exception of a few such as financial services and real estate. The number of formal sector workers shrank by about half from 1.4 million in 1998 to about 700,000 in 2008,[56] about half of whom were employed in the public sector: in the uniformed forces, civil service and parastatals. The twin processes of deindustrialisation and de-proletarianisation in Zimbabwe were perhaps amongst the deepest and most rapid ever experienced in Africa or in any developing country in contemporary times. As observed above, this would not fail to have a direct impact on union membership levels, collective class-consciousness and civic participation.

Let us explore how these have been affected by contraction of the formal sector working class. Fewer formal sector workers mean fewer members of unions. For instance, the teaching and catering sectors witnessed a steep decline in union membership, according to Chagonda. The Zimbabwe Catering and Hotel Workers Union saw its membership contract by half between 1998 and 2008 to about 6,000. The membership of the ZCTU's 36 affiliates declined during this period although there are variances of estimates of the decline from about 320,000 to 200,000.[57] Exceptions to this general trend was the Zimbabwe Banking and Allied Workers Union, which maintained its level of membership during this period.

The diminution of the working class and union membership was widely reflected in the decline of civic and political protests. It is argued that the ZCTU signally failed to protest strongly against Operation Murambatsvina in 2005 and the delay in release of the March 2008 presidential election result, amongst other outrages of the ZANU(PF) government. These were described as 'a sign of lack of leadership' of the ZCTU. Furthermore, the argument stated that:

> The crop of leaders of the ZCTU during Zimbabwe's crisis appeared to have failed to get out of the shadow of the Sibanda and Tsvangirai executive which had been able to tackle the state head-on, on issues that affected the welfare

---

56 UNDP, 2008.
57 Chagonda, 2011, p. 141.

of workers, during the heady days of working class radicalism in the late 1990s.[58]

This line of critique can be misleading for it is clear that the post-1999 leadership faced massive changes in the structure of the labour force as well as intensified state repression. Such conditions would likely have been a challenge for any new leadership.

The multiple crises of 2000-2008 had a demobilising effect on workers and unions as individual and collective actors respectively. Consequently, labour showed signs of low levels of class-consciousness, which is why there were few forms of collective action within the workplace to protest hyperinflation that pauperised the working class. Chagonda argues that instead it was within the socio-economic realm of individual and household survival strategies that workers concentrated their energies for survival. This often entailed a deft but time-consuming straddling of both formal and informal sectors in survivalist responses that were often speculative in nature. Improvising in after-work activities like motor repair, vending of goods obtained through cross-border trade and foreign currency trading were some of those activities to make ends meet.

In addition, through practices of 'dealing' in foreign currency, scarce commodities, fuel and precious gems, dealers were creating a collective habitus of criminality. Through practices that involved extra-legality on the black market, they were able to reshape the social world to some extent as the culture of hustling, corruption and making a quick buck became pervasive.[59] So energy- and time-consuming were such survivalist activities that workers had little time and space to engage in union and civic matters. Most assessments of crises do not delve into such detail about how classes and social forces can be demobilised by an authoritarian regime. This is why the literature on this dimension has been so valuable.[60]

The effects of the above-mentioned processes of deindustrialisation and informalisation are assessed in more recent evaluations.[61] It is observed that between 2011 and 2014, deindustrialisation persisted with about 4,610 firms closing during that period. This resulted in an estimated 55,000 jobs being lost. Informalisation deepened such that the level of

---

58 Ibid., p. 149.
59 Chagonda, 2016, p. 139; Gukurume, 2015.
60 Jones, 2010; Sachikonye, 2012; Chagonda 2016.
61 LEDRIZ, 2016; LEDRIZ and Solidarity Centre, 2016.

informal employment which had increased from 80 per cent in 2004 to 84 per cent in 2011, rose sharply to about 94.5 per cent by 2014. Moreover, as Hammar, McGregor and Landau observe, what was peculiar about the exponential growth of informality in the post-2000 period, was the intersection of informality with 'historically strong bureaucracies geared towards urban control, and the specific urban forms and histories of migration produced through the segregationist past'.[62]

The rapid expansion of the informal sector since the late 1990s and the increasing attention to this sector contrasts with how little attention was paid to it in the 1980s. In the Riddell Commission Report the informal sector constituted only 'some tens of thousands'. Moreover, in setting out its position on the future of the informal sector the Commission observed that in some respects this sector arose as a consequence of the 'lack of alternative employment opportunities', and that the residual nature of this part of the national economy could not be expected to 'provide the solution to employment'.[63] In the current context it would be safe to say that the huge informal sector will be a part of the Zimbabwean economy for some time to come.

More sobering effects of the economic downturn between 2013 and 2015, have been the phenomena of non-payment or irregular payment of wages. This has been particularly prevalent in local authorities such as town councils but also in some parastatals. It is a way in which although workers continue to perform their job tasks, they are not remunerated for it.[64] Sometimes described as 'wage theft', it is a phenomenon that dramatises the social reproduction crisis that results when workers cannot depend on their wages but scrounge or seek informal sources for survival. Mismanagement and corruption in these firms undermined livelihoods of thousands of workers.

Finally, the size and orientation of the working class and unions would not be immune to these deep qualitative and quantitative changes. An additional dimension to the decline in size of the working class was the substantial migration during the post-2000 decade, as we observe in the next section. The outmigration included some of the most skilled and highly qualified workers and professionals from both the public and private sectors. The impact of this brain drain has been so considerable that it requires some assessment.

---

62 Hammar, McGregor and Landau, 2010, p. 270.
63 Government of Zimbabwe, 1981, p. 162.
64 LEDRIZ and Solidarity Centre, 2016.

In summary, the period between 2000 and 2015 has witnessed twin processes of deindustrialisation and de-proletarianisation due to economic crisis, firstly unprecedented hyperinflation and contraction, and secondly stagnation and uncertainty. Research is needed to show how these developments impacted on the composition of the working class and union membership, and by extension, how it resulted in the decline of labour's role in civic and political protest. There is a need to explore to what extent individual and household level survival strategies in a tough economic environment have weakened collective action by workers and their unions.

External migration, the working class and unions

Although migration for employment opportunities began in the 1990s, it accelerated after 2000 as the economic crisis deepened. There is no literature that has systematically assessed the impact of that migration on the skills base, employment patterns, union membership and capacity within Zimbabwe. Some of the early literature considered the numbers of Zimbabweans who had migrated for economic and social reasons including employment. Although no precise figures are available, estimates point to a diaspora of between 1.5 million and 3 million during the post-2000 period.[65] The wide variations in estimates suggest that the methodology of measuring the numbers of migrants may require revisiting.

Earlier literature had a narrower focus, such as on particular categories of migrants; this was the case in the study on professional migrants by Chetsanga and Muchenje.[66] Estimating that about 500,000 skilled Zimbabweans were working outside the country in early 2000s, some 24 per cent of them were trained doctors, nurses or pharmacists; 23 per cent were engineers and scientists; 20 per cent were teachers and about 17 per cent were accountants. In particular, the health sector had witnessed a significant outmigration of skilled professionals. By 2003, Zimbabwe had lost to migration over 2,100 medical doctors, mostly to South Africa, Botswana, Namibia, Australia and the UK.[67] Makina and Kanyenze estimated that the country was losing an average of 20 per cent of its healthcare professionals every year to emigration.[68]

---

65 Makina and Kanyenze, 2010; Crush and Tevera, 2010.
66 Chetsanga and Muchenje, 2003.
67 Chikanda, 2005.
68 Makina and Kanyenze, 2010.

Significantly, Zimbabwean migrants had become an important segment of the workforce in the health sector and care industry in destination countries. For instance, they are one of the four largest contributors of nurses to the British health sector. Nearly 20 per cent of Zimbabwean migrants to the UK were employed as carers or care assistants, sometimes pejoratively called 'bum technicians' or 'British Bottom Cleaners' (BBC).[69]

The literature on migration points out the generally high levels of education and skills amongst the Zimbabwean migrants. For instance, it was observed that the majority of migrants to South Africa were relatively young (72 per cent were under the age of 40) and well educated.[70] While less than 1 per cent had no schooling, over 50 per cent had a post-secondary diploma, undergraduate or post-graduate degree. It was further observed that:

> migrants were employed in a wide variety of skilled, semi-skilled and unskilled jobs outside Zimbabwe. In other words, this is a generalized out-movement of people, not confined to one or two professions or sectors.[71]

In a breakdown of the various sub-categories of migrants, the literature also underlines the deskilling process that occurs when the migrants undertake jobs below their qualifications and experiences. In a survey of migrants in Johannesburg, it was observed that there 'was considerable deskilling with many people being over-qualified for the jobs they did'.[72] Another study concurred that large numbers of Zimbabwean migrants were working in areas that were not commensurate with their skill levels, and many worked in areas other than the professions for which they were trained.[73] The study quotes results of a survey in Johannesburg that showed that 35 per cent of respondents stated that they did work that was not commensurate with their qualifications. Yet another survey that covered both South Africa and UK reported significant unused skills by Zimbabwean migrants in education (17 per cent) and finance, banking and sales (16 per cent).[74]

One outcome of deskilling is the resort to informal sector activities

---

69 Bloch, 2010; McGregor and Primorac, 2010.
70 Crush and Tevera, 2010, p. 12.
71 Ibid.
72 Ibid., p. 32.
73 Makina and Kanyenze, 2010, p. 14.
74 Bloch, 2005.

like vending in South Africa and Botswana by Zimbabwean migrants. Some studies have explored the presence of migrants on farms in the Limpopo province, and as far afield as the Western Cape farms. According to Rutherford, Zimbabwean farm worker migrants in the mid-2000s constituted the vast majority of farmworkers in northern South Africa.[75] Although they were employed in a variety of positions, including supervisory or lower management jobs, their wages on average were lower than the mandatory minimum. On average, the Zimbabwean migrants were more qualified, and had not been driven to work on low-paying South African farms because of a lack of skills. 'The majority were driven there because of the meltdown in Zimbabwe', concluded Rutherford.[76] The contingency and uncertainty of migrant farm workers has also received careful attention in the work of Maxim Bolt, who has studied displaced Zimbabwean labourers working on farms on the Zimbabwe-South African border.[77]

This enormous displacement of people has received substantial academic attention both in its internal and external forms. The disastrous effects of Operation Murambatsvina in 2005 on the livelihoods of workers in both the formal and informal sector has been well analysed by scholars such as Potts, Kamete and Dorman. As Potts has written, the reasons for Operation Murambatsvina included: firstly, a political response to citizens for their support for opposition politics; secondly, a strong ideological attachment by the state to modernist planning and the idea of the modern city, even though there has been less stringent application of planning regulations since the period of ESAP; and thirdly, the inability of the state to provide food and fuel for the growing numbers of poor people in the cities.[78]

Kamete has argued that the invocation of city planning laws and regulations to criminalise the 'unwanted' in the cities was used as the legal premise from which the state launched its authoritarian measures to restore order.[79] In her contribution, Dorman points to the long historical tension between ZANU(PF) and urban movements, given the former's conception of the land and agrarian citizenship as being the sole legitimate signifier of national belonging. Within this context, 'urban citizenship required urban

75 Rutherford, 2010.
76 Ibid., p. 262.
77 Bolt, 2014 and 2016.
78 Potts, 2006, 2007 and 2008.
79 Kamete, 2008, 2010 and 2012.

citizens to conform to certain ways of being and living', but the 'growing informality of the urban areas revealed the state's inability to regulate this', regarding demands for human rights and democratisation as a threat to 'national sovereignty'.[80]

More generally, work on displacement has produced strong analytical recasting in the context of the crisis in Zimbabwe. Hammar's work has set out some of the key questions around the idea of displacement, which include:

> What new forms of commodification are produced; how both old and new resource regimes (such as those related to land, minerals, forests or even finance itself) are reordered; in what ways patterns of access, ownership, labour, production, distribution, exchange, accumulation and differentiation change or persist; and how such conditions affect the dynamic articulation between official or so called 'formal' economies and alternative 'informal' economies.[81]

The literature on migration has several major gaps. First, there is little or no assessment of the impact of migration on the sectors from which migration emanates, including the gender dimensions which remain an important aspect of any discussion on migration. The full cost of migration to the Zimbabwean economy has not been sufficiently examined. However, impressionistic evidence would suggest that a depletion of scarce skills in the public sector undermined the quality of services and the capacity of the bureaucracy in terms of planning and policy implementation. According to Chagonda, a significant number of teachers joined the diaspora to the extent that the 'working class that belonged to the teaching profession was almost totally obliterated during the peak levels of Zimbabwe's hyperinflation'.[82] He quotes the Progressive Teachers Union of Zimbabwe as stating that about 15,000 teachers left their posts for the diaspora in 2008 alone, while the previous decade experienced a total flight of about 45,000. Most schools were affected, especially in rural areas, with hardly any lessons being conducted in 2008.

Second, a more systematic assessment of how the migration of artisans and technicians from such sectors as telecommunications, energy, and transport would illuminate how the hemorrhage severely undermined the capacity of key parastatals and private sector companies. One consequence

80 Dorman, 2016b.
81 Hammar, 2014, pp. 10-11.
82 Chagonda, 2011, p. 192.

33

of the exodus was the employment of persons with lower qualifications and experience in higher grades resulting in a phenomenon of 'grade inflation'. Consequently, it became increasingly difficult to maintain quality standards; furthermore, operating costs were higher because there were no 'experience effects' (learning-curve effects) because of high rates of staff turnover.[83] These issues are absent from most literature on migration. Similarly, there is no information on how unions have been affected by migration of union organisers and members who held positions as artisans, technicians, experts or as professionals. Although admittedly difficult to obtain, such data would illustrate the depth of the effects of migration on specific unions.

There has been more research and literature on the links between migration and the scale of remittances. The perspective that highlights the developmental and welfare benefits has been in the vogue, with international development agencies and some scholars making key contributions.[84] In the context of the Zimbabwean discussion on remittances, the positive dimensions have been explored in relation to support of households that remain behind, investment in education and social services, and even into productive accumulation.[85] The thrust of this literature is that remittances were a godsend.

Maphosa observed that remittances contributed significantly to poverty reduction and development.[86] Remittances in cash and kind cushioned the Zimbabwean economy and society from total collapse. Access to remittances was differentiated: some literature notes that the working classes had much more limited access than middle-class households. For instance, a 2009 report by the Zimbabwe Vulnerability Assessment Committee remarked that remittances contributed a minimal 2 per cent to the income of urban families. The working class households interviewed by Chagonda indicated that most of them did not have relatives sending them money or food from the diaspora.[87]

However, these studies on remittances do not provide comprehensive data on their scale and utilisation. Beyond generalities about their developmental and welfare value, there has not been rigorous research on how the working and middle classes draw on remittances. In addition, there is sparse information on the patterns after 2009. There is a strong

83 UNDP, 2008.
84 OECD, 2005; Maimbo and Ratha, 2005.
85 Bracking and Sachikonye, 2006 and 2010; Cliffe, 2009; Magunha et al., 2009.
86 Maphosa, 2007.
87 Chagonda, 2011, p. 212.

case for updating the literature in this regard; indeed, a comparison with patterns and effects during the second installment of economic downturn of 2014 to 2017 would be illuminating.

In sum, there is a conspicuous gap in the literature on the effects of migration on the size of the formal sector workforce and union membership. There should be a reasonably clear picture of how the exodus of workers has affected the state bureaucracy, parastatals and private sector in terms of numbers involved and quality of their output. There is a need to fill in gaps in information about how migration has affected the membership and technical capacity of unions. Whether remittances have some positive impact on livelihoods of workers is another issue that has not been systematically studied.

Post-2000 labour conditions in agriculture: trends, structures and processes

With about 65 per cent of the population still based in rural areas, agriculture remains a significant sector of the economy and source of livelihoods. Commercial agriculture remains a major contributor. Just before 2000, there were an estimated 320,000 permanent and temporary/casual workers (constituting 20 per cent of the formal sector workforce) on commercial farms that supported nearly 2 million people besides making a substantial contribution to GDP.

The period between 1997 and 2000 was a momentous one for agricultural proletariat, with unprecedented protests over wages and working conditions erupting on some commercial farms.[88] The strikes coincided with peasant occupations of many farms in Mashonaland East and parts of Masvingo. The upsurge in farm worker protests during this period resulted in some important research. Yash Tandon observed that:

> over a period of seven to ten days, farm workers in the Mutoko farming area resorted to direct action to draw attention to their situation. Taking whatever farm instruments came to hand, they ran amok in small groups, slashing fields, burning down tobacco barns, blocking rural roads, setting alight cars belonging to commercial farmers, and looting shops, most of them farm stores. Interestingly, women and children joined in the action alongside male workers... It was, in all likelihood, a spontaneous outburst triggered by desperation.[89]

88 Sachikonye, 1997; Tandon, 2001.
89 Tandon, 2001, p. 222.

In January 1998, farm workers in several districts also joined a nation-wide stayaway organised by the ZCTU against deteriorating living conditions experienced by workers. These stirrings mirrored the spreading ferment that saw land-hungry peasants occupying farms.

The conditions that goaded farm workers into these protests were the difficult conditions of exploitation and repression that undergirded the farm labour regime. Farm workers were victims of a pathological order; although producers of the nation's food and the bulk of its commodity exports, they were the 'last in the chain to receive the fruits of their labour'.[90]

The farm workers' strikes in 1997-98 were a watershed, after which land invasions paved way to the 'fast track reform programme'. This review does not intend to address the land redistribution programme, as it has already received extensive scholarly attention elsewhere.[91]

It is Blair Rutherford's work on farm workers that has perhaps been the most defining intervention. Rutherford produced two important articles on the struggles of farm workers during this period. In 2009 he tracked the ways in which national politics 'forged certain pathways for particular forms of social agency' by farm workers while also pointing to the 'dangers and ambiguities' faced by these workers in relation to their bodily security, the state and social justice.[92] Following this, he explored the ways in which the struggles around human rights and democratisation impacted on farm workers on Upfumi farm in Mashonaland East province in 1999. He demonstrated the ways in which a 'combination of neo-liberal policies, donor-facilitated emphasis on democracy, human rights and good governance' as well as the 'notions of workers' rights and democratisation' espoused by trade unions and other social movements, 'inspired farm workers to face a long legal process and to wring concessions from the farm management, while imagining they were part of wider political changes that were about to occur in Zimbabwe.'[93]

Rutherford's work has also been central to understanding the changing forms of rule over farm workers in both the colonial and post-colonial periods.[94] His central concept of 'domestic government', derived from

90 Ibid.
91 Sachikonye, 2003 and 2004; Hammar et al., 2003; Moyo, 2011; Moyo and Chambati, 2013; Scoones et al, 2010.
92 Rutherford, 2009, p. 391.
93 Rutherford, 2011, p. 510.
94 Rutherford, 2001a and 2001b.

Foucault's idea of 'governmentality',[95] provided a very useful framework through which to understand the forms of dominance of farmers over 'their' labourers:

> Farm workers fell under the authority of state-sanctioned empowerment granted to the white farmer and his family as the means of administering farm workers to form what can be called the 'domestic government' of white farms. This was 'domestic' both in the sense of officially promoting the 'private' over the 'public' domain, and of administratively valuing proper paternalistic and family-like relations between workers and farmers.[96]

The combination of pathology and paternalism made farm workers a precarious social group on the eve of land reform.

While land reform extended tangible benefits to about 170,000 households under A1 and A2 schemes, farm workers were largely marginalised, in that less than 10 per cent of them received land.[97] On top of this, they became subject to far-reaching retrenchments that saw their numbers shrink to less than 100,000 by 2005. As a new group of farmers, this time black farmers, took over expropriated farms, the majority of farm workers were fired and displaced.[98]

Subsequent research noted that differences inevitably existed in the forms and quantities of labour hired by A1 and A2 farms. While wage labour hiring was skewed towards casual labour on A1 farms, the majority of permanent workers were employed in the A2 sector.[99] However, it is important to note that casual labour was the dominant form of hired labour in both sectors. As an indication of relatively low levels of permanent worker hiring, there were an average of about six such workers on A2 farms and about two on the A1 farms. Significantly some of the research shows that most new farmers, notably on A2 holdings, remarked that they could not pay the statutory wages associated with permanent wage work since they were resource-constrained and 'only starting up'.[100] Although it should be acknowledged that farm worker livelihoods were poor before land reform, the post-2000 period has

---

95 Burchell, Gordon and Miller ,1991.
96 Rutherford, 2001a, p. 204.
97 Sachikonye, 2003; Magaramombe and Chambati, 2008.
98 Hartnack, 2005; Magaramombe, 2010.
99 Magaramombe and Chambati, 2008, p. 220.
100 Ibid.

been characterised by 'marked deterioration' in those conditions.

This review acknowledges that just as there has been a sharp debate amongst scholars on the merits and demerits of land reform implementation, so there has also been controversy over whether farm workers are 'better off' or 'worse off' as a consequence. We summarise here the two contending positions on the fate of farm workers following land redistribution. The first begins by extolling the land reform process uncritically while attacking those who have expressed criticism about its mode of implementation. This position describes critics of land reform as purveyors of property rights and of human rights and democracy while devaluing or ignoring the importance of economic rights or second-generation rights generally.[101] Criticism of the use of violence in land occupations as well as cronyism in the subsequent redistribution of land is brushed aside or downplayed, and this literature generally supports the actions of the Mugabe regime as a form of 'radical nationalism', if not a revolutionary agenda.[102] From this position, it is but a short step to talking up the supposed benefits of land reform for farm workers in terms of numbers and qualitative changes in employer-employee relationship in the post-2000 era.[103]

The main exponent of the position that farm workers have been major beneficiaries of new employment opportunities under land reform has been Chambati, who argued that:

> the reversal of monopoly in land ownership via land redistribution affects agrarian labour relations by generating a new agrarian employment structure in which political power is diffused amongst a broad base of many smaller capitalist farms and peasants.[104]

In addition, the redistribution exercise undermined the residual labour tenancy by reducing their authority to compel wage labour in return for residency and labour control.[105] Somewhat shaky findings are then presented to argue that over two-thirds of former farm workers remained on commercial farms; and that there had been an overall gain in livelihoods.[106] This was, as observed above, in the form of 170,000 land beneficiary

---

101   Moyo, 2001; Moyo et al., 2008; Chambati, 2013.
102   Moyo and Yeros, 2007.
103   Chambati, 2011 and 2013.
104   Chambati, 2013, p. 159.
105   Ibid.
106   Ibid.

households who had introduced new types of wage employment.

Perhaps the most contentious part of this 'talking up' of land reform and farm employment is the extrapolation that is then made that by 2010, permanent jobs had risen to 478,000 in comparison to 170,000 in 2000.[107] The claim is then made that redistributed A1 and A2 areas had generated about 680,000 new self-employment jobs representing a huge growth from the situation on commercial farms just before land reform in 2000. According to this analysis, the new agrarian labour structure represented an overall growth in agricultural employment. The methodology used in making calculations of wage employment is open to question. Apparently it lumps together waged workers as conventionally understood, and members of households of the new farmers, but this is unsatisfactory.

The second position in this debate on land reform and its employment effects takes a more sceptical view. It is critical about the mode of reform implementation, particularly the violence that accompanied it and the unfairness and corruption that pervaded it.[108] While this literature does not dispute the case for land reform, it does not downplay the negative outcomes of the process, and it challenges the above claims of massive job opportunities.

First, Chambati's 'talking up' of the employment effects of land reform is based on 'an extremely simplistic, static and crude understanding of labour relations, conditions and power dynamics' in former white commercial farms.[109] Adding to the pioneering work of Rutherford,[110] Hartnack has provided a more nuanced study of the precarious nature of the forms of incorporation and modes of belonging that confront both farm dwellers and farm workers in urban slums.[111] His work has also traced the influences of global, transnational governmentality on the articulations of rights in the narratives and struggles for farm workers' rights.

Second, it is naïve to assume, as Chambati does, that dependencies and power relations can be swept away through massive land distribution, or that labour relations on commercial farms prior to 2000 were inherently

107 Chambati, 2013, p. 168.
108 Sachikonye, 2003; Hammar, Raftopoulos and Jensen, 2003; Marongwe, 2003; RAU, 2009.
109 Hartnack, 2016, p. 112.
110 Rutherford, 2008.
111 Hartnack, 2009.

worse than those now existing on redistributed farms. There was a diversity of working and living conditions on former commercial farms and Chambati's analysis occluded the actual terrain of struggle for farm workers through these power relations prior to and after land reform.[112] Thirdly, the approach represented by Chambati ignored the question of power and politics within the new agrarian relations, and failed to examine critically the actual social relations of precarious dependency and modes of belonging, as well as the power relations involving farm workers, land reform beneficiaries, and local state and party power holders.[113]

Finally, there are several areas in agriculture and labour conditions that have not received attention, despite their importance. These relate to differentiation within agricultural labour itself as well as patterns of unionisation and fragmentation, especially in the post-reform period. As well, the growing phenomenon of contract farming in tobacco and cotton production has not encouraged research interest in labour conditions as foreign capital subcontracts commodity production as a way to minimise risk in the post-reform era.[114] And the changing structural conditions under which agriculture is being carried have not been explored in relation to agribusiness-industry linkages. These developments would helpfully complement research that aims to bring out a more realistic picture of employment conditions and the political economy of a major sector of Zimbabwe's economy.

To sum up, just as there has been a vigorous debate on the merits and demerits of how land reform was implemented, so there has been another debate over whether farm workers were 'better off' or 'worse off' following the reform. Analytical work is necessary to explore this issue. The impact of land reform on the agricultural worker unions, their activities and membership and changing structure of agriculture and agribusiness-industry linkages themselves, need further research.

Post-2000 employment conditions in mining: structures, processes and trends

Mining is an important and strategic sector of Zimbabwe's economy. It is both a significant contributor to commodity exports as well as source of employment for about 40,000 workers. As its contribution to GDP

---

112 Hartnack, 2016.
113 Rutherford, 2011 and 2014.
114 Sachikonye, 2016.

and exports has expanded in the past ten years, so has its capacity for employment declined. At its peak in the mid-1990s, mining employed about 60,000 workers, shrinking to 40,000 in 2014. As one important study observed:

> in the 1980s and early 1990s, Zimbabwe was poised to become a significant force in African mining.... This was due to diverse mineral resources, infrastructure, skilled labour and a relatively stable fiscal and monetary regime. The late 1990s witnessed declining production and loss of investor confidence against a background of macroeconomic instability. In 2000, the mining index dropped to 104 from 116 in 1995. By 2003, the index had fallen to 79. After dollarization, the fortunes of the mining sector have been improving, and the country has been able to take advantage of the commodity price boom.[115]

An assessment of labour conditions in the sector should therefore be set against this wider context of boom, decline and renewed boom of the past 20 years. In particular, in this section, we explore labour conditions in the context of structural changes that have been occurring in the sector during the post-2000 period. Surprisingly, in comparison to other sectors, there have been relatively few studies on labour conditions in formal sector mining. The exceptions include a study of the labour utilisation model,[116] which noted that there had been a failure to bring about a fundamental change in the organisation of production thereby limiting the industry's role in Zimbabwe's political economy. The study also explored the labour utilisation model specifically in relation to wage levels, job colour bar, skill levels and migration.

Foreign labour migration was replaced by a domestic migration in the post-independence period. While wages and skill levels remained low, workers were mostly employed on a permanent basis in the sector. In her study, Dansereau explored the significance of permanent migration between rural areas and mines, observing that this saw families make use of the economic opportunities available to them through their links to rural areas.[117] Low wages made such links essential as a supplementary source of income, but these low wages combined with rising travel costs to make the link difficult, while a lack of savings restricted investment in the rural home.

---

115 LEDRIZ, 2016, p. 16.
116 Dansereau, 2001b.
117 Ibid.

What have been the key structural changes in mining that have shaped labour conditions and employment patterns during the period under review? Hyperinflation as a symptom of a deep underlying crisis made mining an 'early casualty' in the first half of the 2000s. Currency fluctuations, policy vacillation and skyrocketing costs were especially damaging.[118] The viability of most mining houses was put under considerable pressure with the gold sector particularly hard hit. For instance, in 2000-2001, 14 gold mines were closed or placed on a care and maintenance basis due to chronic shortages of power, fuel, capital inputs and skilled labour. Other mineral sub-sectors also were buffeted by rising production costs, materials shortages, degraded infrastructure, skills flight and low returns due to distorted exchange rates. Amongst commodities whose production declined were copper, coal and ferrochrome. Describing the period between 1997 and 2008 as a crisis period, one study provides a list of about 40 mines that closed.[119]

However, there were exceptions to this downward trend. Platinum and diamond production saw a spectacular rise during this period. Some of the firms that spearheaded platinum production were the South African-owned ZIMPLATS and Mimosa. The main factor behind the upsurge in platinum production was that, unlike other minerals, it had unhindered access to foreign currency from offshore accounts.[120] From 2006, diamond production grew in the Marange area of eastern Zimbabwe, first mainly through small-scale artisanal mining, and later under several large foreign companies with domestic partnerships. It is significant that South African and Chinese capital has been prominent in the relatively new areas of platinum and diamond mining respectively.

How were employment levels affected by these post-2000 developments? With the exception of platinum, and later diamonds, there was a general decline in mining employment during the decade. It was observed that:

> those that left employment were hardly ever replaced unless their work could not be shared by those already employed. The loss of skills to the region and beyond had a telling effect on production and safety performance. Many supervisory positions in the industry are currently filled by young people who would

---

118 Saunders, 2008.
119 Matyanga, 2011.
120 Ibid., p. 185.

ordinarily have been under supervision themselves.[121]

In the copper sub-sector, the closure of a major mine such as Mhangura, resulted in major job losses. Similarly, cutbacks in coal production at Hwange caused some retrenchments as happened as a consequence of the cessation of iron and steel manufacture by ZISCO during the 2000s. On the whole, there have been no systematic studies on the decline of employment in the formal mining sector. Nor has there been an exploration of the patterns of employment in the sub-sectors of platinum and diamonds.

However, there has been a growing literature on artisanal mining since the early 2000s. Fueled by activities of small-scale gold and diamond panners, the informal mining sector has experienced unparalleled growth.[122] Artisanal gold mining saved the sub-sector from possible collapse in the mid-2000s, with production doubling in value from 2003 to 2004 due to attractive price incentives by the Reserve of Zimbabwe.[123] One assessment of the artisanal gold sub-sector observed that this period was a high point in the proliferation of mining by 'makorokoza' from Kwekwe and Kadoma to Mazowe.[124] Indeed while official gold output was declining due to 'the scaling down and closure of formal mining operations, artisanal small-scale mining output was rising. It is thus safe to say that formal figures portray an exaggerated picture of receding gold output: rather most gold was channeled into the parallel market. By 2008, some 2 million Zimbabweans were dependent on ASM gold mining'.[125] Out of those, some 500,000 were estimated to be employed informally in the sector.

Following the introduction of dollarisation in 2009, confidence was created in both the formal and informal sectors leading to a major jump in production output in most mineral sub-sectors. For example, mining's contribution to GDP rose to 37 per cent in 2011 before coming down to about 11 per cent in 2013. The improved macroeconomic stability and the global commodity boom prior to 2015 contributed to the good performance of the sector. It was a performance that fueled employment growth of about 6 per cent in 2010, 16 per cent in 2011 and 2 per cent in 2012 before contracting to 5 per cent in 2014.[126]

---

121 Ibid., p. 191.
122 Mawowa, 2014; Nyamunda and Mukwambo, 2012; Chimonyo et al., 2012.
123 Matyanga, 2011, p. 181.
124 Mawowa, 2014.
125 Ibid., p. 926.
126 LEDRIZ, 2016, p. 18.

This account shows that the fortunes of the mining sector have changed significantly during the past 15 years. The decline, boom and slow-down cycles have been caused by both domestic and global factors. This had a direct bearing on conditions of labour and patterns of employment, although detailed research and literature has been sparse. A common similarity with most other economic sectors was the growth of informalisation from the early 2000s. Although this has provided livelihoods for millions, these have been largely precarious. Some studies have shown that violence has been a characteristic of artisanal mining, as when the state moved in to assert its control over the Marange diamond fields in 2008-2009.[127]

In sum, compared to other sectors, there have been fewer studies on labour conditions in formal sector mining, and little data is available on how employment and the mineworkers' union have been affected. In particular, there has been no exploration of employment patterns and labour conditions in the growth areas of platinum and diamond production. These gaps should be filled. In addition, the significance of the upsurge in small-scale mining for employment as well as linkages with the formal mining sector should be explored.

Post-2000 gender dimensions of workers and the labour movement

Although very little literature with a gendered view of the working class and the labour movement is available for review, this study would not be complete without exploring how gender power structures, relations and cultural norms have shaped the working class and labour movement discourse. The gender dimension will be looked at as a crosscutting factor in all the thematic issues, assessing the ways in which working class men and women were not only positioned but how they responded to the crises.

More specifically, the study examines the status and role of working women, their forms of participation in the labour market and the labour movement, and the ways in which such participation changed the structures and identities of labour. The chapter by Naome Chakanya specifically attempts to explore and evaluate the particular experiences of working women in the changing economic, social and political conditions of the post-2000 period. An earlier study of women workers across the formal economy in rural and urban Mashonaland in the late 1980s by Christine

---

127 Saunders and Nyamunda, 2016; Spiegel, 2014 and 2015.

Sylvester provided some valuable insights into the complexities of gender and identity. Sylvester set out the problematic in the following terms:

> We can ask questions of and about gender and identity without trying to sort out a causal path between identity and work, trace the effects of single variables and theories, or endeavour to simplify the multiplicities of meanings and location that may give 'women' and 'progress' their significance.[128]

Given the breakdown of the formal labour force that Sylvester studied, the complexities of gender, identity and work have been compounded.

Conclusion

This review has examined the key literature on Zimbabwe's labour movement and working class in the period after 2000. It does not pretend to be exhaustive. In general, there are gaps in that literature that should be filled through research. The style and focus of the literature review were to highlight the strengths and shortfalls of the texts identified.

Specific attention is paid to the pivotal role of the ZCTU as the anchor of organised labour, and how its strength has been buffeted during the past 15 years. The fortunes of unions and more generally the working class have been tied with those of the economy as a whole, a theme that ties together the different sections of the review. This focus on the political economy of labour conditions and employment is pursued in the sections on agriculture and mining. The review also highlights the need to explore the lasting impact of migration on the density and capacity of unions, and on the working class as a whole.

However, the review also highlights the need to embrace a broad range of theoretical frameworks that include not only the questions around political economy, but also the discourses and cultural issues that affect workers' conceptions of their identities, lives and livelihoods, and their changing modes of belonging. Attention also needs to be paid to other processes such as displacement, urban and rural politics, and the changing narratives and forms of state rule and its constructions of labour questions. Moreover, the impact of global changes in production and labour relations need to be integrated into any study of national labour movements. These are complex interrelations and this study has attempted to draw on the different theoretical insights outlined in this review.

---

128 Sylvester, 2000, p. 24.

Chapter 3

State Politics, Constructions of Labour and Labour Struggles 1980-2000

Brian Raftopoulos[1]

Introduction

This chapter provides an analysis of the first two decades of trade union struggles in post-colonial Zimbabwe. In the first part it tracks two major threads. Firstly, it explains the difficulties faced by the state in developing a new industrial relations regime in the context of both the continuities of the settler colonial state policies on labour, and the tenuous and often hostile historical relations between the nationalist parties and the labour movement. Secondly, it examines the growing problems of the state's attempt to control the labour centre and the movement towards union autonomy and state critique by the end of the 1980s. In the second part of the chapter the analysis moves to the period of economic liberalisation in the 1990s. The predictable decline of labour standards, as in other parts of the African continent subjected to structural adjustment programmes, led to conflict between the state and the labour movement. As the attempts at tripartite dialogue broke down, and the face of the state took on an increasingly repressive expression, the labour movement moved towards the battle for state power through the formation of a political opposition party.

PART ONE: The 1980s labour regime

In Zimbabwe's post-colonial history the 1980s was marked by a particular set of constraints, ambiguities and opportunities. For most Zimbabweans it represented a time of great hope and promise, albeit in the context of

---

1 I would like to thank Ian Phimister and Blair Rutherford for the comments on the draft of this chapter.

a complicated legacy of the liberation struggle that was constructed out of the combined processes of mass mobilisation and coercion, in which the meanings of nationalism and belonging were often contested. The language of inclusivity and unity could be sharply and abruptly interrupted by the violence of exclusionary politics for those who contested dominant nationalist party formation notions of 'the nation'. Thus the 1980s bore the traces of these techniques of mobilisation and disciplining, even as the politics of reconciliation and development dominated the political framing of the policy debates.

As Sara Rich Dorman aptly describes it, while the politics of nation-building was 'disjointed and often superficial, but for the most part ... not discordant', the discourse of development proved a 'less problematic motivating force for government ideology'.[2] Neocosmos describes this form of politics in the broader continental frame as the 'saturation of emancipatory politics' being replaced by 'technical solutions in the form of development'.[3] This process resembled that of many post-colonial states whose leadership attempted to convince workers about the value of 'order and productivity'.[4] Moreover, as a mid-decolonising state marked by both the vestigial promise of a declining socialist vision and the emerging and destructive triumphalism of neoliberalism,[5] the early ideological positioning of the Zimbabwean state was often cast in the contradictory claims of these contested world-views.

In Gramscian terms, the hegemony of a state is constituted through the unity of not only political and economic aims, 'but also intellectual and moral unity, posing all questions around which the struggle rages not on a corporate but on a "universal" plane'. Furthermore, the state should be seen as a structure through which the developmental aims of a particular group are 'conceived of and presented as being the motor force of a universal expansion, of a development of all the "national" energies'.[6] In such a conceptualisation the Zimbabwean state has yet to achieve this political hegemony, except in terms of its widespread use of violence and coercion. In the 1980s the difficulties of establishing more consensual forms of rule that went substantially beyond the violence of the colonial state made some progress in key areas of the development agenda, and in

2 Dorman, 2016a, p. 45.
3 Neocosmos, 2016, p. 120.
4 Cooper, 1996, p. 438.
5 Ndlovu-Gatsheni, 2011, p. 60.
6 Gramsci, 1971, p. 182.

the restructuring of the state. Yet even in the first decade of independence the new democratic spaces that opened up were already shadowed by and 'coexisted uneasily with government authoritarianism'.[7] In the rural areas the modernist attempts to restructure local government rule resulted in an uncomfortable juxtaposition of technocracy, ruling party structures and customary claims that largely failed to democratise the modes of rule in these areas, and resulted in continuities in dual forms of administration in the communal areas and the commercial farming areas.[8]

In the urban areas, in which, up to the 1950s, social forces such as the trade unions had played a key role in anti-colonial struggles,[9] the new state, which had built its support base largely in the rural areas during the liberation struggle, looked on such urban forces with suspicion. Regarded as not having participated fully in the liberation struggle, urban movements such as the trade unions were often treated with a combination of disdain and condescension even as the nationalist government invited them to become part of the new nation. Longstanding questions such as the organisational autonomy of unions from nationalist political parties left a lasting legacy of suspicion between the two.

In theorising the relations between the state and trade unions in Zimbabwe in the post-colonial period several analysts have referred to some form of corporatism as the most appropriate way to describe this administrative rule. From the work of Schmitter, corporatism refers to the involvement of interest groups in policy making in ways that involve mediation and not the suppression of particular groups.[10] Drawing on this framework, scholars have characterised state-labour relations in Zimbabwe as 'corporate paternalist',[11] and 'state corporatism'.[12] Shadur defined the relationship as 'paternalistic state corporatism', in which 'extensive government controls over unions and labour relations' was a combination of authoritarianism and benevolence.[13] Schiphorst, on the other hand, took a more sceptical view of the value of the concept of corporatism. He argued that because of the lack of any 'meaningful

---

7 Muzondidya, 2009, p. 181.
8 Alexander, 2006; Rutherford, 2001b.
9 Raftopoulos and Phimister 1997; Raftopoulos and Yoshikuni, 1999; Scarnecchia, 2008.
10 Schmitter and Lehmbruch, 1979.
11 Wood, 1987.
12 Nordlund, 1996, p. 149.
13 Shadur, 1994, p. 230.

involvement of organised labour in decision making as a *quid pro quo* for a restrained position', it would be more appropriate to refer to state-labour relations as 'benign labour control',[14] or what le Bas refers to as a form of neglect throughout the 1980s.[15] Through this modality, Schiphorst argues, the new state sought primarily to establish political control over organised labour by removing the possibility that any rival political party would gain control over a future labour centre and hence develop an autonomous power outside of the state.[16]

The theoretical framework in this chapter builds on an earlier paper[17] and the work of Schiphorst and Nordlund. Drawing on Foucault's concept of power, discipline and control at the micro level, Nordlund argues that an extension of this concept at the macro level allows for a greater understanding of ZANU(PF)'s rule from 1980 to the early 1990s than the Gramscian concept of hegemony. This is because hegemony implies a good deal of consent, with much less reliance on coercion and violence, and in Norland's reading Zimbabwean politics in this period was characterised by 'very weak or non-existent hegemonic structures on the mass level'.[18] Thus Nordlund concludes that Zimbabwe was ruled by a combination of hegemonic relations, particularly in the rural areas, a political culture of fear, and also by what he calls the 'coordination power working in favour of the government'.[19] Utilising Foucault's conception of disciplinary power at the micro level through forms of 'governmentality' that combine a set of governmental apparatuses and forms of rule, with the capacity to gather information on and 'understand' the subject of state rule,[20] Nordlund defines coordinated power as:

> … the manner in which beliefs are aggregated into structures that govern social interaction. Such structuring of social and political behaviour takes on specific qualities when it forms larger patterns of coordination.[21]

The argument of this chapter is that not only was the hegemonic rule of the Zimbabwean state in the 1980s fragile, as argued by others, but that

---

14 Schiphorst, 2001, p. 349.
15 Le Bas, 2011.
16 Schiphorst, 2001, p. 71.
17 Raftopoulos, 1994.
18 Nordlund 1996, p. 241.
19 Ibid. p. 204.
20 Burchell, Gordon and Miller, 1991, p. 103.
21 Nordlund, 1996, p. 246.

the structures of 'coordinated power' set out by Nordlund were similarly tentative, particularly in the context of the state's attempts to build a new labour regime for urban labour and trade unions. Beckman and Sachikonye conceptualise a labour regime as a 'complex of institutions, rules and practices through which relations between labour and capital are regulated both in the work place and in society at large', as well as denoting the ways in which the 'state and organised interests intervene and mediate those relations'.[22] In this chapter it is argued that the form of labour regime developed by the Zimbabwean post-colonial state in the 1980s was what could be described as a 'tentative governmentality'. This term describes the state's immense challenges in developing a coherent narrative and form of rule for labour relations in the context of a several factors. These included: a lack of state capacity and the often contradictory characteristics of the new industrial relations regime marked by a combination of racial legacies and conflicting constructions of professionalism; a history of strongly contested relations with the labour movement over issues of autonomy, labour rights and the terms of national belonging;[23] and the difficulties of developing a disciplinary framework that sought to both channel and control the demands of labour, while also seeking an accommodation with white capital in the context of the politics of reconciliation of the 1980s.

Further problematising this context, for farm workers on the largely white controlled commercial farms, the dominant form of labour administration, persisting from the settler colonial period, was constituted through what Rutherford calls 'domestic government'. In Rutherford's formulation this is an administrative form that both officially promoted the 'private over the public domain – the rule of the farmer over state officials', and also valued 'paternalistic relations between male workers and their families and between farmers and "their" workers'.[24]

More generally, given the dominantly rural mobilisation of the liberation struggle in the 1970s, the post-colonial state's tentative governmentality was indicative of its long-standing discomfort with urban labour and its organisational history and structures. It also represented a patronising conception of the secondary status of urban labour in the pantheon of the liberation struggle.

---

22 Beckman and Sachikonye, 2001, p. 9.
23 Raftopoulos, 2003.
24 Rutherford, 2001b, p. 14.

Labour upheavals and the new state

The immediate post-colonial period was rocked by a widespread worker strikes throughout the country. Sachikonye estimated that there were 178 strikes in the period 1980-81,[25] while Wood placed the figure at the end of 1980 at approximately 153 strikes.[26] Drawing on regional industrial relations reports from the Ministry of Labour my own projection is that both these figures were underestimates. The Regional Industrial Relations Officer in Mashonaland reported 173 work stoppages for his region,[27] while in Matabeleland it was observed that there were approximately 20 disputes every month during the same year.[28] Thus for Mashonaland and Matabeleland, the two most industrialised provinces in the country, there were approximately 413 work stoppages in 1980 alone. Moreover, in response to increasing criticism from government representatives about these 'illegal strikes', workers also resorted to what labour officials termed 'work-in-strikes'. Labour officers considered these 'the worst of all strikes' as they not only denied employees time to rest but also ensured that Industrial Relations Officers went without their 'precious resting time.'[29]

The causes of the strikes included demands for higher wages and shorter working hours; lighter working loads; payment on time; wage increases similar to civil servants; accommodation allowances and overtime rates; more rations and time off; and action against abusive senior employees and bad management.[30] As Sachikonye observes, for the most part these strikes tended to be 'contagious and spontaneous' and represented an 'attempt to bypass the industrial relations procedures and appeal directly to the government'.[31] The Ministry of Labour received numerous reports of a 'high level of activity' by 'unregistered trade unions', which as a result of the loss of credibility of many of the more established unions, such as the Associated Mineworkers Union of Zimbabwe, led to 'labour

25 Sachikonye, 1986, pp. 268-272.

26 Wood, 1987, p. 67.

27 GOZ Ministry of Labour, Report of the Regional Industrial Relations Officer (RIRO), Mashonaland, for the year 1980.

28 GOZ Ministry of Labour, RIRO, Matabeleland, 1980.

29 GOZ Ministry of Labour and Social Welfare, Report of the RIRO, Matabeleland for the year 1982.

30 GOZ Ministry of Labour and Social Welfare, Summary of Work Stoppages due to disputes Midlands 1980; and Manicaland 1980.

31 Sachikonye, 1986, pp. 252-3.

making greater demands and being far less passive than it has been in the past'. This resulted in, as one labour official described it, an 'epidemic of strikes' which, while often referred to as a 'crisis of expectation', could more aptly be described as the 'grapes of wrath'.[32]

The use of a pathological health metaphor to describe the labour unrest was indicative of the colonial continuities in the labour administration which will be discussed further in the chapter. Most workers 'invariably demanded to see the Minister of Labour and Social Welfare', while the Minister 'complied with relatively few of the demands and left the Industrial Officer to finalise the stoppage and bring about a return to normal working conditions'.[33] Thus much of the emphasis of the workers' actions was to push for more representation in the state and greater state intervention over their demands.

The widespread strikes were largely outside of union structures, and indicated a clear disconnection between existing trade union structures and workers' actions and demands. The inability of these structures to channel the demands of workers provided the state with the opportunity to direct and control the emergence of a new trade union federation in the direction preferred by the state. The ideological framework through which ZANU(PF) attempted to justify its leadership and control of the labour movement was the well-worn concept of the national democratic revolution, an idea often invoked by nationalists with a purported socialist agenda. Moore aptly describes this concept as a stage on the route from socialism to the communist utopia. This would require a developmental state that would create the conditions for the emergence of a national bourgeoisie, or would be a substitute for it.

In order to create the production and ideological conditions for the emergence of a proletariat this would require a strong, left-thinking intellectual and party leadership, which would then 'contrive a judicious combination of rigorous socialist leadership with the requisite amount of democracy allowing the proletariat to develop the capacity to lead the state and society one day in the … future, and simultaneously to build up the forces of production'.[34] In deploying this concept, a ZANU(PF) document in 1978 described the role of labour in the struggle against settler colonial rule in Zimbabwe as follows:

32 GOZ Ministry of Labour and Social Welfare, Report of the RIRO, Mashonaland for the year 1980, Paul E. Toovey.

33 GOZ Ministry of Labour and Social Welfare, Annual Report of the Assistant RIRO, Manicaland for the Year ended 31 December 1980, D.J. Butterworth.

34 Moore, 2012, p. 120.

In this total context of national oppression and exploitation, the question of equal rights in Labour matters can thus only be meaningfully addressed within the context of the on-going national democratic revolution aimed at the total overthrow of the Smith settlerist regime.[35]

The document further declared that:

We therefore recognise that the principal form of struggle in the conditions of Zimbabwe is the revolutionary armed struggle. All other forms of struggle (strikes, sabotage, diplomatic and political action etc.) complement and supplement the revolutionary armed struggle.[36]

This position was reiterated by the Minister of Labour, Manpower Planning and Social Welfare in July 1985 when he stated that 'it is important that workers and their organisations work under, and take direction from, a revolutionary party – in our case Zanu PF'.[37] This injunction was followed by a narrative locating trade unions struggles as, historically, largely outside of the liberation movement, and in need of ruling party tutelage:

Historically, Trade Unions in this country, particularly in the 1960's and 1970's, have operated outside the mainstream of our political life. For example, the labour movement was not directly involved in the liberation movement. Naturally, this important situation has resulted in tendencies like opportunism, economism and divisiveness.... Granted that the labour movement operated under extremely difficult conditions under colonialism where they were suppressed and not allowed to associate themselves with political parties; granted too that after the 1950's there was no labour movement to talk of in the country. For that reason the party and government have strenuously worked to promote the formation, growth and development of the ZCTU.[38]

In this ruling party construction, trade unions, and indeed urban labour in general, were treated as aspirants to the new nation, still lacking in their patriotic duties and yet to deserve their role in the theatre of nationhood.

35 ZANU(PF), 1978, p. 2.
36 Ibid., p. 3.
37 Speech by the Minister of Labour, Manpower Planning and Social Welfare at the Zimbabwe Congress of Trade Unions Congress, 27-28 July 1985.
38 Ibid.

As a senior labour official described it, the psychological weakness of the labour movement in the early post-colonial years 'arose from the workers' failure to relate adequately to the liberation struggle'. This in turn led to the 'inhibitions' of workers who 'tended to leave the initiative in labour matters to those who had distinguished themselves during the liberation struggle'.[39] In the context of the theory of the national democratic revolution (NDR), this narrative translated into an indefinitely deferred subservience to ruling party domination. As ZANU(PF) and the state became conflated in the decades that followed, the NDR, as in other so called radical African states, became the long-term conceptual resting place for authoritarian nationalism.

The state and the creation of the Zimbabwe Congress of Trade Unions

When, in 1980, ZANU(PF) moved to establish a new trade union centre, there were already moves underway by older trade unions centres to establish a new formation. Following the abortive 'internal settlement' of 1978 between Ian Smith, Bishop Muzorewa and Ndabaningi Sithole, unions supporting the latter two leaders organised a federation of unions called the United Trade Unions of Zimbabwe (UTUZ). The three organisations that came together to form UTUZ were the Zimbabwe Federation of Labour (ZFL), the African Trade Union Centre (ATUC), and the Trade Union Congress of Rhodesia, the old white-led trade union. Soon after independence the acting General Secretary of UTUZ wrote to the Minister of Labour formally announcing its presence and its intention to play a coordinating role in union matters. As one of the key justifications for its role, UTUZ noted that it would coordinate the policies of its affiliates and act on their behalf with national trade union bodies of other countries such as the British TUC and international organisations such as the AFL-CIO. UTUZ also made clear that the future of assistance from such outside organisations would be dependent on such offers being channelled through a recognised national trade union centre.[40]

Following this letter, at a meeting attended by the Minister of Labour, ZANU(PF) officials, UTUZ and other union representatives, the UTUZ member once more presented the organisation's case. He stated that the proposal of the Minister to establish a new trade union centre

39 *The Herald*, 23 March 1985.
40 GOZ ZCTU File 18/03/10 Letter from Brian Holleran, Acting General Secretary of UTUZ, to the Minister of Labour, Kumbirai Kangai, 28 April 1980.

was a 'complete departure from the plans that were afoot to establish a united trade union organisation', and that while 'there would have to be acceptance' of such a state-imposed structure, this new body would not have the support of the trade unions who had not been invited to the meeting.[41] The Minister's reply was that UTUZ 'did not have the interests of the people' in mind, and that the new trade union centre proposed by the state 'would have the whole hearted support of the government as it was a trade union organisation for the people'.[42] This position followed an earlier 'suggestion' from the Minister that UTUZ 'should work to establish a viable trade union, not united trade unions'.[43]

The Minister then announced that a coordinating committee of a new trade union centre, the Zimbabwe Congress of Trade Unions (ZCTU), was to arrange a convention to create one trade union centre.[44] UTUZ complained that this committee, personally invited by the Minister, contained eight individuals 'who had not worked in industry or represented a trade union movement as such, but were appointees of the political party in power'.[45] Even as the ruling party was marginalising those union centres that had been associated with the 'internal settlement', it also kept an eye on those unions, such as the Zimbabwe African Congress of Unions (ZACU), that supported the rival liberation movement, ZAPU.[46] As increasing numbers of 'union entrepreneurs'[47] joined the state-controlled process around the new union centre, these individuals, assisted by the ruling party, promoted the development of splinter unions that would support the state project. The UTUZ complained to the ILO that those unionists who were part of the emerging state-controlled union centre were 'starting splinter unions in industries where registered unions have been recognised for years and have created a most divisive atmosphere'. The union further requested

---

41 Ibid.

42 GOZ ZCTU File, 18/3/10 Minutes of the meeting held in the Board room of, Compensation House, 25 July 1980.

43 GOZ ZCTU File 18/3/10 Letter from Minster of Labour and Social Welfare Kumbirai Kangai to Brian Holleran, UTUZ, 9 April 1980, Ref: 18/239.

44 GOZ ZCTU File 18/3/10 Reply by MJ Thompson, Secretary for Labour to EEA, 22.10.80, Ref: 18/3/10/16.

45 GOZ ZCTU File 18/3/10 Letter from Aaron Ndlovu, Acting General Secretary of UTUZ to the Director ILO 9/12/80.

46 GOZ ZCTU File 18/3/10 Memo: Ministry of Labour June 1980, Ref. 18/239/10.

47 Wood, 1987, p. 65.

the ILO to withhold recognition of any Zimbabwean trade union centre until such time as it had been able to 'authoritatively determine that such a centre does reflect the views and aspirations of the Zimbabwean workers'.[48] In making this demand, UTUZ was drawing on a long-held trade union strategy of appealing to a universal language of labour rights as a 'reference point outside of particular power structures', where such structures are perceived as constraints on the application of rights in the case of nation state projects.[49]

When the inaugural congress of the ZCTU took place in February 1981, it was, as Woods argues, a 'fairly stage managed affair',[50] with unionists loyal to ZANU(PF) in the forefront. The new leadership was eager to prove its subservience to the state, duly providing proof of its supplication:

> Zanu PF is the only last salvation left before us if we are to succeed
> in our endeavour to achieve a genuine socialist society.[51]

Thereafter, the state was to face the consequences of its creation not only in the form of maladministration, corruption, ethnic politicking and a range of undemocratic practices,[52] but also in the form of using the authority of the ruling party's official 'commitment' to workers to undermine the legitimacy of the emerging industrial relations regime. The growing evidence of incompetence, corruption and lack of representativeness of the new ZCTU leadership began to mount very quickly. The Administrator of the ZCTU appointed by the state to help resolve the problems of its creation reported in 1984 in terms that left little doubt about the weakness of this state project:

> The ZCTU has a General Council of 29 but is effectively controlled by five people, Makwarimba, Kupfuma, Mashavira, Soko and Moyo. Mashavira runs a splinter union in the Clothing industry. This union competes with the registered union led by Pasipanodya. Makwarimba who is the ZCTU President is the General Secretary of the Commercial and Allied Workers Union. This union is on the verge of packing up. Soko's union has problems too. This is

48 GOZ ZCTU File 18/3/10 Letter from Aaron Ndlovu Acting Secretary General of UTUZ to the Director of the ILO 9/12/80.
49 Cooper, 1996, pp. 467-468.
50 Wood, 1987, p. 37.
51 GOZ ZCTU File 18/3/10 Minutes of the ZCTU Meeting held on 11/10/82.
52 Government of Zimbabwe, National Trade Union Survey 1984.

because Soko and Mutema are General Secretary and President respectively of the Textile Union and are also top executives in their companies. The membership generally feel that the union is being disadvantaged.

As for Carlton Moyo his trade union role is not clear now. He used to be General Secretary of Domestic Union, and administrator of ZCTU. He has relinquished those posts and is now associated with ZAWU. He was sent there by the ZCTU 5 who feel he cannot be abandoned as he accepted to be used as a scapegoat in the bicycles scandal.

It appears that Moyo, Soko, Kupfuma, Mashavira and Makwarimba do not have the capacity to reform. [53]

Criticisms of the ZCTU leadership were also increasingly made by trade unionists themselves. In October 1984, ten of the major unions in the country sent a petition to the Ministry of Labour demanding the suspension of the whole Executive and General Council of the ZCTU for their 'shameful and corrupt activities'. The unions complained that the ZCTU had been 'infiltrated by businessmen', who should 'leave the workers association alone and join the Employers Association in respect of their business interests'.[54] A similar resolution was passed by 23 unions in Bulawayo.[55]

As criticism mounted, the ZCTU leadership attempted to defend itself by recourse to an attack on ZAPU officials in the Ministry of Labour at a time when the state was carrying out the Gukurahundi massacres in Matabeleland. In a letter to the Prime Minster, the ZCTU leadership made the following accusations:

> The staff situation in the Ministry of Labour, Manpower Planning
> and Social Welfare is such that no matter how much we re-structure

---

53 GOZ ZCTU File 18/3/10 ZCTU Report: Week ending 27 October 1984, ZCTU Administrator.

54 GOZ ZCTU File 18/3/10 Petition to Suspend the ZCTU Corrupt Administration to Minister Shava 28/10/84. The Unions included: National Union of the Clothing Industry; Zimbabwe Explosives and Chemical Workers Union; National Engineering Workers Unions; Zimbabwe Motor Industry Workers Union; United Food and Allied Workers Union; Railway Associated Workers Union; Air Transport Workers Union; General Agricultural and Plantation Workers Union; Radio and Television Workers Union; Zimbabwe Graphical Union.

55 GOZ ZCTU File 18/3/10 Draft Resolution from Meeting of all Trade Unions in Bulawayo, 1/11/84.

ZCTU, progress will be difficult. The PS (Permanent Secretary) is a ZAPU member, the CIRO (Chief Industrial Relations Officer) is ZAPU, and the Mashonaland Industrial Relations Officer is a ZAPU man who was their representative in Moscow.... The Minister has constantly listened to ZAPU members within the ZCTU.[56]

The ZCTU leadership also accused the Bulawayo leadership of helping ZAPU to 'win all the Local Government elections in Matabeleland North and South'.[57] By the mid-1980s, the problems of legitimacy of the ZCTU were immense and pressure was growing for changes in the leadership and structures of the organisation. The members ZANU(PF) had supported to lead the organisation had been greatly discredited, even as its own mass membership was weak in the urban trade union structures as a whole. As ZANU(PF)'s Harare Central District reported, most of its members were domestic servants or unemployed, and the District appealed to the party to provide greater opportunities for employment in the Harare City Council.[58]

The challenges of establishing a new industrial relations system

While dealing with the growing challenges of establishing and attempting to control a new labour federation, the state also had to make changes to the industrial relations system and discourse that would increase its legitimacy while not alienating the capitalist structures it was reconciled to working with. The first policy response in this direction, in July 1980, was to legislate a minimum wage of $50 per month for domestic and agricultural workers. Workers in urban areas and those covered by industrial agreements would receive $70 per month, rising to $85 per month in January 1981. As Sachikonye points out, this was long overdue and demonstrated the capacity of the state to intervene on behalf of workers while not undermining the 'general prevailing conditions of capitalist production, reproduction and accumulation'.[59] In 1980, the government set up the Riddell Commission of Inquiry into Incomes, Prices and

---

56 GOZ ZCTU File 18/3/10. Letter from A Kupfuma (General Secretary) and A.Makwarimba (President) to Prime Minister 17/10/84.

57 GOZ ZCTU File 18/3/11. Report of ZCTU for the first week ending 9th November 1984 by E.N. Matsika.

58 Voice of Harare Central (2) District, the Organ of Harare Central (2) District ZANU(PF) No 3. March 1987.

59 Sachikonye, 1986, p. 258.

Conditions of Service. Its key terms of reference were to inquire into and make recommendations on the 'conditions of employment and service and the remuneration of and other benefits for all categories of workers', consistent with 'an equitable system of employment' and a 'free and egalitarian society'.[60]

Adding to these interventions the government passed a new Labour Relations Act in 1985 which made significant strides in setting down, amongst other areas, fundamental workers' rights and unfair labour practices, the scope and enforcement of collective bargaining agreements, and the functions of workers' committees. However, there were limitations in the legislation regarding severe proscriptions on the right to strike, particularly in what were termed essential services, as well as the vastly extended role of ministerial intervention.[61] As Cheater points out, whereas in the colonial system the decision making authority of civil servants was dominant in the area of industrial relations, in the post-colonial period the more 'fully politicised state system' greatly subordinated this role to state political figures.[62] This often led to disputes over the lack of professionalism of the new public service, which, given the colonial legacy of senior white civil servants still in the public sector, often contained racialised assumptions about the incapacities of the Africanised public sector.

The intensified politicisation of the industrial relations system quickly became apparent. The Ministry of Labour, Manpower Planning and Social Welfare had to deal with ruling party politicians who sought to usurp the functions of both the trade unions and the Industrial Relations Department. In 1986, officials of the Ministry complained about members of parliament who 'disappointingly assume the role of professionals by interfering in things which are specifically meant for civil servants'.[63] This particular complaint concerned an MP,

> ...who dares to go about without any reference to the Labour
> Relations Department, calls Workers Committees, addresses
> grievances, writes letters to management giving directives as to what

---

60 Report of the Commission of Inquiry into Incomes, Prices and Conditions of Service 1981, p. 1.
61 Sachikonye, 1986, pp. 260-261.
62 Cheater, 1992, pp. 9-10.
63 GOZ Ministry of Labour, Manpower Planning and Social Welfare, Monthly Report of the Acting Regional Hearing Officer Manicaland Region for the Month Ending 31 August 1986.

they must do purporting to be using the country labour legislation.[64]

Trade unionists were also accused of the 'use of Zanu PF membership in self-defence'[65] when they had to account for their activities, and of interfering in the domestic affairs of commerce and industry by giving out 'arbitrary and erroneous information'.[66] In relatively non-unionised sectors such as agriculture and domestic work, 'trade union entrepreneurs' also used the role of the state in the ZCTU to push their agendas, in the process impersonating Industrial Relations Officers and threatening employers with deportation,[67] and also 'forcing employers and employees alike to pay fees'.[68] To support their often corrupt fee collection schemes these individuals accused senior civil servants from the colonial period of being a 'stumbling block' because of their 'anti-African Unionist attitude'.[69]

Some of the trade union leaders thus used the new government's black advancement discourse and programme to push their more particular agendas,[70] while senior civil servants, both from the Rhodesian period and newly appointed black civil servants, insisted on the need for professionalism and correct procedures. While many former Rhodesian civil servants may have tried to conceal their racialised conceptions of labour issues beneath the language of professionalism, it would be too easy to dismiss their professional concerns as racist behaviour, as many key black senior officials in the post-1980 labour Ministry shared their concerns. As Alexander's work shows, the values of many nationalists were shaped by the unfulfilled hopes of the Federation period and while they criticised black civil servants of this era for their 'subservience',

---

64 Ibid.

65 GOZ Ministry of Labour and Social Welfare, Report of the Department of Industrial Relations-IT Chigwedere Chief Industrial Relations Officer, 6 May 1982.

66 GOZ, Ministry of Labour and Social Welfare Annual Report of the RIRO, Victoria Region for the year ending December 1980-H.D.H. Van Verden, Regional Industrial Relations Officer.

67 GOZ Ministry of Labour and Social Welfare, Annual Report of the Acting RIRO, Manicaland Region for the year 1982.

68 Ibid.

69 GOZ ZCTU File 18/3/10 October 1981-March 1983, Letter from Carlton Moyo, Admin Secretary ZCTU TO Secretary for Labour, 15/10/82.

70 This needs to be distinguished from the more genuine concerns of many sectoral trade unionists who for much of the 1980s criticised the hiring of expatriate workers by white employers and viewed this as a blockage to black advancement in the private sector. See Ndakaripa, 2017, chapter 4.

'they also recognised and valued both their aspirations and their utility; their professional skills would be needed to construct a new state in the future'.[71] That sense of professionalism certainly carried over into debates about the public sector in the post-colonial period.

The problems of state capacity presented the new state with several challenges in its attempts to build a more legitimate industrial relations structure. Firstly, the loss of experienced staff was a cause of concern. In 1980, the Mashonaland region reported 'numerous staff changes during the year with an exodus of senior and experienced staff',[72] while in Matabeleland it was also noted that the first year of independence 'has been a year of resignations'.[73] Secondly, operational problems such as transport shortages, were a regular complaint. In Manicaland it was noted that that the Department of Labour 'operates without a single vehicle', and that a department engaged in arbitration between workers and employers was 'forced to be begging for transport assistance' from employers.[74] In Matabeleland it was reported that it was a 'matter of concern' that the office received urgent cases which could not be attended to 'promptly because of lack of transport'.[75] Thirdly, problems arose from the inadequate training of new labour officers on 'how they should interpret and implement the labour regulations'.[76]

The result of these capacity constraints was that the actual reach of the state in labour issues was, at the very least, seriously limited, which opened up spaces for a series of compromises and evasions, where both workers and employers could push their own initiatives, but with workers usually in the weaker position. This problematic was aptly captured in the following narrative:

---

71 Alexander, 2017, p. 6.
72 GOZ Ministry of Labour and Social Welfare, Report of the RIRO, Mashonaland for the year 1980.
73 GOZ Ministry of Labour and Social Welfare, Report of the RIRO, Matabeleland for the year ended 1980.
74 GOZ Ministry of Labour Manpower Planning and Development, Regional Hearing Officer Report, Manicaland, for the Month ending 31 October 1986, F.M. Dhlamini.
75 GOZ Ministry of Labour, Manpower Planning and Social Welfare, Monthly Report of the Principal Labour Relations Officer Matabeleland for the Month of September 1986.
76 GOZ Ministry of Labour, Manpower Planning and Social Welfare, Monthly Report of the Acting Provincial Labour Relations Officer, Mashonaland for the Month ending 30 April 1986.

It is becoming apparent that the minimum wage in all its forms is not operative amongst the African community. It has become the rule rather than the exception for both parties in the 'employment' relationship to come to a mutual agreement on wages much less than the stipulated minimum. The question is should this office recognise this type of arrangement.[77]

This evasion of the minimum wage regulations was particularly apparent in the least unionised sectors such as domestic work and agriculture. In the latter, so lucidly set out in Rutherford's conceptualisation of 'domestic government', one employer was reported to the labour ministry for using abusive language and assault on workers while carrying a 'revolver on his hip and a whip'.[78] However, the issue of non-payment and underpayment of wages was a broader problem covering other sectors as well.[79]

In the face of these challenges state officials sought to develop a discursive and disciplinary structure that combined an appeal to a practice of reconciliation to mimic the officially espoused political project at national level, an appeal to the patriotism of new labour officers, and a developmentalist reminder of the imperatives of labour productivity. In the first appeal, notably from a civil servant from the Rhodesian era, labour officials called on management to 'exercise care and communication ... to avoid endless costly labour difficulties', and to 'engage in constructive dialogue, so that the average worker can see that he is no longer treated as a second class citizen in industry'.[80] In a call for patience and dedication, labour officers were told that leaving the department would be 'the most cowardly solution' and that they should 'right the wrong wherever you find it and prove yourself a patriot'.[81] The third part of this assemblage was driven by an appeal to workers' committees to 'strive very hard to educate the workers making them aware of their responsibilities and obligations

---

77 GOZ Ministry of Labour, Manpower Planning and Social Welfare, Monthly Report for the Principal Labour Relations Officer, Matabeleland, for the Month of September 1986.

78 GOZ Ministry of Labour, Manpower Planning and Social Welfare, Monthly Report for the Principal Labour Relations Officer for the Month of September, 1986.

79 Ibid.

80 GOZ, Ministry of Labour and Social Welfare, Report of the RIRO, Mashonaland, for the Year 1980, W. Gillies.

81 GOZ Ministry of Labour, Manpower Planning and Social Welfare, Monthly Report of the Regional Hearing Officer, Manicaland Region for the Month ending 31st October 1986.

particularly in relation to production levels'.[82] In one case involving a clothing company in which a work stoppage resulted in the disruption of export orders, the Ministry of Labour were involved in an investigation of the stoppage and threatened that 'whoever will be found to have instigated the labour unrest will be brought to justice'.[83]

The ZCTU – Breaking with the state

By the mid-1980s it was clear, as Schiphorst and others have written, that ZANU(PF)'s central objective was political control of the labour movement. The strategy deployed to bring this about combined the marginalisation of both white trade unionists and those associated with ZAPU.[84] However, this had resulted in the creation of a corrupt labour centre which had little or no credibility within the trade union movement, and which in the end proved an embarrassment to the state itself. Moreover, the creation of the ZCTU, in addition to the broader problems of state capacity and the difficulties of creating a sustainable discourse around state-capital-labour relations, meant that there was little basis for a legitimising corporatist structure. The result was what I have called a 'partial governmentality' that provided the ground for the emergence of an increasingly critical labour centre that sought greater autonomy from the patronising subterfuge of the state.

As a result of the lack of the legitimacy of the early ZCTU, resulting from the manner of its creation and the corruption that ensued, funding was a problem from its inception. Early financial reports noted that the ZCTU 'had no income from unions but was able to get money from interested International Organisations'. This support included furniture for the head office from the Friedrich-Ebert-Stiftung; a donation of US$3,600 from the ICFTU for rent; US$17,640 from the African American Labour Centre; and US$5,000 for the Congress and US$8,100 for education seminars from the ICFTU.[85] By 1983 funding from the ICFTU was frozen because

---

82 GOZ Ministry of Labour, Manpower Planning and Social Welfare, Monthly Report of the Acting Regional Hearing Officer Manicaland Region for the Month ending 31 August 1986.

83 GOZ Ministry of Labour, Manpower Planning and Social Welfare, Monthly Report for the Acting Principal Labour Relations Officer Mashonaland Region for the Month of December 1986.

84 Schiphorst, 2001, p. 87.

85 GOZ Ministry oF Labour and Social Welfare, ZCTU File 18/3/10, October 1981–1983.

the ZCTU could not provide the receipts for the money spent,[86] and the ZCTU treasurer reported in 1983 that the financial position 'is continuing to go down every month and the centre cannot operate at all'.[87] With union membership estimated, optimistically, anywhere between 200,000 in 1981 (including registered, unregistered and public sector members)[88] and 219,015 in 1984,[89] the struggling labour centre was desperate for the state 'to make it compulsory for the employer to deduct and remit such funds to the ZCTU directly'.[90]

In the face of these intensifying problems of corruption and financial sustainability calls from concerned and established trade unions for a new congress to change the ZCTU leadership intensified, and by late 1984 a new Minister of Labour made an urgent call for the congress. In March 1985, an interim committee comprising 12 trade unionists and led by the President of the Associated Mineworkers Unions, Jeffrey Mutandare, was established, which together with the administrator appointed by the ministry oversaw the preparations for the second congress in 1985. As a prelude to that congress key members of the first leadership of the ZCTU, including Soko, Makwarimba, Kupfuma and Mashavira, were suspended.[91] Despite advice from the administrator that the state should think very seriously about appointing a Secretary General 'who is a member of the Zanu PF Central Committee who is flexible and approachable',[92] the Minister was insistent that the government should refrain from further interference,[93] probably in the knowledge that loyalty to the ruling party would continue without too much intervention. Nevertheless, it was clear that by the mid-1980s state attempts to construct a labour centre that was suitable to its requirements resulted in increasing problems not only for the labour movement but for the state itself.

---

86 Minutes of the Meeting with ZCTU delegation called by the Acting Chief Industrial Relations Officer, 12 July 1983.

87 ZCTU, The General Treasurer's Report to the National Executive and General Council Members, 12/02/83, Mhungu.

88 Report of the Commission of Inquiry into Incomes, Prices and Conditions of Service, 1981, p. 260.

89 National Trade Union Survey 1984 pp. 81-82.

90 GOZ Ministry of Labour and Social Welfare, ZCTU File, 18/3/10 March 1983-November 1984.

91 ZCTU General Council Meeting, 23/03/85.

92 GOZ File 18/03-October 1984-05/02/1986: Memo from Matsika to Minister on ZCTU 08/02/85, on the appointment of a Secretary General.

93 Schiphorst, 2001, p. 73.

A new ZCTU executive was appointed in July 1985 with Jeffrey Mutandare as its President. Notwithstanding the removal of the key figures who had been responsible for corruption, the new executive quickly reaffirmed its subordination to the ruling party. In August 1985 Mutandare made the following pledge to the Labour Minister, Frederick Shava:

> May I assure you that the labour movement as a whole is deeply appreciative of the Party and Government's consistent and sympathetic approach to the aspirations and interests of workers. The ZCTU therefore believes that the conditions are propitious for enhanced and stronger relations between itself and the party.[94]

By 1988, despite growing criticism of state policy by the ZCTU, Schiphorst correctly observes that ZANU(PF) felt that it had 'sufficiently neutralised the ZCTU once and for all as a political factor'.[95]

The continuing problems around administration and political subordination of the ZCTU led to the election of a new leadership in 1998. With Morgan Tsvangirai as Secretary General, supported later by Gibson Sibanda, the new leadership committed itself to supporting and providing services to affiliate unions.[96] The subsequent campaigns of the ZCTU addressed a range of issues, including wider tripartite consultations on the changes in the Labour Relations Act, pressure to distance the state from the collective bargaining process, demands for more clarity and commitment from the government around its purported socialist programme, and a growing critique of the government's move towards economic liberalisation. The new ZCTU leadership also linked its campaigns around the economy to demands for greater democratisation in the polity.

Thus the ZCTU added its voice to opposition against a one-party state, severely criticised the growing corruption in the party/state and challenged the continuing use of the State of Emergency to deal with dissent. By the end of the first decade of independence the labour movement had moved from being a subordinate appendage of the ruling party to becoming a more critical force, in alliance with other forces in civil society such as the student body.[97] As a result of this move the ZCTU leadership also

---

94 GOZ File 18/3/10: October 1984 to 06-02-86: Letter from J.Mutandare (President) ZCTU to Minister Shava 06/08/85.

95 Schiphorst, 2001, p. 88.

96 Sachikonye, 2001, p. 98.

97 Raftopoulos, 2001, p. 7.

experienced the repressive force of the state, in the form of detention of and violence.

PART TWO: Trade unions in the period of liberalisation[98]

After the government launched the Economic Structural Adjustment Programme (ESAP) in 1991 the ZCTU led the critique of the move towards economic liberalisation.[99] By the mid-1990s there were clear indications of the negative effects of liberalisation on workers. Real wages declined from an index of 122 in 1982 to 67 in 1994 rising to 888 in 1997. The share of wages in the gross national income fell from 54 per cent in 1987 to 39 per cent in 1997, while that of profits increased from 47 per cent to 63 per cent. Employment growth declined from an annual average of 2.4 per cent in the period 1985-1990 to 1.55 per cent in 1991-1997, and a study carried by the government in 1995 found that 61 per cent of Zimbabwean households were living in poverty.[100]

The challenges of sustaining autonomy

As the ZCTU struggled to confront these deteriorating conditions it had to address issues of capacity and financial sustainability. In dealing with these challenges it faced similar problems to other African union centres that had to balance the tensions between autonomy and political engagement while setting out an alternative vision of social transformation.[101] Very soon into the liberalisation period the ZCTU had its first confrontation with the state over changes in labour legislation. In 1992 the government introduced the Labour Relations Amendment Act that set out to deregulate labour relations in line with ESAP. The Act placed constraints on union power at the shop floor, while at the same time ensuring that the Ministry of Labour retained wide-ranging powers over collective bargaining and the industrial relations process. It did not apply to public servants, who were governed by the Public Services Act.

The control of trade unions was further increased by the Law and Order Maintenance Act, the Miscellaneous Offences Act and the Unlawful Organisations Act.[102] In response to the 1992 Amendment, the ZCTU organised an anti-ESAP demonstration that was banned and

---

98   This section draws from Raftopoulos (forthcoming 2019).
99   Yeros, 2013a, p. 221.
100   Kanyenze, 2000.
101   Beckman and Sachikonye, 2010, p. 11.
102   Madhuku, 2001, p. 108.

broken up by the police. Six unionists were arrested and charged under the Law and Order Maintenance Act. A subsequent High Court judgment acquitted the six and affirmed their constitutional right to public assembly. While affirming the importance of the role of the labour movement in the democratic struggle, this event raised the concerns of the ruling party about the political ambition of the ZCTU. Chiluba's rise to power in Zambia through the labour movement loomed large in the thinking of ZANU(PF).[103]

In its struggles to develop its capacity and financial viability, and to maintain a momentum of struggle against both economic liberalisation and state repression, the ZCTU faced great challenges. In terms of financial viability, union subscriptions showed a persistent decline in 1997: Z$114,000 in January, Z$95,000 in February, Z$67,000 in March, Z$30,000 in April and Z$13,000 in May.[104] By the end of 1998 the figure for outstanding union subscriptions had reached Z$1,135,635.[105] Given this decline, the ZCTU came to rely heavily on donor assistance,[106] which came to represent 75 per cent of its income by 1997.[107] The ZCTU recognised this dependency as an 'unhealthy situation' and that it threatened the independence of the organisation.[108] Nevertheless, in the years that followed, the ZCTU leadership also acknowledged that the movement 'managed to pull through due to the solidarity' of cooperating partners.[109]

The ZCTU faced several other problems in the late 1990s, including the need to strengthen effective coordination and communication between the central body and its affiliates; a lack of openness, trust and transparency within the leadership; weakness of capacity and shop floor presence of affiliate unions; and the absence of coordinated action with other civic organisations.[110] Additionally, ZANU(PF) became increasingly worried by the ZCTU's move towards greater autonomy, and responded

---

103 Raftopoulos, 2001, p. 8; Larmer, 2011.
104 ZCTU, Minutes of the Emergency General Council Meeting, New Ambassador Hotel, Harare, 7 June 1997.
105 ZCTU Minutes of the General Council Meeting, Matopos, 10 April 1999.
106 Yeros, 2013a.
107 ZCTU Financial Report, 1997.
108 ZCTU Financial Report, 1997.
109 ZCTU Treasurer's Report 2000-2005 to the 6th General Council Conference, 19-20 May 2006.
110 ZCTU Minutes of the Emergency Council Meeting, Harare, 16 December 1997.

by sponsoring the establishment of an alternative labour centre that would once again place a labour movement under its control. In 1998, the Zimbabwe Federation of Trade Unions (ZFTU) was established. With the support of the state and ruling party structures it worked to establish its presence within factories, while also sponsoring splinter unions. In the years that followed, this splintering strategy affected many sectors: engineering; catering; leather; clothing; commercial industry; agriculture; sugar plantations, and construction.[111] It is of interest that in the current narrative of the ZFTU, as it faces similar state challenges as the ZCTU, it regards its origins as having been located in the 'ideological dissection' of the path of ZANU(PF). In this construction the alternative federation was set up because its founders were 'critical of the state'. [112]

The ZCTU was aware that its own and its affiliates' organisational weaknesses, and their inability to deal with the grievances of members, were contributing to the splintering process.[113] These developments were unfolding within a broader structural crisis in the economy, as the decline in formal sector employment was accompanied by an increase in the number of informal sector workers from tens of thousands in the 1980s to 1.6 million (27 per cent of the labour force) by the early 1990s,[114] reaching a majority share by the 2000s. These structural changes took their toll on the membership figures of the ZCTU, which fell from around 200,000 – representing 16 per cent of the 1.2 million formal sector workers – in 1990, to 165,000 – 12 per cent of the formal labour force – in 2000.[115]

Towards political opposition

A central motivation in the ZCTU's turn to political opposition was the lack of progress on tripartite consultations. The National Economic Consultative Forum (NECF), an initiative recommended by the ZCTU in the mid-1990s, failed to establish any substantive level of consultation. By 1997 the ZCTU complained about the ways in which the composition of the forum had moved from organisational to individual representation,

---

111 ZCTU Organising Department Annual Report for the year ended 2004, November 2004.
112 Interview with the Secretary General of the ZFTU, Mr. Shamuyarira, Harare, 19 April 2017.
113 ZCTU Minutes of the General Council Meeting, Harare, 12 February 2000.
114 FES/LEDRIZ, Strategies for Transitioning from the Informal Economy to the Formalisation in Zimbabwe, Harare, 2015.
115 Kanyenze and Chiripanhuru, 2001, p. 33.

resulting in the weakening of consultative traction.[116] In addition to the frustration at working conditions in the private sector there was also growing dissent over the plight of public sector workers.

The public sector strike in 1996 sent shock waves through the state and was, as Chagonda notes, 'a rehearsal for the upcoming economic struggle'.[117] The strike was the result of low wages and benefits, declining public expenditure on services, poor working conditions and unfair labour practices.[118] While, as Saunders points out,[119] the strike provided an opportunity for the ZCTU and public sector workers to collaborate and to push for the harmonisation of the labour legislation to cover both sectors, it also exemplified the continued challenges of consultation in the labour centre. In an attempt to build on the momentum of the public sector strike, the ZCTU called for a general strike in November 1996. The result was a disappointing level of mobilisation. General Council members questioned the leadership for not giving unions sufficient time and notice 'to organise their members for the strike instead of sending a circular and leaflets into the industry avoiding the National Unions which constitute the ZCTU'.[120]

The outcomes of the general strike in December 1997 and the stayaway in March 1998 over the new taxes and levies introduced to pay for the war veteran pensions and gratuities, proved to be much more successful. Learning from the failure in 1996, the ZCTU improved communication with its affiliates. By August 1998, when the ZCTU leadership were reporting back to their membership on the lack of progress on its demands to the state president for changes to the policy on levies and tax, most members called for another stayway.[121] The process was carried out in the context of the ZCTU's efforts since the mid-1990s to present an alternative to the government's neoliberal economic policies.[122] This policy framework sought to oppose the neoliberal model with 'another that stressed a strong developmental role for the state and equity'.[123] Attempts to develop a

---

116 ZCTU Minutes of the General Council Meeting, Matopos, 6 December 1997.
117 Chagonda, 2011, p. 102.
118 Saunders, 2001, pp. 151-2.
119 Ibid., p. 153.
120 ZCTU Minutes of the Emergency General Council Meeting, Masvingo, 16 November 1996.
121 ZCTU Minutes of the Special General Council Meeting, Harare, 29 August 1998.
122 ZCTU, *Beyond ESAP,* Harare, 1996
123 Matombo and Sachikonye, 2010, p. 113.

framework of consultation with the state and employers through the NECF and later the Tripartite National Forum (TNF) proved largely fruitless. As Mugure writes, from the mid-1990s neither the state nor employers were 'serious about social dialogue given their predisposition towards negotiating in bad faith'.[124] Thus by the late 1990s 'strikes became a regular feature of the industrial relations scene' with 231 being recorded in 1997 alone.[125] The ZCTU reached out more to other groupings in the civic movement and crafted a message that began to articulate a connection between labour questions and more national democratic issues. In 1997, it played a central role in the creation of a constitutional movement, the National Constitutional Assembly, that linked the growing concerns of the labour movement on labour rights and economic policy with the need for constitutional reform and the opening up of democratic spaces. This movement led a mass campaign for constitutional reform that resulted in the defeat of the government's attempt to impose a state-led reform process in a referendum in 2000. As McCandless observes in her comprehensive study, the accusation that the NCA was 'donor created' or 'donor-led' were baseless.[126] The organisation had a strong local constituency and donors supported a nationally formulated agenda and programme of action. This dynamic was similar to the support received by the ZCTU. While the strong reliance on donor support was a problem for the ZCTU, and was clearly recognised as such, none of its activities, including the ongoing critique of the structural adjustment programme, could have been realised without this support.

As the momentum of opposition began to build up in 1997 and the labour movement started to build a broader alliance with other civic organisations, it was jolted by ZANU(PF)'s quick move to stop any possible linkage between the war veterans' demands and those of the labour movement. Since the 1980s the ruling party had been concerned about the possible threats of an autonomous labour movement and the potential for an opposition politics. This concern grew after the coming to power of Frederick Chiluba in Zambia in 1991 on the back of the Zambian trade union movement and an 'uneasy.... coalition of social forces that opposed UNIP for a variety of reasons'.[127] In 1997, the ZCTU Secretary

---

124 Mugure, 2008, p. 45.
125 Kanyenze, Kondo, Chitambara and Martens, 2011, p. 266.
126 McCandless, 2011, p. 69.
127 Larmer, 2011, p. 250.

General, Morgan Tsvangirai, met with the war veterans' leader, Chenjerai Hunzvi. The two agreed that the government should not levy workers to pay war veterans' compensation and that other policy options should be pursued. There were no further meetings between the two, as Mugabe moved quickly to cement his relations with the veterans.[128] This move was not surprising given the close relations between the ruling party and the veterans. As Kriger has chronicled, just as in the first years of independence ZANU(PF) and the ZANLA war veterans collaborated to build power in the military, bureaucracy and urban workforce, so in the post-2000 period this collaboration, despite the sometimes different agendas of the veterans, was deployed against the forces of opposition including the trade unions.[129]

The events of 1997 opened up further discussion on the future political commitments of the ZCTU. Many in the leadership made the call for 'genuine trade unionists with no political interests'. While some suggested that labour 'pronounce their political interest to government', and advocated for labour representation in parliament, the majority stated that 'they had no political interests and that the moment labour enters the political arena the trade union agenda will be compromised'.[130] From this position, the ZCTU called for the land to be 'distributed to the landless (the peasants, unemployed and the workers)' as the main objective of the liberation struggle, and criticised the amassing of land by senior government officials.[131] It stressed the need take up the land issue for 'economic empowerment' reasons, rather than political ones.[132]

After food riots took place in January 1998 against a steep rise in basic food prices, the labour leadership contemplated whether these eruptions represented 'short term anger at the people's deteriorating economic situation or a return to more profound resistance to changing economic and political uncertainty'.[133] From this position the movement asserted that the fundamental issue confronting Zimbabwe was 'how the rules of democratic governance were set' given the increasing centralisation

128 Raftopoulos, 2001, p. 12.
129 Kriger, 2003.
130 ZCTU Minutes of the Emergency General Council Meeting, Harare, 16 December 1997.
131 Ibid.
132 ZCTU Minutes of the Special General Council Meeting, Harare, 29 August 1998.
133 ZCTU Minutes of the Special General Council Meeting, Harare, 20 January, 1998.

of political and economic decision making and the ineffectiveness of parliament. From its standpoint, people from all walks of life were 'crying out for salvation to the labour movement' and there was therefore a need to 'seriously consider going beyond the worker and integrating the ordinary people.' The strategy to follow would then be to involve the ZCTU in 'all levels of change at the same time' with workers linking their particular demands with community issues and networking with other civic groups.[134] This analysis echoed the conceptualisation around 'social movement unionism' developed in South Africa in the 1980s,[135] through which unions connected their shop-floor struggles to those in the townships.

The ZCTU then began to consider the move to national political action, and the logic of this progression was clearly explained by Morgan Tsvangirai two years after he entered opposition politics:

> The politics of the stomach cannot be separated from the politics of the state. These promises cannot be achieved without the state. We understood in the 1990's that we could not achieve our wage, price and cost of living goals by restricting ourselves to industrial relations, and had to engage at national level. We protected our right to do this even as the head of state was telling us to go back to our schoolrooms and train-cabooses. Neither can we deal with these national issues without state authority to make the change. And because of the extremely skewed nature of our constitution in Zimbabwe, this means presidential power.[136]

In pursuit of this objective, the ZCTU coordinated a National Working People's Convention in February 1999, the purpose of which was to build a consensus around the central challenges facing Zimbabweans and agree on a way forward. The gathering brought together people from urban, peri-urban, and rural areas representing trade unions, women's organisations, professional bodies, development organisations, churches, human rights organisations, representatives from the informal sector, communal farmers, industry, the unemployed and the student movement. In its deliberations the convention identified the economic and political problems facing the

---

134 ZCTU Minutes of the Special General Council Meeting, Harare, 29 August 1998.
135 Webster, 1988.
136 MDC President's Speech to the ZCTU Congress, Masvingo, 24-25 February 2001.

country and made several recommendations, including the need for a basic needs strategy on food security; shelter, clean water, health and education; the equitable distribution of resources; and constitutional reform. At a strategic level the movement resolved to build consensus on the need to establish a 'vigorous and democratic movement for change'.[137]

Following the February Convention another gathering was held in May 1999 which gave the ZCTU a mandate to form a political party. At a special congress of the labour movement in August of that year, the ZCTU voted to facilitate the process, and the Movement for Democratic Change (MDC) was launched in September 1999. In the aftermath of the 2000 constitutional referendum, which the ruling party lost, and the MDC's impressive results in the 2000 election, state violence fell heavily on MDC and civic structures. In this process trade unions were greatly affected by the repressive actions of the state because, as Matombo and Sachikonye point out, 'they were viewed as bedfellows of the MDC and were accused of having provided infrastructure and other forms of support for it'.[138] This state violence intensified against the Zimbabwean opposition and citizenry in the context of the Fast Track Land Reform programme in the 2000s.

From the inception of this political process there were voices in the leadership that were concerned about the central role of the ZCTU in the formation of the MDC. The issues of concern included finding a balance between maintaining a focus on collective bargaining questions and a national political presence,[139] the contractual benefits that were due to trade union leaders who had gone into politics,[140] and a great deal of 'tension' and 'fissures' in the movement before the congress that brought in the leadership that followed the exit of Tsvangirai and some of his colleagues into the MDC. This resulted in a 'no proper handover-takeover' process between the old and new leaderships.[141] In the 2000s the voices of concern grew louder over the lack of unity because of divided political affiliation between the MDC and ZANU(PF),[142] which

137 ZCTU Report of the National Working People's Convention, Harare, 1999.
138 Matombo and Sachikonye, 2010, p. 117.
139 ZCTU Report of the Special General Council Meeting, 30 January 1998; Minutes of the General Council Meeting, Harare, 22 April 1998.
140 ZCTU Minutes of the General Council Meeting, 28 July 2000.
141 ZCTU General Council Report to the 6th Ordinary Conference, Harare, 19-20 May 2006.
142 ZCTU Organising Department Annual Report for the year ended 2004, November 2004.

in turn affected the very slow progress in the amalgamation of splinter unions, and the need to maintain the 'independence' of the trade unions.[143]

Conclusion

The first twenty years of post-colonial politics marked decisive shifts for the labour movement, which transformed itself from a subservient tool of the ruling party to the most formidable presence in civil society. From the late 1980s the ZCTU and its affiliates led the fight for broader and deeper democratisation in a series of struggles that ranged from more substantive and wide-ranging labour legislation and a more labour responsive industrial relations system, to constitutional reform that galvanised the nation into a seismic debate on the nature of the post-colonial state in Zimbabwe. In a further move, the ZCTU took the lead in the formation of a formidable opposition party that would change the terrain of Zimbabwean politics and challenge the central narratives of the party of liberation around the question of what it meant to be Zimbabwean. In the process, it was confronted with new challenges around its structures, forms of accountability, and relations to international partners. It also had to face the limits of certain forms of democratic struggle when confronted by the disruptions of a redistributive land programme that constructed the narratives of the labour movement as an attack on national sovereignty in the service of foreign powers. More will be said about these issues in the next chapter.

For the ruling party and state, questions around labour proved to be a persistent problem. The historical tensions between nationalist parties and trade unions persisted and were further exacerbated in the first two decades of independence. Protagonists in the largely rural liberation war for the most part viewed urban resistance as marginal to the liberation struggle, and this condescending attitude remained a central feature of the ruling party's approach to trade unions. By the end of 2000 the stage was set for a longer-term confrontation between the ruling party/state and the labour movement. Moreover, the forthcoming changes in employment structure would present the trade unions with an enormous set of challenges, the massive scale of which they did not foresee.

---

143 ZCTU Minutes of the Silver Jubilee Congress, Harare, 19-20 May 2006.

Chapter 4

Economic Crisis, Structural Change and the Devaluation of Labour

Godfrey Kanyenze

1. Introduction

This chapter explores the structural changes emerging in Zimbabwe since the turn of the new millennium, the deepening economic crisis, culminating in the hyperinflation period of 2007-08. This period was the most turbulent since independence in 1980; no country outside a war situation has gone through such a sustained downturn.

The signing of the Global Political Agreement on 15 September 2008 which led to the Government of National Unity (GNU) in March 2009, the adoption of a multi-currency regime (partial dollarisation) in January 2009 and liberalisation of the pricing regime resulted in a short-term economic rebound over the period 2009-12. This rebound ended with the weakening of international commodity prices beginning in 2013, which coincided with the end of the GNU following the elections of July 2013. The post-2013 period was characterised by a return to fiscal indiscipline and mismanagement. As foreign currency receipts failed to meet demand, a liquidity crisis emerged.

As the succession fights within ZANU(PF) escalated post-GNU, this culminated in the ouster of the long-serving President Mugabe in November 2017 and the ascension of Mnangagwa to the presidency. The chapter traces the direction and pattern of structural change, and the associated devaluation of labour during the period 2000-17.

2. The conceptual framework

Studies on economic development have postulated that economic growth is often associated with far-reaching changes in social and economic structure that are necessary for continued growth. The development process is based on a set of interrelated processes that lead to the transformation of essentially rural, agricultural societies into more urban, industrialised nations. These changes typically involve demand, production, employment and the structure of external trade and capital flows. Of central importance to this transformation are the processes of industrialisation, urbanisation and the sectoral redeployment of labour. These changes define the transformation of a traditional economy into a modern economic system. The pace and character of structural change varies across countries depending on their size, resource endowments, demographic trends, socio-political contexts and, most importantly, the development policies pursued. [1]

As the processes unravel, some broad patterns emerge, beginning with changes in the composition of production as per capita income increases. As countries develop, an emerging feature is the increase in the share of industry in total output and the corresponding decline in the share of primary production (agriculture and mining). While poor countries in Asia and Africa are in the early part of the transformation, in the industrialised countries, where income per capita is highest, the rising share of services is associated with the stabilisation and eventual decline in the share of industry.

The reallocation of jobs across sectors is central to the process of structural change and productivity upgrading. Growth in labour productivity can occur either through changes in labour productivity within sectors, when for instance new machines and innovative technologies that raise output with the same amount of labour input are implemented, or from the reallocation of jobs across sectors ('structural change') as workers move from low to high productivity sectors (e.g. from agriculture to industry or services). Instructively, structural change is central and necessary to sustainable improvements in living standards, allowing more people to benefit from higher productivity levels in more advanced parts of the economy (the structural bonus).

Consequently, structural change is the most effective driver of growth that lowers rates of vulnerable employment in developing economies, in both the short and long run, especially given that vulnerable employment is predominant in the agricultural sector. Hence a growth model based

---

1   Chenery and Syrquin, 1975; Chenery, 1979; ILO, 2013, among others.

on structural change brings down the share of workers in vulnerable employment faster than other growth models in the context of a reallocation of labour away from agriculture into industry and service sectors. In this way, labour markets benefit from structural change.

Before examining the outcomes in terms of the extent to which the expected structural change ('bonus') was experienced in Zimbabwe, it is important to discuss the underlying socio-economic context, governance and performance of the economy during the period under review.

3. Economic meltdown and descent to hyperinflation, 2000-2008

As its hegemony was under threat, the government increasingly resorted to 'authoritarian populism,'[2] jettisoning the neoliberal policies of the 1990s, with the decisive break occurring after it lost the February 2000 referendum on the proposed new constitution. The response to the threat of an emerging opposition movement involved recourse to 'patriotic history',[3] recasting the party's liberation credentials, and connecting the Fast Track Land Reform Programme (FTLRP) to the new struggle against 'white imperialists' and their local supporters, namely, the MDC and its civil society allies. Given the centrality of the land question after February 2000, ZANU(PF)'s campaign in the June 2000 parliamentary elections was based on the slogan 'Land is the Economy; the Economy is Land'.

The language and narrative of the liberation movement was revamped ('patriotic history'), with supporters tagged as 'revolutionaries' while opposition groups were branded as 'sell-outs'.[4] For anyone familiar with the liberation movement, it becomes clear what fate befalls those labeled 'sell-outs'. This narrative and discourse created a polarisation between an anti-authoritarian, urban-based opposition movement and an authoritarian, anti-neoliberal regime with a rural base, riding on its contentious but popular FTLRP. The labour-led dual agenda against both neoliberalism and political authoritarianism of the 1990s became more problematic as these two forces were now separated as the state pursued a polarising 'authoritarian populism'.

2　Mamdani, 2008.
3　Ranger, 2004, argues that 'patriotic history', 'a coherent but complex doctrine', was designed to suggest the continuity of Zimbabwe's revolutionary tradition.
4　Ranger, 2004; Sutcliffe, 2013. President Mugabe made it clear at the December 2000 ZANU(PF) Congress that: 'No self-respecting black man must ever support the MDC because it is just a front for the white man.'

Economic management was increasingly characterised by fire-fighting, knee-jerk measures to deal with emerging crises. To manage its indebtedness, government introduced a policy of suppressed interest rates, which was combined with a fixed exchange rate and a foreign currency surrender requirement on exporters from the start of 2001. While repressing interest rates temporarily subdued interest payments on the national debt, this was at high cost to the economy since, given high levels of inflation, negative real interest rates encouraged over-consumption and speculation. In the context of severe shortages of foreign currency, the parallel exchange rate depreciated rapidly, creating a premium for those able to access foreign currency at the official exchange rate and trade it at the black market value or import luxury items for resale on the domestic market.

Meanwhile, Zimbabwe's international isolation escalated as the country defaulted on its debt repayment obligations in 1999. The IMF declared Zimbabwe ineligible to use its general resources and the country was no longer eligible to borrow from its Poverty and Growth Facility from autumn 2001. This was followed by the issuing of a formal declaration of non-co-operation, with all technical assistance to the country suspended in 2002. Since Zimbabwe defaulted on its debt repayment obligations, total foreign payment arrears rose from $109 million in 1999 to $2.5 billion by end of 2006. As a result of international isolation, foreign direct investment declined from $444.3 million in 1998 to $50 million by 2006. Donor support, including to critical sectors such as health and education, fell to an all-time low.

Box 1: Aborted Attempts at Negotiating a Social Contract[5]

During the period under review, the three social partners signed a Declaration of Intent Towards a Social Contract on 19 January 2001, outlining the obligations of the parties. The parties agreed to negotiate and conclude sector-based protocols.

However, shortly thereafter, the ZCTU withdrew from the negotiations, citing continued violence. The 70 per cent increase in fuel prices of June 2001 prompted the ZCTU to organise a two-day stayaway in July 2001, which resulted in the reconvening of the Tripartite Negotiating Forum (TNF). The parties negotiated and agreed on national minimum wages for agriculture, and industry and commerce in line with the June 2001 Poverty Datum Levels of Z$4,000 and Z$8,900 respectively. The agreement to negotiate viable prices with producers was set aside when the government imposed price controls

---

5   For a useful discussion of social dialogue in Zimbabwe, see Mtapuri, 2006.

on all basic commodities, which, however, created shortages. At the TNF meeting held on 20 August 2001, the social partners agreed to address the totality of the macro-economic problems, including the Country Risk Factor. By November 2001, a technical team from the TNF had consolidated the position papers of the social partners into a draft Kadoma Declaration: Towards a Shared National Economic and Social Vision.[6] However, the Declaration was not signed following misunderstandings between government and labour over continued violence, and especially the facilitation of a rival trade union body, the Zimbabwe Federation of Trade Unions (ZFTU) by government.

As had become the trend, the session of the TNF that commenced in 2003 broke off following a unilateral increase in fuel prices by government in February and April of that year. It was agreed that the TNF would only resume after an ILO workshop to clarify the roles and obligations of stakeholders in negotiating a Social Contract. However, it resumed its meetings around October 2005, but did not yield much. In an attempt to address the deteriorating economy, the social partners adopted three protocols, on Incomes and Pricing Stabilisation; Restoration of Production Viability; and Mobilisation, Pricing and Management of Foreign Currency. These were to be signed on 1 June 2007, but the ZCTU only signed the protocol on Incomes and Pricing Stabilisation, arguing this was the one most relevant to its constituency.

Source: Tripartite Negotiating Forum (TNF) reports.

In an attempt to address the economic decline, the government launched an 18-month Millennium Economic Recovery Programme (MERP) in August 2001, to run concurrently with the Millennium Budget. Of note was the anti-Western narrative, with MERP assessing the unfolding crisis in the context of '…deleterious effects of neo-imperialist machinations aimed at limiting national sovereignty over the redistribution of national assets such as land in favour of indigenous Zimbabweans. These machinations are aimed at frustrating national efforts to transform the Zimbabwean economy so that it cannot reach higher levels of development as well as withstand acts of economic destabilisation'.[7]

The private sector was also seen as a convenient scapegoat, blamed for alleged profiteering and unfair business practices, with business cartels singled out as part of the problem. In the government's view, well-meaning economic reforms were '…exploited by crime syndicates and corrupt businesses who illegally externalise funds, destabilise foreign exchange

6　Country risk was defined as 'a premium that is attached by nationals, residents, foreigners and international bodies on residing in, visiting and/or doing business with a particular country' (p. 2).

7　Zimbabwe Millennium Economic Recovery Programme (MERP), 2001, Harare, p. 13, 1.3.

markets through speculative behaviour which in some cases is foreign inspired in order to frustrate economic stabilisation efforts by government. Amidst these challenges, the Zimbabwean people have proved to be very resilient. The country is united under a visionary leadership'.[8]

As was the case with its predecessor, ZIMPREST,[9] MERP was replaced by an ad hoc approach to economic management. While the target of MERP, as that of the 2000 budget, was to reduce the budget deficit to 3.8 per cent of GDP, the outcome was an unsustainable 23.7 per cent. The official position saw the country as if it was engaged in a war, and therefore took the suspension of the rule of law as a useful tool for dealing with discontent. This view also saw price and other controls as the only way of dealing with the crisis. It is from this template that the President, in a direct rebuttal of his Finance Minister's stance, labelled those calling for the devaluation of the Z$ enemies of the State.[10] Predictably, the outcomes flowing from this framework were a disaster.

In an address to parliament in August 2002, the president announced that government was now implementing a ten-point strategy which was agriculturally-driven. This surprised the then Minister of Finance, Simba Makoni, who insisted that MERP was still operational. The anti-business approach continued as the president declared at the opening of the 52nd ZANU(PF) central committee meeting in Chinhoyi on 11 December 2002, that: 'While many manufacturers and traders want to blame it on production costs, it is clear that the consumer is being ripped off, abused and taken advantage of by avaricious heartless business people, several of whom would want to politicise production processes in sympathy with white landed interest'.[11]

The launch of a 12-month stabilisation programme, the National Economic Revival Programme (NERP), in February 2003, failed to address the deepening crisis. As with MERP, NERP blamed 'sanctions' for the economic woes, while continuing with the detrimental ad hoc interventions. The reliance on price controls was contradicted in the 2003

8   Ibid., p. 14, 1.7.

9   Zimbabwe Programme for Economic and Social Transformation (1996-2000).

10 Officially opening the Third Session of the Fifth Parliament of Zimbabwe on 23 July 2002, President Mugabe publicly attacked his finance minister for proposing the devaluation of the overvalued local currency, insisting that 'Devaluation is sinister and can only be advocated by our saboteurs and enemies of this government ... Devaluation is thus dead!' (see *The Daily News*, 24 July 2002; *Financial Gazette*, 29 May 2009).

11 *The Herald*, 12 December 2002.

national budget statement, which criticised them for undermining business viability and creating shortages and job losses. In a move that contradicted the budget statement, government extended the list of items covered by the price freeze on 15 November 2002 for a period of six months.[12]

The appointment of Gideon Gono as the Governor of the Reserve Bank of Zimbabwe (RBZ) in November 2003 marked a fundamental shift in the conduct of monetary policy in Zimbabwe. The RBZ rapidly departed from the traditional central bank mandate over monetary and exchange rate policy, usurping the fiscal function of the Ministry of Finance through its quasi-fiscal expenditures, and extending its reach to policy and funding decisions of other ministries, particularly agriculture.[13] To fund its quasi-fiscal (off-budget) activities and provide loans to economic actors, the RBZ started printing more money. Since the loans were doled out at derisorily low interest rates under high inflationary conditions, they were effectively subsidies.

Even the context where financial institutions had resorted to non-core business such as purchasing physical assets using short-term funds in order to hedge against rising inflation, Dr. Gono's first monetary policy statement of 18 December 2003 had to deal with such errant activities, resulting in eight banks being shut down. Since all the affected institutions were locally-owned, this stigmatised indigenous financial institutions, especially as people lost their deposits.

The riskiest and boldest policy statement taken was with respect to the exchange rate, which had just been negotiated at Z$628 to the US$ under the TNF. Beginning in January 2004, the RBZ placed the exchange rate on a controlled auction system. The exchange rate depreciated substantially, reflecting the wide gap between the bids and what was available, such that by the end of the system in October 2005, the weighted average auction rate was Z$26,000 to the US$. The exchange rate policy was adjusted during the Third Monetary Policy Statement of 2005 (on 24 October 2005) by being based on an interbank market rate. The major weakness of this system was that it was prone to perpetual depreciation because even if US$1 was traded in a day, the rate adjusted. However, the significant

---

12 During the TNF meetings that commenced in December 2002, government tried unsuccessfully to have stakeholders buy into the idea of a price and wage freeze.

13 Governor Gono justified these measures on the premise of 'Extraordinary Measures for Extraordinary Challenges,' the sub-title to his book (Gono, 2008).

depreciation of the exchange rate not only fuelled inflation, but also failed to curb the parallel market.

Apart from the March 2005 parliamentary elections having not been budgeted for, following the elections a more bloated government was appointed, with the irony that it was presented as a 'development' cabinet. Worse still, the October Senate elections had also not been budgeted for. This created real problems for both the fiscus and monetary policy as the budget deficit, which stood at 4.4 per cent of GDP in 2004 and was projected at 4.6 per cent of GDP in 2005, shot to 23.9 per cent of GDP by July 2006. To finance the deficit, government resorted to printing money and increased domestic borrowing.

Instead of reining in fiscal expenditure and the associated printing of money to reduce inflationary pressures, the government launched Operation Dzikisa Mutengo (Reduce Prices) under the National Incomes and Pricing Commission (NIPC) established in July 2007 to approve adjustments of prices, school fees and levies. Manufacturers, wholesalers and retailers were directed to reduce their prices by half when inflation was running at 4,500 per cent. However, the public euphoria over reduced prices quickly turned into panic as the impact of the operation dawned, with shelves becoming empty, and severe shortages of basics such as cooking oil, soap, sugar and bread. Shortages of fuel created a transport crisis.

The quasi-fiscal operations of the RBZ, which were implemented supposedly to resuscitate production in targeted sectors, exacerbated the distortions in the economy, creating huge opportunities for arbitrage profits. For instance, total subsidies to the agricultural sector amounted to 19 per cent of GDP in 2005, more than its contribution in terms of value added to the economy at 18 per cent of GDP.[14] The consequences of such fiscal imprudence were entirely predictable. Inflation accelerated from 57 per cent in December 1999 to over 1,000 per cent by 2006, an average of 12,563 per cent in 2007 and 231.2 million per cent at the last official count in July 2008. The IMF's 2009 Article IV Consultation Staff Report on Zimbabwe estimated the hyperinflation rate at 489 billion per cent by end of September 2008.[15] The high levels of inflation were caused by excess government expenditure which was financed through the printing

---

14 Zimbabwe Institute, 2007.
15 Steve H. Hanke argues that Zimbabwe's episode of hyperinflation did not end, as the IMF asserts, at the end of September, but roared away for another month and a half, until 14 November 2008, when the hyperinflation blow-off

of money in an economy where real GDP had been declining since 1997.[16]

As a result, the value of the currency moved quickly from millions (six zeros) to billions (nine zeros), trillions (12 zeros), quadrillions (15 zeros), quintillions (18 zeros), and sextillions (21 zeros). For transactional convenience and to address the inability of IT systems to handle the digits, a total of 25 zeroes were administratively removed from the ZW$ during the period August 2006 to February 2009 (three zeros on 1 August 2006, 10 zeros on 1 August 2008, and 12 zeros on 2 February 2009). The slashing of 25 zeros failed to resolve the challenges of transacting under hyperinflationary conditions. In fact, at the time of dollarisation in January 2009, the highest denomination was a one-trillion-dollar note, introduced on 16 January, then worth US$30. In the madness that ensued, the ZSE closed on 17 November 2008 and only reopened on 19 February 2009.

With no resolution in sight, the economic situation deteriorated rapidly in 2008. To keep pace with hyperinflation, the RBZ had to print bank notes in higher denominations, from millions to billions to trillions.[17] The situation was such that as quickly as government printed money to pay shrinking public sector employees, this fed into runaway inflation, rendering their pay worthless. Without any incentive to work in the form of meaningful remuneration, the social sectors, especially health, collapsed. Teachers and nurses left their stations in droves, and clinics had no medicines. It is estimated that out of 100,000 teachers only 55,000 remained, with only around 30 per cent of government health workers reporting for duty. Several hospitals and sections of many others closed down in 2003 for lack of personnel, equipment, medicine and other facilities.

Even though the prevalence of HIV/AIDS amongst 15-49-year-olds declined from a peak of 24.6 per cent in 2003 to 20.1 per cent in 2005, 18.1 per cent by September 2006 and 15.9 per cent by 2008, it was amongst the highest in the world. The situation was exacerbated by the re-emergence of diseases that had been controlled (malaria, TB,

occurred when it peaked at 89.7 sextillion per cent, the second-highest episode of hyperinflation in world history after Hungary, where hyperinflation peaked in July 1946 at a monthly rate of 41.9 quadrillion per cent. See Hanke and Kwok, 2009.

16 Technically, hyperinflation sets in when the increase in the price index is in excess of 50 per cent per month on a continued basis. It can therefore be inferred that Zimbabwe was technically in a hyperinflationary mode from March 2007 to February 2009.
17 In July, a loaf of bread cost nearly 100 billion.

cholera etc.). As a result, life expectancy rates declined steeply from a peak of 61.9 years in 1985 and 1986 to a low of 40.7 years in 2002 and 2003, before rising to 45.8 years by 2008 as a result of the drug roll-out programme. As the health sector collapsed, a cholera epidemic, the largest and deadliest in the history of Zimbabwe, broke out in August 2008. The 2008–09 cholera epidemic resulted in 98,585 reported cases and 4,287 reported deaths. While the initial outbreak was notable for its high cumulative case fatality rate (4.3 per cent) that persisted over a protracted duration of 10 months, a second wave of infections lasted through June 2011.[18]

As a result of the political and economic instability, large numbers of Zimbabweans left the country. South Africa had the largest number of Zimbabwean migrants, estimated to be 2.12 million at the end of 2009, followed by the UK, with an estimated 300–500,000 and Botswana, with an estimated 200–300,000.[19] This level of out-migration adversely affected the country's human capital base, resulting in an acute shortage of skills.

While remittances officially recorded by the Reserve Bank were as little as US$5.2 million in 2006 and US$23.9 million in 2007, these are way below the levels reported by the International Fund for Agricultural Development (IFAD) at US$361 million (7.2 per cent of GDP) in 2007 (excluding transfers in kind).[20] Makina and Kanyenze report that total remittances through both formal and informal channels into Zimbabwe increased from under US$200,000 in 2001 to nearly US$1.4 billion by the end of 2009.[21] It is therefore critical to observe that such huge inflows of remittances provided private social protection for Zimbabweans at home, which was particularly important in the absence of public social security, hedging against complete collapse.

Paradoxically, Zimbabwe's economic decline coincides with a period of strong growth elsewhere in Africa. During the period of persistent negative growth in Zimbabwe (1999-2008), real GDP declined by a cumulative 64.6 per cent, compared to a cumulative gain of 47.6 per cent

---

18 Cuneo et al., 2017. See also 'Zimbabwe: Untreated sewage makes its way into drinking water', IRIN Humanitarian News and Analysis, 23 August 2007.

19 See Makina and Kanyenze, 2010.

20 This is particularly so given that most remittances to Zimbabwe came through informal channels in order to take advantage of the premium offered by the thriving parallel market.

21 Makina and Kanyenze, 2010; Magunha et al., 2009, estimated that US$0.94 billion was sent from the UK alone in 2007.

for Sub-Saharan Africa and 31.5 per cent for the world average during the same period (World Bank data). The steepest decline in GDP was in 2008, at 14.1 per cent. During 2008, owing to unviable prices, production hit a nadir, with industrial capacity utilisation below 10 per cent. Per capita GDP declined from US$720 during 1997-2002 to US$265 by 2008. The country declined from being the second largest economy in SADC at the turn of the millennium to eleventh by 2008. Effectively, therefore, the period 1997-2008 was characterised as a 'lost decade' of development.

Follow-up economic programmes adopted after NERP, such as the Macroeconomic Policy Framework (2005-06) and the National Economic Development Priority Programme (NEDPP) (2007), were ineffectual, effectively shepherding the crisis rather than reversing it. The last programme under this crisis period, the Zimbabwe Economic Development Strategy (ZEDS) (2008) was aborted at formulation.

Realising the untenability of the situation, towards the end of September 2008 the RBZ introduced foreign exchange licensed warehouses and shops (FOLIWARS), on a trial period of 18 months to 31 March 31 2010. Under this programme, a number of retail and wholesale outlets were licensed as foreign currency denominated shops that were allowed to sell goods and services in foreign currency. Unlicensed shops and critical service providers such as commuter transporters had to charge in local currency. Those entities with access to it were allowed to pay their employees in hard currencies, provided they also remitted their taxes in that currency.

Hence, instead of growing the economy and reducing poverty, the macroeconomic policies pursued during this period, including unsustainable budget deficits and unmanageable public debt, the fixing of the exchange rate resulting in volatile and unpredictable exchange-rate systems (multiple exchange rates) and fiscal indiscipline, became the main binding constraints. Clearly, the crisis could no longer be redressed without a comprehensive programme of political and economic reform.

4. Period of the Government of National Unity (GNU): 2009-2013

In the aftermath of the contentious March 2008 national elections and violent presidential run-off of June, it became difficult for ZANU(PF) to form a government, in the context of economic paralysis and the threat of social unrest as soldiers mutinied. In September 2008, President

Mugabe and heads of the MDC formations, Morgan Tsvangirai and Arthur Mutambara, signed the Global Political Agreement (GPA) which led to the establishment of the Government of National Unity (GNU) on 13 February 2009. Mugabe remained as President while Tsvangirai assumed the position of Prime Minister.

To ease pressure on payment systems, promote the smooth flow of transactions, and kill off hyperinflation, the government adopted use of a multi-currency system in the budget statement of 29 January 2009 and the monetary policy of February 2009.[22] The basket of currencies in the system included the Euro, UK Pound Sterling, South African Rand and Botswana Pula, with the US dollar as the anchor currency. The monetary policy statement of January 2009 also ended the RBZ's quasi-fiscal operations and ensured that the Bank reverted to its core mandate of fostering price and financial sector stability. The use of multi-currencies spelt the demise of the Zimbabwean dollar, which had become worthless.[23] However, the new regime resulted in the RBZ losing its monetary and exchange rate policy tools. The measures adopted in the January budget statement, especially the liberalisation of the domestic pricing regime, and price stability, resulted in the rebound of output.

In order to stabilise the economy, the GNU launched the Short-term Emergency Recovery Programme (STERP 1) on 19 March 2009, to run from February to December 2009. To build on STERP 1, it adopted the three-year Macro-Economic Policy and Budget Framework (STERP II), to run for three years to 2012. In an effort to revert back to medium-term planning, the GNU launched the Medium Term Plan (MTP) (2011-15) on 7 July 2011, the target of which was to achieve an average growth rate of 7.1 per cent during the period 2011-2015.

Real GDP rebounded by 5.4 per cent in 2009, 11.4 per cent in 2010, 11.9 per cent in 2011 and 10.6 per cent in 2012; it averaged 9.8 per cent during the period 2009-12, above the MTP target of 7.1 per cent. The economic recovery during the GNU period was buoyed by the mineral sector, riding on high global prices such that it became the leading export

---

22 Government adopted partial dollarisation because full dollarisation would have entailed the RBZ buying the deposits of the banks and financial system as a whole, and converting them to US dollars, which was not feasible without external assistance.

23 However, formal demonetisation of the Zimbabwe dollar was only effected in 2015, with the government choosing to use an unofficial (UN) exchange rate of ZW$35 quadrillion to US$1 to meet the bank balances at conversion.

sector, replacing agriculture. Inflation declined to minus 7.7 per cent in 2009, increased to 3.1 per cent in 2010, 3.5 per cent in 2011 and 3.7 per cent in 2012, against an MTP target of 4-6 per cent indicating a process of price discovery.

Unbudgeted adjustments in the payroll of January and July 2011 saw employment costs rising from 45 per cent of the budget in 2009 and 2010 to 63 per cent. Given the context of cash budgeting, the government had to cut back on total expenditures by 10 per cent from US$4 billion to US$3.64 billion in the July 2012 mid-term budget statement. This reprioritisation meant suppressing key funding for social and physical infrastructure, further compromising the fragile economic situation. Taking into account the adjustment to the civil service salary levels by 5.5 per cent in 2013, the overall wage bill accounted for 75 per cent of total expenditure, leaving under 25 per cent for both operations and the capital budget. No other country in Sub-Saharan Africa deploys such a high level of its expenditures towards employment costs.

While Zimbabwe's domestic debt had been wiped out during the period of hyperinflation, the country had to worry only about its external debt situation. Bizarrely, the exact extent of the external debt had been lost, and yet continued accumulation of external debt payment arrears seriously undermined the country's creditworthiness, and severely compromised its ability to secure new financing from both bilateral and multilateral sources. Furthermore, resolution of the debt overhang was seen as key to normalising relations with the international financial institutions and bilateral creditors. Hence in November 2010, government approved the Zimbabwe Accelerated Arrears Clearance, Debt and Development Strategy (ZAADDS), as a basis for negotiating debt relief and the clearance of arrears.

As part of the ZAADDS programme, the Zimbabwe Aid and Debt Management Office (ZADMO) was established in December 2010 in the Ministry of Finance. ZADMO initiated the validation and reconciliation exercise of the external debt database in 2011 with the assistance of UNCTAD and the Macroeconomic and Financial Management Institute of Eastern and Southern Africa (MEFMI), a process which was completed by 2012. As at 31 December 2012, total external public and publicly guaranteed debt (excluding Reserve Bank and private sector external debt) stood at US$6.077 billion (49 per cent of GDP). The stock of accumulated arrears accounted for US$4.72 billion (78 per cent of total debt stock).

Since Zimbabwe's debt overhang was seen as an impediment to medium-term fiscal and external sustainability, a debt-resolution strategy was therefore critical to resolving external payment arrears and re-engaging the international community to unlock international credit lines. Addressing this issue would require a comprehensive arrears clearance framework underpinned by a strong macro policy framework, the Zimbabwe Accelerated Re-engagement Economic Programme (ZAREP).

It was in this context that Zimbabwe entered into a Staff Monitored Programme (SMP) with the IMF in June 2013.[24] The SMP was approved by the IMF in June 2013 for the period April–December 2013 and was later extended to 30 June 2014 at the authorities' request to allow time for them to strengthen their policies and deliver on outstanding commitments. However, a rift emerged in the GNU, with the MDC insisting on following the IMF and World Bank's Heavily Indebted Poor Countries (HIPC) Initiative, while ZANU(PF) preferred securitising the debt using mineral resources. The result was a compromise hybrid approach, ZAADDS, which combined elements from HIPC and securitising mineral resources.

It is therefore not far-fetched to suggest that the opposition MDC lost the trust of its erstwhile allies in the civil society partly as a result of its pursuit of neoliberal policies under the GNU. One clear area of concern was with respect to the promotion of labour market flexibility, which was fiercely resisted by the ZCTU. The 2012 national budget statement presented to parliament by the then Minister of Finance, Tendai Biti, on 24 November 2011 proposed '…a comprehensive review of the labour legislation with a view of making it flexible and consistent with business realities' (paragraph 489, p. 128).

Delivering a solidarity message at the MDC's National Policy Conference in May 2013, ZCTU Secretary General, Japhet Moyo, raised the labour movement's concern with the policies pursued by some of the MDC party's ministers in the GNU. He singled out Minister of Finance Tendai Biti and Energy Minister, Elton Mangoma, declaring: 'How do you defend a minister who says he will not sign a collective bargaining agreement? I am talking about the Energy Minister here…. How do you defend a minister who talks of labour market flexibility which allows employers to fire people willy-nilly?' He warned them: 'Mind your

---

24 An SMP is an informal agreement between country authorities and Fund staff to monitor the implementation of the authorities' economic programme and does not entail financial assistance or endorsement by the IMF Executive Board.

language, you are not yet in power. It is the poor who vote, not investors. If you call yourself social democrats let that be reflected in the policies'.[25]

A major achievement of the GNU was the crafting of a new constitution, spearheaded by the Constitution Parliamentary Select Committee (COPAC) comprising the three political parties represented in parliament. COPAC issued the finalised draft constitution on 31 January 2013, and it was approved on 16 March 2013 in a nationwide referendum with 94.5 per cent of those who voted affirming. This new constitution, generally seen as progressive, has a strong Bill of Rights.

With the five-year coalition parliament expiring on 29 June, parliamentary and presidential elections were scheduled to follow within 90 days of that date. President Mugabe and his allies wanted the polls to go ahead as scheduled, while the opposition parties insisted on reforms first. They also observed that the country was not ready for polls, which required a budget of $130 million. In a twist of events, the Centre for Elections and Democracy in Southern Africa (CEDSA), led by Jealousy Mawarire, filed an urgent Supreme Court application in May 2013 seeking an order compelling President Mugabe to immediately proclaim election dates. The Constitutional Court ruled that President Mugabe had violated Mawarire's rights as a voter by not proclaiming an election date and ordered him to set a date 'as soon as possible' and that elections be held no later than 31 July 2013. This ruling helped Mugabe circumvent attempts by SADC to postpone the elections to allow for reforms as per the GPA.[26]

At midnight on 29 June 2013, the seventh parliament of Zimbabwe was dissolved, paving way for elections scheduled for 31 July. In elections held with little violence, ZANU(PF) resoundingly won and formed a new government. Analysts highlighted some key factors that led to the

---

25 'ZCTU warns MDC', *The Zimbabwean*, 17 May 2013,
26 For instance, the Report by President Zuma to the SADC Troika Organ on Politics, Defence and Cooperation of 9 March 2013 had made 'extremely urgent' recommendations for security sector reforms to secure confidence in the elections, a position that was reaffirmed at the SADC special meeting in June 2013. Earlier, at the launch of ZANU(PF)'s election campaign in July 2013, President Mugabe dismissed Zuma's special envoy on Zimbabwe and the SADC mediator, Lindiwe Zulu, who had pushed vigorously for reforms before elections, as a 'street woman.' Mocking his main rival Morgan Tsvangirai, he said, 'Did such a person (Tsvangirai) think that we, as a country, would take heed of this street woman's stupid utterances?' Mugabe went on to threaten to pull out of SADC. The SADC meeting in Maputo of June 2013 could only request Mugabe to petition the Constitutional Court to postpone the elections to allow time for better preparations.

disastrous results for the MDC, such as lack of traction with its social base, and the absence of an ideologically resonant message. It is also argued that in 2013, the MDC campaign was much more complacent than in previous elections, especially in the absence of violence.[27] Of course, the perennial issue of rigging also reared its ugly head, with the MDC alleging the involvement of the Israeli IT company, Nikuv, in voter registration.

5. Economic performance in the post-2013 election period, 2013-17

In the aftermath of the 2013 elections, Jonathan Moyo, then chairman of the policy drafting committee, presented the draft economic blueprint, Zimbabwe Agenda for Sustainable Socio-Economic Transformation (Zim Asset) (October 2013-December 2018) to the party Politburo for adoption on 16 October 2013. Ostensibly guided by the ZANU(PF) manifesto and the president's inauguration speech delivered on 22 August 2013, Zim Asset is a cluster-based, results-oriented agenda. The four strategic clusters identified were: (i) food security and nutrition; (ii) social services and poverty eradication; (iii) infrastructure and utilities; and (iv) value addition and beneficiation.

However, a major challenge in its design was the lack of broad-based consultations during its formulation, as it had been driven in the main by the ruling party. Tellingly, its adoption when its predecessor MTP was still in midstream implies that the latter was abandoned before its expiry in 2015. This apparent lack of policy continuity and coherence reflected the inconsistency and reversals that defined past policies. More importantly, Zim Asset was adopted at a time when the economic rebound of 2009-12 was weakening against deteriorating international commodity prices.

In the absence of stronger policies, recovery of the mining sector proved short-lived, as it was limited to a temporary rebound associated with stronger external demand, but with weak downstream effects on the rest of the economy. Having averaged 10 per cent during the period 2009-2012 (10.6 per cent in 2012), real GDP growth declined to 4.5 per cent in 2013, 3.8 per cent in 2014, 1.5 per cent in 2015, 0.7 per cent in 2016, and a projected 3.7 per cent in 2017, averaging 2.8 per cent for the period 2013-17, against the Zim Asset target of 7.3 per cent.

Figure 1 captures the growth trends in Zimbabwe, Sub-Saharan Africa

---

27 Chan and Gallagher, 2017.

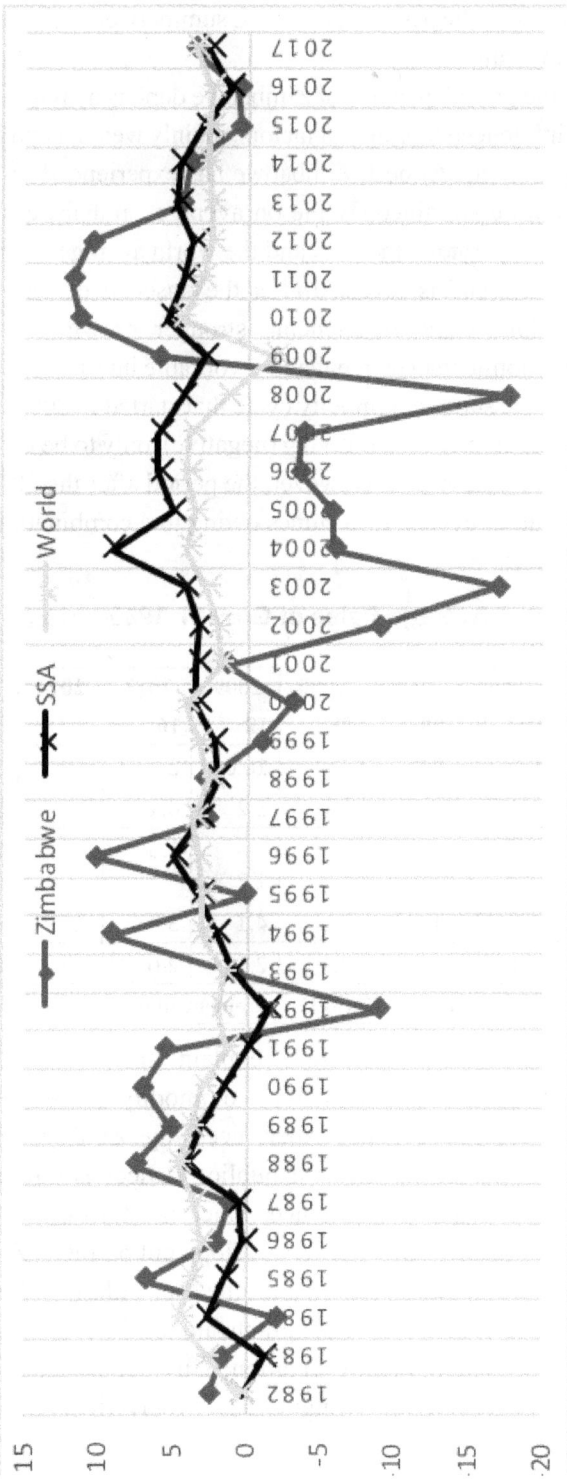

Figure 1: Real GDP growth trends (annual %), 1980-2017

Source: Derived from World Bank data.

and the world over the period 1980-2017, summarised in Table 1 to include regional comparators.

Clearly, the growth pattern for Zimbabwe depicts a highly erratic trend, quite often influenced by external factors, mainly weather and international commodity markets. At best, Zimbabwe has experienced 'growth spurts' that could not be sustained. While on average Zimbabwe outperformed its regional comparators, the SSA and the world average during the 1980s and 1990s, the trend is reversed after the onset of the crisis. Tellingly, as other regions were experiencing stronger growth associated with improved economic management and favourable international commodity prices during the super-commodity cycle that started in 2000, Zimbabwe's performance is atypical and outlying (negative), only to be reversed during the GNU period (2009-13). However, the period after the 2013 election is associated with a reversal of fortunes owing to a combination of external and internal factors.

Table 1: Annual Average Rates of Growth, 1980-2016 (%)

Period	1980-89	1990-99	2000-08	2009-12	2013-16	2014	2015	2016
Zimbabwe	5.2	2.9	-7.1	10.0	2.4	3.9	0.5	0.6
Zambia	1.4	1.3	6.6	8.2	4.1	4.7	2.9	3.6
South Africa	2.2	1.4	4.2	1.7	1.3	1.6	1.3	0.3
SSA	1.7	1.9	5.0	4.1	3.4	4.6	3.0	1.2
World	3.1	2.7	3.1	2.1	2.6	2.7	2.6	2.5
Source: Calculated from World Development Indicators, World Bank.								

While a number of factors explain this anaemic economic performance, including weakening commodity prices, they do not explain the steeper decline experienced by Zimbabwe relative to comparators. The management of public finances is one area that has undermined economic performance. Since the turn of the millennium and the disengagement of external development partners, Zimbabwe has not had the advantage of accessing all the four pillars of the fiscal space diamond that include: (i) external grants/aid, or debt relief; (ii) domestic revenue mobilisation, mainly taxation; (iii) deficit financing through domestic and external borrowing; and (iv) reprioritisation (expenditure switching) and raising efficiency of expenditures.[28]

In the absence of re-engagement with the international community, official aid is off-budget. Zimbabwe has therefore relied on domestic resource mobilisation as the major source of budgetary financing. As such, fiscal space remains severely constrained due to poor performance of revenues against rising recurrent expenditures and a shrinking tax base owing to company closures, retrenchments and the informalisation of the economy. Since tax rates are already high, the focus should be on growing the economy, broadening the tax base and minimising the cost of administration.

While revenues are severely strained and have been progressively declining, expenditures have grown to levels inconsistent with revenue collection. Apart from the impact of company closures and retrenchments, severe leakages have been identified as a challenge. The mid-term 2015 Fiscal Review Statement indicated that the government was losing US$1.8 billion annually through illicit outflows that included smuggling, illegal dealing in gold and precious stones, corruption, fraud, tax evasion, and externalisation. The non-remittance of revenues from the diamond sector to the Treasury was highlighted in the 2016 Budget Statement as '…this is a resource that seems to have not benefitted the generality of our people, notwithstanding that the diamond industry has potential to uplift our population, especially as we fully exploit the diamonds value chain' (paragraph 357, p. 81).

Furthermore, as noted in the 2016 Mid-Term Fiscal Review Statement, '…the scourge of corruption, in both the public and private sectors, has reached alarming proportions and is now stifling growth and revenue mobilisation efforts' (paragraph 1033, p. 240).[29] Curbing corruption was hampered by the culture of impunity, with the Zimbabwe Anti-Corruption Commission (ZACC) being compromised.[30]

---

28 The 'fiscal space diamond' is an analytical tool, a visual representation of the sources, and potential increases or decreases in resources derived through fiscal instruments. Plotted over four axes signifying different key components of revenue, with each axis scaled as a percentage of GDP, the diamond illustrates the aggregate fiscal space available to governments.

29 In the 2016 Transparency International Corruption Perception Index, Zimbabwe ranked 154 out of 176 countries.

30 In July 2016, then Vice President Phelekezela Mphoko reportedly stormed Avondale Police Station in Harare, ordering the release of Zimbabwe National Road Administration (ZINARA) executives arrested for corruption ('Mphoko releases arrested officials', *Zimbabwe Independent*, 16 July 2016. The then

Fragmentation of the public sector posed considerable fiscal challenges, exacerbated by the limited oversight of many public institutions and parastatals. Government guarantees to State Enterprises and Parastatal (SEP) debt, and the contingent liabilities they generate, increasingly strained the public finances. The challenges facing public enterprises and parastatals were well articulated by President Mugabe in his State of the Nation address to the joint sitting of parliament and Senate on 25 August 2015:

> It is very clear that, over many years and due to a variety of reasons, the level of compliance with good corporate governance principles at many, if not most of our parastatals/State enterprises, has fallen to levels well below what might be regarded as even 'minimally acceptable.' The extravagance of the remuneration packages and associated benefits which boards and management have blithely awarded themselves, borders on the obscene reflecting avarice and greed, instead of the commitment to serve which we expect, indeed demand, of those appointed to such strategic positions. The launch, in April 2015, of the National Code on Corporate Governance and the current process of integrating the principles therein in the amendments to the Companies Act, indicate Government's serious intent in this regard.

Tellingly, the estimated total external debt of public enterprises guaranteed by the government of USD$2 billion as at end June 2016 was called up as these entities failed to service their debt. This contributed to an increase of government arrears by US$1.75 billion (25 per cent of total external debt). At the end of October 2016, called up guarantees represented 15.8 per cent of the total external debt stock. Hence the need to strengthen public debt management by increasing oversight on the contingent liabilities of public entities to minimise the moral hazard implications on guarantees issued by the government and on-lending by government to public institutions. By end of 2017, the contribution of public enterprises to the economy had declined precipitously from around 60 per cent to about 2 per cent, with 70 per cent of these entities technically insolvent.

First Lady, Grace Mugabe made it a habit of castigating ZACC at the Youth Interface rallies for trying to arrest Jonathan Moyo and his deputy at the Ministry of Higher Education, Science and Technology for abusing Zimdef funds, protesting their innocence.

A related issue is the role of institutions in growth and development. Literature points to the importance of 'strong' institutions in sustaining growth beyond the initial take-off phase.[31] Zimbabwe has for a long time been caught in a 'weak institutions trap', contributing to its poor long-run growth record and weak poverty reduction.[32] Even though Zimbabwe's policies and institutions strengthened, as measured by the World Bank's Country Policy and Institutional Assessment, from a score of 2.2 in 2012 to 2.3 in 2013, 2.7 in 2014, and 2.9 by 2015, before declining to 2.7 in 2016, the economy remained in the fragile state category. The quality of Zimbabwe's policies and institutions are below the SSA International Development Association average score of 3.2 during the period.

Table 2 shows the trend in government revenues, expenditures, deficits and borrowing requirements for the period 2009-17. Clearly, while the country experienced fiscal surpluses during most of the GNU period as a result of strict adherence to cash budgeting and fiscal discipline,[33] after 2013 the spectre of fiscal indiscipline re-emerged, reminiscent of the first decade of the new millennium, with the budget deficit escalating from 0.1 per cent of GDP in 2012 to almost 10 per cent by 2017, double the average for SSA. As UNICEF observed, 'The Government has abandoned the cash budgeting approach it had adopted as a safeguard measure in 2013'.[34]

Since 2015, a combination of factors, including subdued revenues, severe drought and the slow pace of reforms, resulted in unsustainably high expenditure levels and the associated large public financing requirements. Owing to limited access to foreign inflows, the fiscal deficits had to be financed through domestic borrowing, which put the financial sector under considerable pressure, leading to liquidity shortages in 2016. The sudden rise in the fiscal deficit in 2016 is related to the Reserve Bank Debt Assumption Act of July 2015, which required government to take liability of an estimated $1.35 billion debts incurred by the RBZ before 31 December 2008.

---

31 Acemoglu et al., 2005; Birdsall, 2007; Acemoglu and Robinson, 2010. Acemoglu and Robinson argue (2010, p. 2) that 'institutions, broadly construed, ...are the fundamental cause of economic growth and development differences across countries'.

32 Ndlela and Kanyenze, 2017.

33 GNU Minister of Finance Tendai Biti's dictum was 'you eat what you kill', implying living within one's means.

34 UNICEF, 2017, p. 1.

Table 2: Budget Deficit & Borrowing Requirements

	2009	2010	2011	2012	2013	2014	2015	2016	2017*
Revenue (US$m)	933.6	2339.1	2921.0	3495.8	3741.0	3727.2	3737.1	3502.2	4338.5
Expenditure (US$m)	898.1	2143.0	2898.9	3505.3	3987.4	3911.6	4119.6	4923.2	6045.0
Budget deficit	35.5	196.1	22.1	-9.6	-246.4	-184.4	-382.5	-1421.0	1706.5
Deficit/GDP (%)	0.4	1.9	0.2	-0.1	-1.6	-1.2	-2.3	-8.5	9.9

Source: Budget Statements, various years.

Notes: Asterisks * denotes estimate.

The financing of the Reserve Bank debt, payment arrears for services supplied, increased agriculture-related spending under the Special Maize Programme for Import Substitution (Command Agriculture Programme),[35] and the unbudgeted thirteenth month pay for civil servants forced the government to issue Treasury Bills and have recourse to the Reserve Bank overdraft. Of the US$2.1 billion Treasury Bills and bonds issued in 2016, only US$356.3 million (17 per cent) was to finance the budget deficit, with US$1.7 billion (81 per cent) for outstanding legacy debt. Worryingly, the budget deficit increased to $1.7 billion in 2017 from a target of $400 million, to be mainly financed through Treasury Bills and recourse to overdraft at the Reserve Bank.

As a result of the expansionary fiscal stance, government debt to the banking sector increased steeply after 2015, culminating in a prolonged financial crisis that severely limited credit to the economy and resulted in cash shortages, prompting banks to limit cash withdrawals and import payments as they had depleted their US dollar reserves.[36] In May 2016, in response to persistent liquidity challenges, the government introduced capital and current account controls and quasi-currency instruments (see below).

However, an overvalued real exchange rate of 4 per cent in 2011, rising to 24 per cent in 2012, 32 per cent in 2013, 40 per cent in 2014 and 45 per cent by 2015, continued to undermine external competitiveness.[37] Using the Old Mutual Implied Rate, which compares prices between the London Stock Exchange share prices in sterling to the Zimbabwe Stock Exchange share price in (Zimbabwe) U.S. dollars, the IMF estimated that the intrinsic value of the dollar in Zimbabwe was 50 per cent lower than the US dollar. Although Zimbabwe's ranking at 124 out of 137 countries improved slightly in the 2017/18 World Economic Forum Global Competitiveness Index from its position of 126 out of 138 countries in 2016/17, the

---

35 While command agriculture has resulted in surplus maize production at 2.2 million metric tonnes, against domestic grain requirement of 1.8 million tons for both human and livestock consumption, concern has been raised with respect to the design and financing of the programme, especially the commitment to buy grain at above market prices which may not be cost-efficient (IMF, 2017).

36 As indicated in the 2018 budget statement, Treasury bills have assumed the form of surrogate [for the IMF, 2017, a 'quasi-'] currency to settle government expenditure.

37 Reserve Bank of Zimbabwe data.

economy was still uncompetitive. The main factors responsible for this include policy instability (24.6 per cent), access to financing (14.5 per cent), corruption (12.7 per cent), inefficient government bureaucracy (11.2 per cent), inadequate supply of infrastructure (10.1 per cent), restrictive labour regulations (6.4 per cent), tax rates and foreign currency regulations (6.1 per cent each).

The introduction of new bond notes in November 2016 failed to ease the liquidity shortages.[38] According to the January 2017 Monetary Policy Statement, the country remained with US$250 million in the nostro accounts and only US$120 million in physical cash at banks against imports of US$6.4 billion. As Gresham's law would predict, if there are two forms of commodity money in circulation, which are accepted by law as having similar face value, the more valuable commodity will disappear from circulation – 'bad money drives out good'.

However, an inflationary development occurred wherein three exchange rates emerged, between the bond note and the US$, electronic transfers and mobile money. Significantly, annual inflation, which had dropped from 3.7 per cent in 2012 to 1.6 per cent in 2013, slumped into a deflation at -0.2 per cent in 2014 and -2.4 per cent in 2015, largely reflecting a depreciating South African rand and weakening domestic demand. However, it trended upwards throughout 2016, averaging -1.6 per cent in 2016 and 0.9 per cent in 2017 owing to growth in money supply arising from issuance of TBs, restrictions on imports, and foreign exchange rate premiums associated with the mis-match between electronic bank balances and available foreign currency.

The precarious external position, reflected in the large current account imbalances and low international reserves at just 0.6 months of import cover, against an optimal level of three months, leaves the country exposed. Exports, which account on average for 60 per cent of foreign exchange inflows, amounted to US$3.5 billion in 2016, against imports of US$6.4 billion. Worryingly, the unsustainable current account deficit is being financed through loans contracted by both the public and private sectors. Formal remittances, which account on average for 30 per cent of foreign currency earnings (2009-16), and which had increased consistently since the level of US$300.7 million in 2009, peaking at US$935 million

---

38 Bond notes are a locally tradable currency backed by a US$200 million facility from the Afreximbank that was introduced by the government as an incentive to exporters and remittances as well as for providing liquidity to the market. They are officially based on a 1:1 exchange rate with the US Dollar.

in 2015, declined to US$780.1 million in 2016 and a projected US$785.3 million by 2017.

Reliance on local borrowing resulted in the domestic debt rising to US$3.7 billion as at October 2016, US$4 billion as at March 2017, and an estimated US$6 billion by year-end 2017.[39] At US$6 billion (33.3 per cent of GDP), the risks are high that the government will not be able to repay the TBs when they fall due, requiring roll-over, which will further dampen confidence in the financial sector as well as government's future borrowing plans. Critically, as highlighted in the 2018 budget statement of 7 December 2017: 'The room for domestic financing of the large fiscal deficit has now been fully depleted, and additional monetary financing of the deficit can only lead to inflation and further economic deterioration' (paragraph 96, p. 32).

In addition, the public service wage reviews were always above growth in output and revenues.[40] Unfortunately, the bulk of the expenditures were employment costs, which accounted for 91.7 per cent of total revenues in 2016.[41] No other country in SSA has deployed such a high level of expenditures towards employment costs.[42] Part of the escalation was associated with the rising levels of employment in the public sector, despite the policy of a general freeze on recruitment adopted by the government in 2011. The manpower audit conducted by Ernest and Young (India) in 2009 had identified 75,000 civil servants who were irregularly employed.

In 2015, Patrick Zhuwao, then Minister of Youth, Indigenisation and Economic Empowerment, vowed that 10,000-plus ward youth officers employed by his ministry would not be retrenched. Finance Minister Patrick Chinamasa had insisted that they were 'ghost workers' who should not be receiving salaries from Treasury. The response from the Minister of Youth was emphatic; 'The youth officers will not go away despite attempts by some people to have them dismissed from government'.[43]

---

39 It is instructive to note that having been eroded by hyperinflation, there was hardly any domestic debt by 2011, and it was below US$500 million by 2014 (less than 3 per cent of GDP).

40 UNICEF, 2017.

41 At 20.6 per cent of GDP, employment costs were higher than regional levels of 7 per cent (UNICEF, 2017).

42 See IMF, 2013 Article IV Consultation Report, Zimbabwe.

43 See *Zimbabwe Situation*, 4 October 2015; 'Zimbabwe: 10,000 Youth Officers Going Nowhere, Zhuwao Vows'. *Bulawayo24News* of 27 October 2015 quotes the Minister of Youth as saying: 'Some are saying we are going to fire youth officers. Who do you think you can fire? It might be you who will go

After 2000, youth and gender officers had their salaries terminated by Treasury, but President Mugabe ordered their reinstatement.[44] The Civil Service Commission (CSC) announced the freezing of the public service rationalisation exercise aimed at cutting government's wage bill by retiring 3,187 youth officers, reversing a Cabinet decision of November 2015.[45]

The unsustainable expenditure mix leaves little room for operational and capital expenditures, and reliance on external partners to support key social sectors of the economy. The situation where total consumption takes up 116.8 per cent of GDP in 2012, 106.8 per cent in 2013, 103.9 per cent in 2014, 110.3 per cent in 2015, and 101.8 per cent in 2016 is untenable.[46] At over 100 per cent of GDP, the consumption ratio implies that the country is dissaving. Within such strictures, the budget has failed to allocate not less than 5 per cent of national revenues raised in any financial year to provincial and local authorities as is required in terms of Section 301(3) of the Constitution.

The emerging and escalating domestic debt exacerbates an already difficult debt position. The economy is already in debt distress, with a high debt overhang estimated at US$11.3 billion or 79 per cent of GDP, of which US$7.3 billion is external debt, as at 31 December 2016. The total debt stock is estimated at US$13.6 billion (74.9 per cent of GDP) in 2017, of which US$7.5 billion is external debt. Clearly, the debt stock is beyond the requirement that total outstanding Public and Publicly Guaranteed Debt should not exceed 70 per cent of GDP at the end of any fiscal year.[47]

Following the end of the implementation of the IMF Staff Monitored Programme in December 2015, and its endorsement by the IMF Board on 2 May 2016, Zimbabwe designed an Arrears Clearance and Debt Resolution strategy that was approved by the IMF and World Bank in Lima, Peru in October 2015. While the requirement was for Zimbabwe to clear its arrears to the IMF, World Bank and AfDB totalling US$1.8 billion by end of April 2016, only arrears to the IMF of US$107.9 million were paid off on 20 October 2016 through a set-off. The country committed to resolve the outstanding arrears to the AfDB (US$610 million), the World Bank (US$1.16 billion), the European Investment Bank (US$212 million)

---

home first. If it is an MP who is saying that, then we should go and sit down with him.'

44 'President orders reinstatement of 2 000 youths', *The Herald,* 1 August 2017.

45 'Govt freezes retrenchments', *The Herald,* 8 August 2017.

46 The consumption ratio averages 107.5 per cent over the period 2009-2016.

47 See Section 11(2) of the Public Debt Management Act [Chapter 22, p. 21].

and other multilateral institutions and bilateral official creditors.

However, with no progress in this regard, re-engagement stalled, even though the country adopted the Interim Poverty Reduction Strategy (I-PRSP) (2016-2018) in September 2016. In the absence of progress towards the clearance of the arrears and implementation of the required structural reforms, Zimbabwe cannot access the much needed new lines of credit. While President Mugabe tacitly endorsed the reform agenda, he maintained his radical and often contradictory rhetoric and when necessary applied hard power to keep in check the pro-change forces.[48]

Interestingly, as Mandaza (2016) observes, over time, policy issues were no longer being made in Cabinet, but between the president and individual ministers. It is reported that even after Cabinet meetings, ministers would queue outside the president's office with their files to have their respective policy issues cleared. This gave room for the 'divide and rule' tactic increasingly deployed by President Mugabe to derail reforms, as evidenced by the often divergent interpretations of the indigenisation law and the contradictions and policy reversals on rationalisation of the public service, as well as review of civil service pay and, in particular, the issue of the bonus.

For many years, Zimbabwe has not been an attractive destination for Foreign Direct Investment (FDI), lagging behind its regional comparators for a number of reasons, including the indigenisation law requiring foreigners investing more than US$500,000 to surrender 51 per cent of shares to indigenous Zimbabweans. FDI inflows amounted to a paltry US$387 million in 2011, US$400 million in each of 2013 and 2014, US$545 million in 2014, US$421 million in 2015 and US$319 million in 2016. Mozambique, South Africa and Zambia received inflows of US$3 billion, US$2.3 billion and US$469 million, respectively, in 2016. Figure 2 traces the trends in FDI inflows to Zimbabwe, Zambia and Mozambique during the period 1980-2015.

Clearly, while the economic crisis required urgent attention, the underlying challenge was first to deal with the political crisis. The prevailing political climate was not conducive to the evolution of the required stakeholder consensus, or the political will to resolve the economic crisis. Owing to the concentration of power in the presidency, failure to deal with the succession issue would entail serious and far-reaching implications for incumbency and the sustenance of the ruling party, hence the 'governance

---

48 Masunungure and Shumba, 2012.

Figure 2: Trends in FDI inflows (US$ millions), 1980-2015

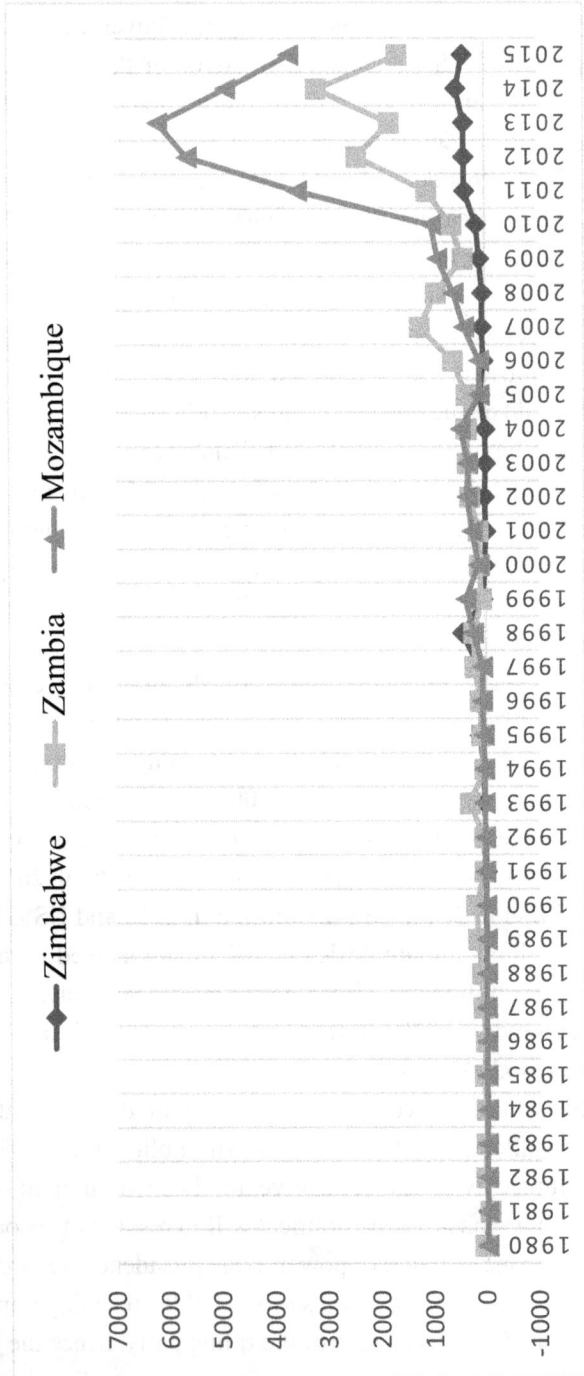

Legend: Zimbabwe, Zambia, Mozambique

Source: Derived from UNCTAD data, various years.

crisis' manifesting itself in incessant factionalism and succession wars.[49]

In the context of the 'securocrat state' and concentrated power, the military-security factor became intricately entrenched in the succession battles. The nature of the securocratic state described by Mandaza explains the lack of transition to a developmental discourse, and the failure to transition to a 'developmental state' through a 'hegemonic project' enticing key stakeholders to embrace it voluntarily.[50] Ironically, the very 'securocrats' Mugabe had relied on to retain power turned against him as they supported then Vice-President Mnangagwa's faction, culminating in the military intervention of 14 November and the ascension to power of Mnangagwa on 24 November 2017. This marked the end of Mugabe's 37-year reign and the emergence of a 'new' political dispensation.

6. Structural change and the devaluation of labour, 2000-2017

6.1 Structural change in the economy

Earlier, structural change was discussed as the process through which underdeveloped countries transform their domestic economic structures from reliance on traditional subsistence agriculture to a more modern, more urbanised and more industrially diverse manufacturing and service economy. This section traces the nature and direction of structural change in Zimbabwe since 2000, and its impact on labour.

Table 3 indicates the trends in the percentage distribution of GDP (current prices) by sector for the period 1980-2016.

The contribution of agriculture to total output declined from an average of 20.6 per cent during the crisis period 1997-2008 to an average of 10.4 per cent during 2009-16, reflecting the impact of the FTLRP and the crisis. The mining sector increased its contribution to total value added from 5.8 per cent to an average of 7.5 per cent during the same periods. The manufacturing sector, however, which is expected to increase its share in output as the structure of the economy is transformed, experienced a persistent decline in its contribution to total output from 21.4 per cent during 1980-90, a peak of 26.9 per cent in 1992, to 8.5 per cent by 2016. This decline is associated with the deindustrialisation of the economy after ESAP. Disturbingly, 'Industries in Zimbabwe are under serious threat. Deindustrialisation has reached catastrophic levels, with dire

---

49 RAU, 2016.
50 Mandaza, 2016.

Table 3: Percentage Distribution of GDP by Sector, 1980-2016 (current prices).

Percentage Distribution of GDP by Sector (current prices)

Sector	1980-90	1991-96	1997-2008	2009	2010	2011	2012	2013	2014	2015	2016
Agriculture	14.0	14.1	20.6	12.4	11.5	10.1	9.8	9.0	10.7	10.3	9.7
Mining & quarrying	4.8	3.4	5.8	6.7	8.0	8.3	7.6	7.8	7.3	6.8	7.3
Manufacturing	21.4	21.1	13.5	12.7	11.0	10.7	10.1	9.6	9.1	8.7	8.5
Electricity & water	2.2	2.8	3.4	3.3	3.6	3.6	3.2	3.2	3.4	3.3	1.7
Construction	3.1	2.5	1.6	1.6	1.8	2.4	2.7	2.6	2.7	2.7	2.7
Finance & insurance	5.7	7.4	8.0	6.8	6.2	5.8	6.7	7.0	6.0	5.5	6.5
Real estate	1.7	2.1	1.3	1.3	1.3	1.6	2.2	2.2	2.4	2.6	2.5
Distribution, H & R	14.2	16.6	16.6	14.4	13.7	11.6	11.4	12.5	12.1	12.3	13.3
Transport & comm.	6.1	5.4	6.7	12.9	11.3	10.9	9.5	9.0	9.3	9.3	9.1
Public administratio	6.3	4.6	4.3	3.9	5.4	7.5	9.0	8.5	9.1	9.3	9.7
Education	5.8	5.7	5.0	3.6	6.5	7.9	9.4	10.0	10.6	11.4	11.4
Health	1.6	1.4	2.0	0.8	1.3	1.7	2.0	2.1	2.2	2.5	2.5
Domestic services	1.5	1.1	1.3	0.4	0.4	0.3	0.3	0.3	0.3	0.3	0.3
Other services	4.6	3.7	4.6	4.1	3.9	3.8	3.0	2.6	2.5	2.6	2.9

Source: Zimstat National Accounts, various years.

consequences to the state of the economy'.[51]

Industrial capacity utilisation, which had peaked at 76 per cent in 1996, declined sharply to its lowest level of below 10 per cent by 2008, before improving to 33 per cent in 2009, 43.7 per cent in 2010, 57.2 per cent in 2011, and climbing down to 44.2 per cent in 2012 and 39.6 per cent in 2013, 36.3 per cent in 2014, 34.3 per cent in 2015 and up to 47.2 per cent in 2016, before declining to 45.1 per cent in 2017 (see Figure 3).

Central to the process of structural change and productivity upgrading is the reallocation of jobs across sectors associated with the strongest speed at which vulnerable employment is reduced, thereby raising living standards sustainably by exposing more people to higher productivity and income levels in more advanced parts of the economy. Expectedly, as GDP collapsed in all sectors between 1999 and 2008, labour productivity also declined. Labour productivity growth was modest from 1991 to 1999, and experienced slow recovery since 2004 in industry and services, remaining lower now than it was in 1999.

However, since 2008, GDP rebounded, as labour productivity stabilised. Average labour productivity in agriculture in 2014 was 45 per cent lower than the 1999 real value, while in services it was 79 per cent of the real 1999 value. Average agricultural labour productivity declined by 55 per cent between 1999 and 2014. Labour moved into agriculture where labour productivity was 6 per cent of the industry average and 11 per cent of the services average in 2014.[52] Hence structural change in Zimbabwe was productivity reducing, implying that Zimbabwe needs to create more higher productivity (decent) jobs.

Table 4 tracks the distribution of formal employment by sector for selected periods between 1980 and 2014. Data integrity issues for agriculture make it difficult to rely on ZimStat statistics for the period since the land reform programme. While mining has seen its contribution to total output rise, its share in total formal sector employment declined to 3 per cent by 2014, reflecting its capital intensity.

Manufacturing sector employment declined from 16.5 per cent of formal sector employment in 1990 to 14.7 per cent in 2000, and 8.4 per cent by 2014. Ironically, it is the public sectors – public administration, education and health – that increased their contribution to total formal sector employment, with the attendant fiscal challenges discussed above.

---

51 CZI, 2015, p. 6.
52 World Bank, 2018.

Figure 3: Capacity Utilisation 1994-2017

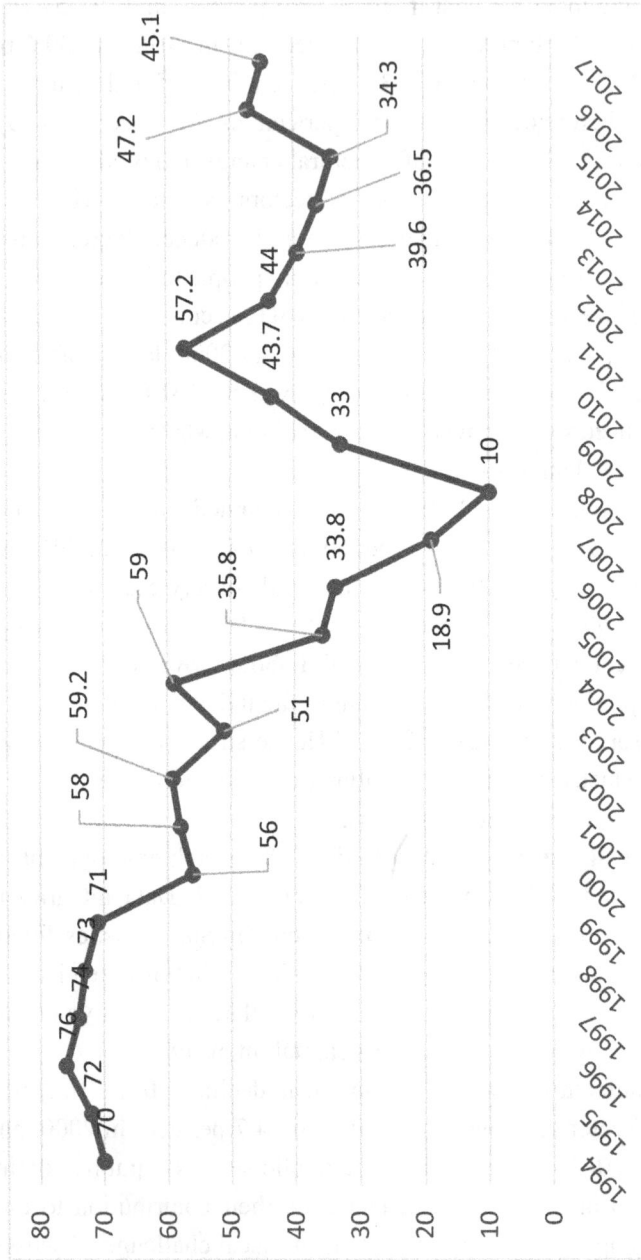

Source: CZI State of the Manufacturing Sector Surveys, various years.

Table 4: Sectorial Distribution of Employment, Selected Periods, 1980-2014

Sector/Year	1980	1985	1990	1995	2000	2005	2010	2014
Agriculture	32.4	26.3	24.3	26.9	26.3	-	32.9	29.6
Mining	6.6	5.2	4.3	4.8	3.6	5.0	3	3.4
Manufacturing	15.8	16.1	16.5	15.0	14.7	18.8	11.5	8.4
Electricity & Water	0.7	0.7	0.7	0.8	0.9	1.5	1.3	1.7
Construction	4.2	4.3	6.4	5.8	4.3	3.8	1.8	1.8
Financial Services & Real Estate	1.2	1.5	1.5	1.7	2.8	7.6	6	4.6
Distribution	7	7.4	8.1	8.1	8.4	0.8	6.5	7.4
Transport & Communication	4.5	4.8	4.5	4.1	3.5	4.2	2.4	3.2
Public Administration	7	8.6	7.8	6.2	4.7	8.9	7.9	9.9
Education	4.1	8.5	9.1	9.3	11.3	15.5	10.2	13.3
Health	1.5	1.9	2.1	2.1	2.3	4.7	4	4.2
Private Domestic Services	10.7	9.4	8.6	8.2	8.3	1.6	8.1	7.6
Other	4.3	5.5	6.2	6.9	9	7.7	4.3	5
Total	100	100	100	100	100	100	100	100

Source: Calculated from ZimStat data.

Hence, even as the economy recovered after 2009, 4,610 firms closed down, retrenching 55,443 workers between 2011 and 2014.[53]

Table 5 illustrates the trends in ever-retrenched employees for the period 2000-2013. Data from the 2004 Labour Force Survey suggests that a total of 193,076 employees were once retrenched between January 1995 and May 2004, 86 per cent of whom were males. The ever-retrenched employees were divided almost equally between rural and urban areas. For the period January 1995 to May 2004, the highest number of retrenchments (14 per cent or 27,378) occurred in 2000. Between June 2004 and May 2011, 248,186 were at least once retrenched, with the highest number (40,587) recorded in 2008.

Table 5: Ever-Retrenched Employees 15 years and above, 2000-2013.

Year	Employees Retrenched	Year	Employees Retrenched
2000	27,378	2007	35,310
2001	22,821	2008	40,587
2002	22,242	2009	31,102
2003	22,532	2010	38,946
2004*	9,229	2011	56,459
2005	31,064	2012	63,483
2006	22,158	2013	84,789

Source: 2004, 2011 and 2014 Labour Force Surveys, ZimStat.

Notes: Asterisk* denotes January to May.

During the period June 2011 to May 2014, a total of 227,369 employees were once laid off, with males constituting 72 per cent and females 28 per cent of the ever-retrenched population. The highest retrenchments were in 2013, at 84,789. The highest percentage of the ever-retrenched population during the period May 2011 to May 2014 was in the agriculture, forestry and fishing sector (19.8 per cent) followed by the manufacturing (17.8 per cent), wholesale and retail trade (14.4 per cent), construction (8.9 per cent), mining and quarrying (7.4 per cent), administrative and support services (5.4 per cent). education (4.5 per cent) and transport and storage (4.4 per cent). The highest percentage of the ever-retrenched population

---

53 See 2015 Budget Statement.

(42.3 per cent) were own-account workers (communal, resettlement and peri-urban farmers), followed by the own account worker (other) category at 24 per cent and the paid employee (casual /contract/seasonal) category with 22 per cent. Clearly, the retrenchment levels worsened over time.

To assess the impact of the crisis on employment, LEDRIZ (2016) estimated the fitted employment levels for the period 2000-2014 on the basis of the historical (1964-99) trends and found a gap of 400,000 jobs in 2014 (see Figure 4). This means that 400,000 manufacturing jobs were lost as a result of the crisis.

Figure 5 traces the trends in the indices of manufacturing output (value added) and employment for the period 1965-2016.

Value added in the manufacturing sector peaked at an index of 136.6 in 1992, declining (with some annual variations) to 44 by 2016. Manufacturing employment peaked at an index of 143.5 in 1999 when it employed 200,700 employees, declining persistently to an index of 61 by 2016 with a workforce of 88,200, implying 112,500 lost jobs over the period 1999-2016.

The wrenching structural change the economy has undergone is best illustrated through tracing trends in export earnings by sector (see Figure 6). Clearly, the mining sector, whose contribution to export earnings was as low as 15.7 per cent in 2002, increased sharply to an estimated 60 per cent by 2016 and 58.6 per cent by 2017. Agricultural exports, which were as high as 44.2 per cent in 1999, declined to a low of 15.8 per cent in 2010, before recovering to 28.8 per cent in 2016 and 29.3 per cent by 2017. Meanwhile, manufactured exports, which peaked at 41.4 per cent in 2003, plummeted to as low as 8.7 per cent by 2016 and 9.5 per cent by 2017. This implies that Zimbabwe is now a typical SSA economy based on primary exports, where agriculture and mining accounted for 88.8 per cent of total exports by 2016 and 87.9 per cent by 2017. Instead of enjoying the 'structural bonus' associated with industrialisation, Zimbabwe is experiencing a structural regression, and has lost its position as the second most industrialised country in Africa after South Africa.[54]

Zimbabwe's population is young, with 52.9 per cent of the population aged below 20 years in 2014. This youth bulge points to the scope to harness the 'demographic dividend' associated with falling fertility rates, increased employment opportunities and declining dependency ratios.[55]

---

54 Besada, 2011, Table 5.2.
55 The 'demographic dividend' is associated with a demographic transition when

Figure 4: Actual, Projected and Employment Gap (Formal Sector Employment), 2000-2014

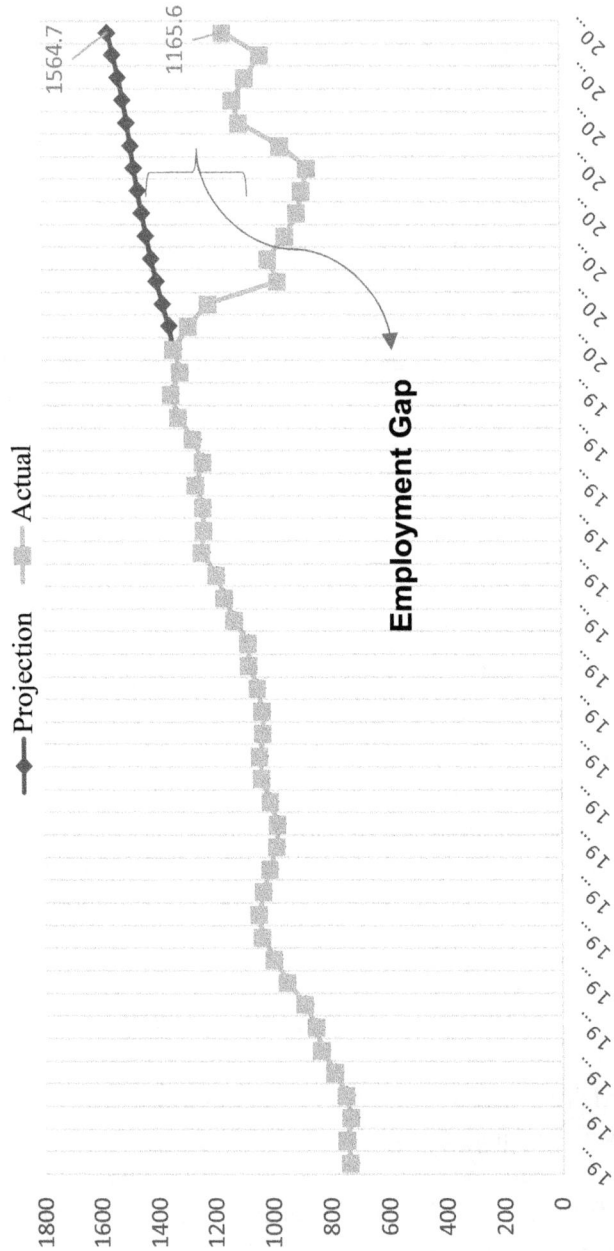

Source: LEDRIZ, (2016), Figure 4 page 21.

110

Figure 5: Indices of manufacturing output and employment (1965-2016), 1980=100.

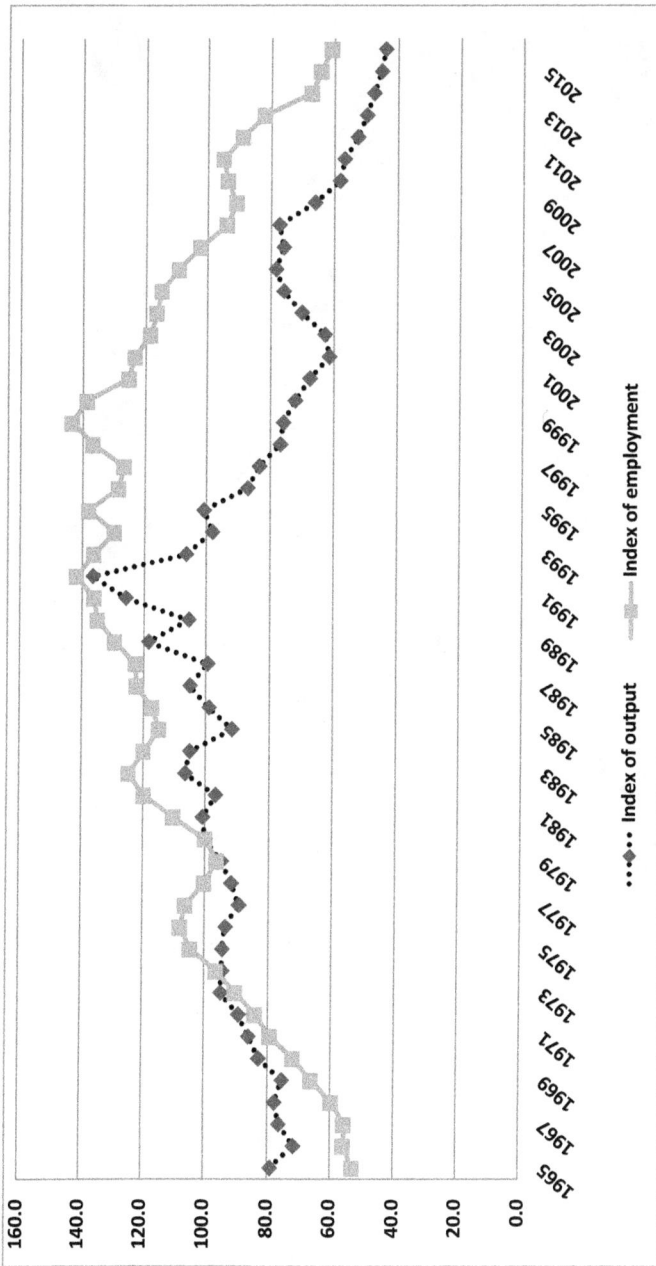

Source: Derived from output data from the World Development Indicators (World Bank) and Zimstat employment figures.

Figure 6: Sectoral Share to total Exports (per cent)

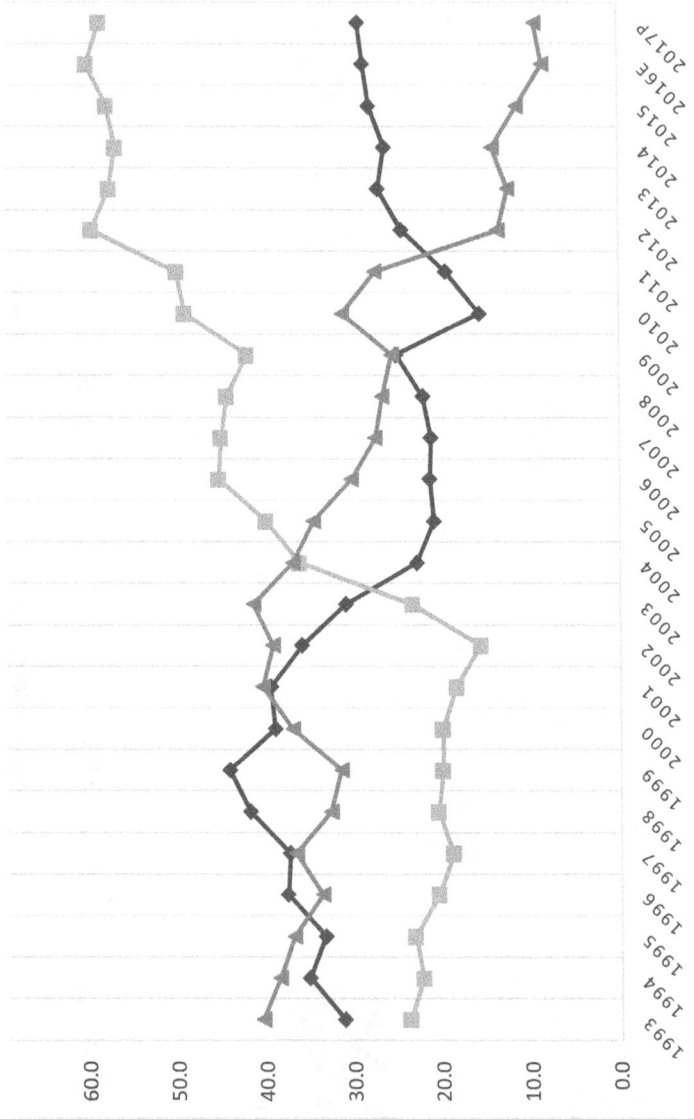

Source: Calculated from Unpublished Reserve Bank of Zimbabwe Data.

A key challenge in Zimbabwe is that 94.5 per cent of jobs are informal. To harness the demographic dividend requires that labour productivity is increased and that new entrants find job opportunities at a rate higher than average productivity. This should be reinforced by increased urbanisation, which offers opportunities for increased off-farm employment.[56]

6.2 Devaluation of labour

As labour moved from urban to rural areas in the context of the land reform programme and limited job opportunities in urban areas (see below), the employment rate in rural areas increased from 82 per cent in 2004 to 90 per cent in 2011 and 94 per cent in 2014, while that in urban areas declined from 73 per cent in 2004 to 60 per cent in 2011 and 59 per cent in 2014.[57] The decline in urban labour force participation is greatest amongst women, especially those who did not complete secondary education.[58] While most unemployment and non-participation in the labour market in 1999 was rural, it is now urban, implying that unemployment and non-participation are increasingly urban challenges.[59] While the overall employment rate increased from 79 per cent in 2004 and 78 per cent in 2011 to 80.5 per cent in 2014, the major challenge is the quality of the jobs.[60]

Young workers aged 15-24 fared the worst, with their employment rate, which initially increased from 47 per cent in 1999 to 68 per cent in

---

falling birth rates change the age distribution of a country such that fewer investments are required to meet the needs of the dependent population. As such, during this period the labour force grows more rapidly than the population dependent on it, thereby releasing resources for investment in economic development and family welfare, resulting in faster per capita income growth. This dividend period is estimated to last for five decades or more.

56 See also World Bank, 2018.

57 According to the international definition used by ZIMSTAT, it is sufficient for a person to be engaged in an economic activity for at least one hour during the reference period to be classified as employed. If one was actively seeking for employment but provided goods and services, then the person is considered employed during the reference period. As Zimstat observed, 'In the labour force framework, unemployment is considered to be an extreme situation of total lack of work. In many developing countries there is either none or a very limited number of workers covered by unemployment insurance or other public relief schemes. Under these conditions, very few people can afford to be unemployed for any period of time. As such most people would be engaged in some economic activity, i.e. they get employed although it may be inadequate. Therefore the employment status cannot be fully described by unemployment data alone; underemployment data also plays a role' (2006, p. 70).

58 World Bank, 2018.

59 Ibid.

60 Data from the 2004, 2011 and 2014 Labour Force Surveys.

2004, declining to 66 per cent in 2011, before strengthening to 70 per cent in 2014. This compares unfavourably to the employment rates for older workers, aged 25-64, which remained constant at 87 per cent during the respective years, with the exception of 2011 when it declined slightly to 86 per cent. While the employment rate for rural youth increased from 49 per cent in 1999 to 72 per cent in 2004, 83 per cent in 2011 and 90 per cent by 2014, that for their urban counterparts increased initially from 42 per cent in 1999 to 59 per cent in 2004, before declining to 33 per cent in 2011 and 32 per cent in 2014. Clearly, urban youth, especially young and less educated women in urban areas, tend to be less active in the labour market. The shift from urban to rural employment, especially amongst the youth, reflects low demand for labour in urban areas and hence they accounted for 78 per cent of all inactive workers and 86 per cent of unemployment.[61]

Using the international definition of employment, employed persons increased from 5,136,087 in 2004 to 5,431,026 in 2011 and 6,265,869 by 2014. The majority of these (61 per cent in 1999, rising to 64.8 per cent in 2004, 65.8 per cent in 2011 and 67.2 per cent in 2014) are in agriculture, forestry and fishing, where productivity and incomes are low.[62] This rising share of agricultural employment is associated with the net migration from urban to rural areas of 1.142 million from 1994 to 2014, much of which is from 2001, as the land redistribution programme gained momentum. A much higher proportion of women than men are employed in agriculture: 71.1 per cent (58.8 per cent) in 2004, 71.6 per cent (59.9 per cent) in 2011 and 71.6 per cent (62.7 per cent) in 2014. A very small proportion is employed in the manufacturing sector, declining from 8.7 per cent in 1999 to 5.9 per cent in 2004, 5 per cent in 2011 and 4 per cent by 2014, reflecting the deindustrialisation of the economy.[63]

Not surprisingly, the level of skills among the employed population is very low; the unskilled proportion of the employed was 78.7 per cent, 82.9 per cent and 83.3 per cent per cent in 2004, 2011 and 2014 respectively. The proportion of the employed that are skilled declined from 8.3 per cent in 2004 to 5.5 per cent in 2011 and 5.4 per cent by 2014. A related issue is that the largest proportion of the employed had secondary education: 46.6

61 See analysis of the 1999, 2004, 2011 and 2014 Labour Force Surveys in World Bank, 2018.
62 The majority of the population (68 per cent) live in rural areas where their livelihood is directly derived from agriculture, while 32 per cent is urban.
63 Data from the 1999, 2004. 2011 and 2014 Labour Force Surveys.

per cent in 2004, 55 per cent in 2011 and 51.1 per cent in 2014. Only a small proportion had tertiary education: 8.2 per cent in 2004, 11.2 per cent in 2011 and 9.9 per cent in 2014.

Table 6 reports the percentage distribution of currently employed aged 15 years and above by status in employment and sex for the periods 2004, 2011 and 2014.

Only a very small proportion of the employed have paid permanent jobs, declining from 20.9 per cent in 2004 to 15.5 per cent in 2014. The majority of the employed are in vulnerable employment, 70.9 per cent in 2004, rising to 74.6 per cent in 2011 and 74.7 per cent by 2014.[64] A total of 81.1 per cent of youth aged 15-24 are in vulnerable employment in 2014. Whereas 1,200,549 (23.4 per cent of the employed, 72.7 per cent of whom were male) were employed in the formal sector in 2004, they declined to 963,444 (15.4 per cent of the employed of whom 69.5 per cent were male) in 2014. Clearly, the majority of jobs are characterised by a high level of precarity.

Owing to persistent deindustrialisation and economic decline, the economy has rapidly informalised. The share of informal employment in total employment increased from 80 per cent in 2004 to 84.2 per cent in 2011 and 94.5 per cent in 2014.[65] The worst affected are the youth, who have little labour market experience. The 2014 Labour Force Survey shows that 98 per cent of the currently employed youth aged 15-24 years and 96 per cent of currently employed youth aged 15-34 years were in informal employment. As pointed out above, owing to a lack of employment in urban areas, youth have moved to rural areas. The FinScope survey of 2012 indicated that 85 per cent of the 3.4 million Micro, Small and Medium Enterprises (MSMEs) were unregistered.

Such high levels of informalisation are striking given that 5.7 million people were working in MSMEs in 2012, 2.8 million as business owners and 2.9 million as employees. The majority of workers in the informal economy are at the bottom of the economic and social ladder, working under precarious conditions without access to any form of social protection, with their work suffering from decent work deficits, being casual, 'unprotected,' 'excluded,' 'unregistered,' or 'unrepresented'. Insecurity on the labour market has grown, creating a sea of extremely

---

64 The ILO definition of vulnerable employment includes own account workers and contributing family members.
65 See The Labour Force Surveys of 2004, 2011 and 2014.

Table 6: Percentage distribution of currently employed aged 15 years and above by status in employment and sex; 2004, 2011 & 2014

Status in employment	2004			2011			2014		
	Male	Female	Total	Male	Female	Total	Male	Female	Total
Paid employee (permanent)	28.9	12.6	20.9	21.8	9.2	15.5	20.7	10.4	15.5
Paid employee (casual/temporary/contract/seasonal)	9.2	6.4	7.8	11.6	7.3	9.4	11.7	6.3	9.0
Employer	0.5	0.1	0.3	0.6	0.3	0.4	1.1	0.4	0.7
Own account worker (communal & resettlement farmer)	24.7	42.7	33.4	52.5	68.4	60.5	51.5	66.2	58.9
Own account worker (other)	12.5	14.4	13.5	12.8	13.6	13.2	13.4	14.7	14.1
Unpaid contributing family worker	24.3	23.8	24.0	0.6	1.2	0.9	1.2	1.8	1.5
Member of producer cooperative	0.0	0.0	0.0	0.0	0.0	0.0	0.3	0.1	0.2
Not stated	0.0	0.1	0.0	0.1	0.1	0.1	0.0	0.1	0.1
Total per cent	100.0	100.0	100.0	100.0	100.0	100.0	100.0	100.0	100.0
Total employed persons	2,639,251	2,496,837	5,136,088	2,704,060	2,726,967	5,431,026	3,091,318	3,174,551	6,265,859

Source: 2004, 2011 & 2014 Labour Force Surveys, ZimStat.

unstable, low-paid employment where there is no possibility for career planning. A major structural shift is evident, from an economy driven by comparatively large, stable, formal enterprises to one based on fragmented, fragile, informal enterprises (Balkanisation).

The period of hyperinflation rendered employment and earnings meaningless. Transacting became not only difficult, but the experience of earning a salary not adequate to cover the cost of transport to and from work resulted in public employees, especially in the health and education sectors, failing to turn up to work. The devaluation of labour is reflected partly in the collapse in real average earnings, which peaked at an index of 116.5 in 1982, before collapsing to 10 by 2004, and the real per capita GDP index from a peak of 106 in 1998 to as low as 46.6 by 2008 before strengthening to 72.1 by 2016 (see Figure 7). It is an indictment of the post-independence era that both real per capita and real average earnings are below pre-1980 colonial levels.

The 2007 CZI Manufacturing Sector Survey observed that the collapse in real wages had adverse effects on the economy as it eroded disposable incomes resulting in falling demand for products as well as inducing a loss of skills through emigration. It called for a review of the earnings structure to ensure that those at the bottom are paid living wages. The 2008 Survey noted that the situation had deteriorated further, such that salaries at the lower end were below requirements for transport, resulting in workers absconding from work. The Prices, Income, Consumption and Expenditure Survey (PICES) (2011/12) reveals that due to low incomes, households in Zimbabwe were selling financial assets more than they were buying them, suggesting that they were dissaving to fund current expenditures.

It is also instructive that between 2013 and 2016 the main constraint on industrial capacity utilisation was low local demand for products, only to be supplanted in 2017 by cash/raw material shortages (CZI State of the Manufacturing Sector Surveys). Further, only 2.1 per cent of the population were receiving a monthly pension or some social security funds by 2014. In terms of medical aid cover, 9.4 per cent of the population were members of a medical aid scheme, up from 8 per cent in 2011 (see 2014 Labour Force Survey).

Workers also lost considerable value during the period of hyperinflation through the erosion of pensions and real investment returns, and the wholesale termination of individual life, retirement and savings insurance

117

Figure 7: Trends in the index of per capita GDP (constant 2010 prices) and total formal sector real average earnings (1990=100), 1975-2016

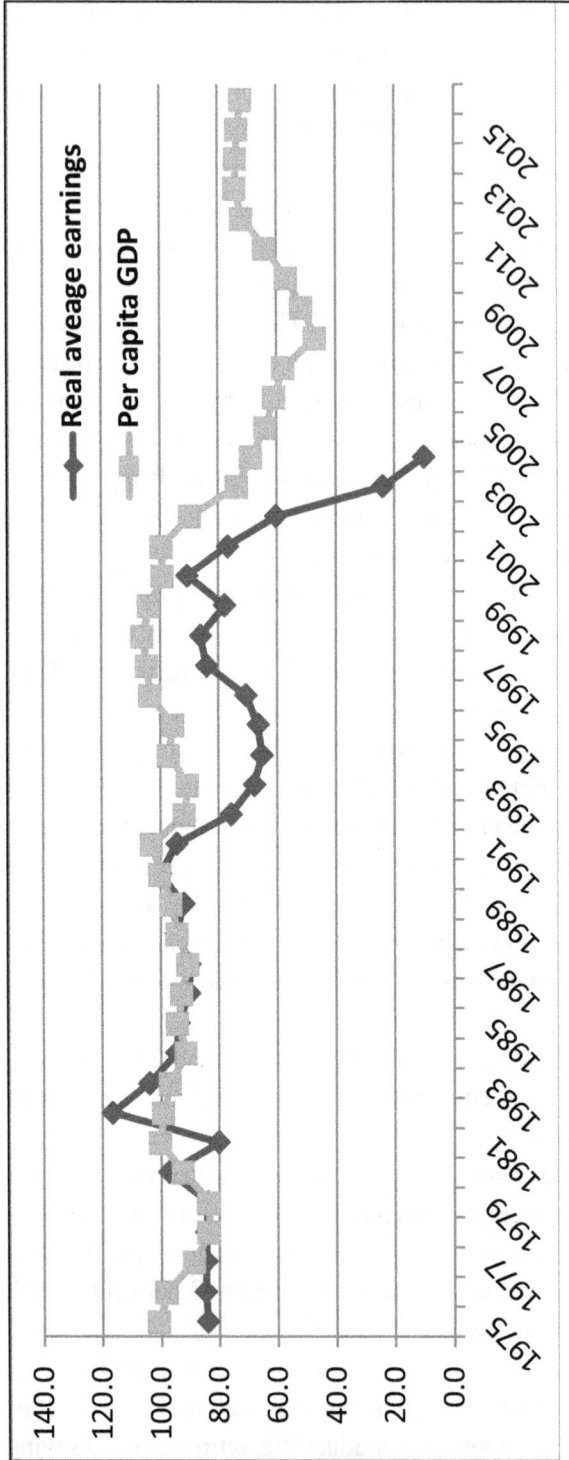

Source: Per capita data from World Development Indicators, World Bank, and Real average earnings derived from ZimStat data.

Notes: Average earnings data were available up to 2004 in the Zimbabwe dollar era.

products. The loss was also accentuated through the removal of 25 zeros from the currency between August 2006 and February 2009 which resulted in insurance companies and pension funds extinguishing insurance and pension liabilities without having to pay anything.[66] Moreover, the conversion of insurance and pension liabilities did not receive regulatory guidance to ensure equity and fairness, resulting in arbitrary benefit payments.

Due to the high number of complaints received from insurance policyholders and pension contributors, a Presidential Commission of Inquiry[67] was set up to look into the conversion of insurance and pension values from Zimbabwe dollars to United States dollars in August 2015. Having completed its work in March 2017, the Commission submitted its findings to President Mnangagwa on 18 December 2017 and the Report has now been gazetted. The Commission confirmed the prejudice suffered by insurance policyholders and pensioners during the period before and during dollarisation, and recommended a computation of rightful benefits by the respective insurance companies and pension funds.

Furthermore, when the government decided to demonetise the local currency in 2015, seven years after the conversion to multi-currencies, they used an arbitrary parallel and hence illegal exchange rate of 1USD to 35 quadrillion Zimbabwe dollars (the UN rate) to compensate non-loan bank balances as at 31 December 2008, which resulted in most workers being reimbursed only US$5.[68] The choice of exchange rate was deliberate, to minimise the government's liability. The erosion of value through decimating the currency was well noted earlier by John Maynard Keynes: 'Lenin was right. There is no subtler, no surer means of overturning the existing basis of society than to debauch the currency. The process engages all the hidden forces of economic law on the side of destruction, and does it in a manner which not one man in a million is able to diagnose'.[69]

In the current scenario of a debilitating crisis, a growing number of workers are not being paid for work done. In their aptly titled study,

66 A total of three zeroes were removed in August 2006, ten in August 2008 and 12 in February 2009.
67 Report of the Commission of Inquiry into the Conversion of Insurance and Pension Values from the Zimbabwe Dollar to the United States Dollar under the Chairmanship of Retired Justice L.G. Smith, March 2017.
68 The official exchange rate in December 2008 was US$1 to ZW$3,641,246.
69 Lenin's argument was that through a continuous process of inflation, governments can secretly and arbitrarily deprive their citizens of an important part of their wealth and impoverish them. See Keynes, 1919, pp. 235-248.

'Working Without Pay: Wage Theft in Zimbabwe', LEDRIZ and Solidarity Center (2016) found that workers in several sectors are averaging more than 20 months without being paid, in violation of international labour standards and national legislation. Furthermore, the cash shortages in the economy suggest that workers cannot access their savings in the banking sector, which were used to finance the fiscal deficit. The emergence of parallel exchange rates for cash, bond notes, electronic transfers and mobile money implies that workers' earnings, which are often deposited into their accounts, are being eroded, since such quasi-currency does not earn a premium which applies to physical cash. The emergence of a parallel market for foreign currency has spawned inflation, which increased from a deflation of -1.6 per cent in 2016 to 0.9 per cent in 2017.[70]

Table 7 traces the percentage share in the distribution of Gross Domestic Income (GDI) by Factor Income, 1985-2016. The distributive effect of inflation away from wages towards profits is aptly illustrated in the fall in the share of wages and salaries in GDI from 49.4 per cent in 1985-90 to 35.3 per cent during the crisis period 2000-2007, only to recover to an average of 49.8 per cent during the multi-currency period 2009-2016. Similarly, the share of profit increased from 50.7 per cent in 1985-90 to 65.3 per cent during the crisis period 2000-2007, before declining to an average of 29.5 per cent in 2009-2016.

Inevitably, the low and erratic levels of growth in Zimbabwe failed to create productive employment and reduce stubbornly high poverty levels. As Karl Marx observed, the surest way to discipline labour is to ensure the existence of a reserve army of the un- and under-employed. Clearly, labour has been systematically devalued and debased over the years. The 'new economy' is characterised by the decline of full-time permanent employment and is dominated by precarious and vulnerable forms of employment. Consequently, poverty levels have remained above 70 per cent of the population since the mid-1990s (see Table 8 below). This is atypical as the percentage of the population living below the poverty line in SSA declined from a peak of 60.8 per cent in 1993 to 46.9 per cent by 2011.

---

70 Annual inflation, which had dropped from 3.7 per cent in 2012 to 1.6 per cent in 2013, slumped into a deflation at -0.2 per cent in 2014 and -2.4 per cent in 2015, largely reflecting a depreciating South African rand and weakening domestic demand.

Table 7: Percentage share in the distribution of Gross Domestic Income (GDI) by Factor Income, 1985-2007

	1985-90	1991-96	1997-07	2000-07	2009-16
Wages & salaries	49.4	41.5	37.2	35.3	49.8
Rent	2.3	2.2	1.5	1.3	19.4
Profit	50.7	58.4	63.8	65.3	29.5
Financial Interest Services	-2.4	-2.1	-2.5	-1.8	1.4
GDI	**100.0**	**100.0**	**100.0**	**100.0**	**100.0**

Source: Calculated from National Accounts, ZimStat, various years.

Table 8: Household and Individual Measured Prevalence of Poverty, 1995, 2001 & 2011 (%)

	Household		Individual	
		Extreme		Extreme
	Poverty	Poverty	Poverty	Poverty
PICES 2011/12				
Rural	76.0	22.9	84.3	30.4
Urban	38.2	4.0	46.5	5.6
Zimbabwe	62.6	16.2	72.3	22.9
ICES 2001				
Rural	73.0	42.3	82.4	52.4
Urban	33.8	10.5	42.3	14.5
Zimbabwe	60.6	32.2	70.9	41.5
ICES 1995				
Rural	76.2	50.4	86.4	62.8
Urban	41.1	10.2	53.4	15.0
Zimbabwe	63.3	35.7	75.6	47.2

Source: ZimStat (2013) and Poverty and Poverty Analysis in Zimbabwe, 2011/13

7. Conclusion

This chapter has traced the structural changes that the Zimbabwean economy has undergone since the turn of the millennium. Economic progress is associated with structural change through which factors of production, especially labour, are redeployed from less productive towards the more advanced parts of the economy, a process that sustainably improves livelihoods and rapidly reduces poverty. This hypothesis is tested for Zimbabwe.

Intriguingly, the period since 2000 emerges as the most turbulent in the country's history, with economic management based on ad hoc, knee-jerk interventions. The pursuit of 'authoritarian populism' culminated in the hyperinflationary experience of 2007 and 2008. As a result, the economy virtually collapsed after a decade of economic downturn. Social conditions deteriorated to an extent that an estimated 2-3 million Zimbabweans emigrated. Following violent and contentious elections in 2008, a Government of National Unity emerged as the best way to stabilise the political and economic situation in the country. The adoption of a multi-currency regime, as well as the liberalisation of prices, resulted in a short-lived economic rebound between 2009 and 2012.

The weakening of international commodity prices since 2012 coincided with elections in July 2013 that were resoundingly won by ZANU(PF). However, the post-GNU period mirrors the crisis of the pre-2008 period. Fiscal indiscipline re-emerged as government expenditures strengthened aainst weakening revenues. The government resorted to domestic borrowing from the banking sector to finance the budget deficit, effectively crowding out the private sector. Treasury Bills were rolled out such that they became a surrogate currency, with the risk of the government failing to meet its liabilities on maturity. Furthermore, this period was marked by intense succession fights driven by the advanced age and ill-health of the incumbent president. These struggles culminated in the military intervention of 14-15 November 2017, which resulted in the resignation of President Mugabe and his replacement by Emmerson Mnangagwa, marking the end of an era and the emergence of a 'new' dispensation.

Against this background, the expected structural transformation driven by industrialisation did not happen. Instead, the economy experienced persistent deindustrialisation and unprecedented levels of informalisation. The decimation of the manufacturing sector saw the economy increasingly dependent on primary commodities such that the pre-2000 economy was barely recognisable. This structural regression was associated with a reversal in the deployment of labour, from the formal to the informal and agricultural sectors. In the context of weak public social protection mechanisms, the scourge of un- and under-employment became predominant. Employment, even in the formal sector, became increasingly informalised. Even during the economic rebound, retrenchments actually increased.

In a context of hyperinflation, the erosion of earnings was unprecedented as remuneration became meaningless. There was hardly any incentive to work, and speculative activities and open corruption emerged. Pensions and insurance products were rendered valueless by hyperinflation and the crossover to multi-currencies lacked guidance, leaving the conversions to the whims of individual service providers. Insurance contributors and pension funds lost value and were prejudiced, as was established by the 2015 Commission of Inquiry into the Conversion of Insurance and Pension Values from Zimbabwe Dollars to United States Dollars. Clearly, the net effect of the crisis and structural regression was the devaluation and debasing of labour. A form of 'wage theft' has emerged in several sectors where workers in some sectors have gone for more than 20 months without being paid.

As precarious and vulnerable employment has become the norm rather than the exception, with the attendant huge decent work deficits, poverty levels have remained above 70 per cent since the mid-1990s.

Chapter 5

Labour, State and Crises in the post-2000 era

Lloyd Sachikonye

Introduction

This chapter explores the relationship between labour and state in Zimbabwe in the post-2000 crisis-ridden period. It builds on the analysis and narrative of that relationship as explained in considerable detail in the chapter on developments from 1980 to 2000[1]. During the era from 2000 to 2017, the contest between the state and labour became more intense and protracted in a context of deepening economic and political crises. Compared with previous decades, these crises were unprecedented. Not only were the stakes high but the survival of the regime in power, and that of the labour movement, was under threat. The most acute phase of the crises was between 2000 and 2008. This was followed by a period of recovery during the Government of National Unity (GNU) from 2009 to 2014, although the fortunes of labour did not improve. Indeed, since 2014 the economy has stagnated, with negative consequences for labour. In addition, there are echoes of a fiscal and currency crisis as well as commodity shortages reminiscent of the 2000s.

Political and economic crises and the state

While the narrative on the economic crisis is more extensively assessed elsewhere in this volume, it is still necessary to show how it was inextricably intertwined with momentous political developments from 2000. The formation of the Movement for Democratic Change (MDC) in 1999 was the culmination of the groundwork of the labour movement in consultation with some civil society organisations. To illustrate how

---

1   Raftopoulos, 2018.

powerful and popular the democratic movement was at that juncture, it had succeeded against all expectations to impose a referendum defeat on a draft constitution in February 2000. Several months later, in June 2000, the MDC won almost half of the directly contested parliamentary seats.

The conjuncture in 1999-2000 was a fertile one for political reform, and even for regime change, if the electoral system had been credible and fair. The political system was authoritarian and stacked against both constitutional and regime reform. The labour movement was caught in this vicious contest to the extent that it was viewed as the handmaiden of the opposition. The years between 2000 and 2003 witnessed an unprecedented onslaught on labour as the regime resorted to repression, electoral manipulation and renewed mobilisation by ZANU(PF).

The political crisis stemmed from the isolation that the Mugabe government faced from international institutions and western countries. The isolation was in protest against electoral irregularities and political violence, particularly in the 2000 and 2002 elections. Economic measures, also described as 'sanctions', were applied against the regime as a penalty for carrying out a land reform riddled with disorder, violence and cronyism. While this was an immediate context for economic crisis, the structural roots of decline had been sown in the late 1990s.[2] The use of patronage in the form of gratuities and pensions for war veterans had caused a severe devaluation of the Zimbabwe dollar in 1997, while intervention in the war in the Democratic Republic of Congo in 1998-2003 had been a substantial drain on the fiscus. In combination with incompetent economic management, these developments enabled 'the chickens to come home to roost' for the regime.

By the mid-2000s, Zimbabwe was in the throes of a deep economic crisis. Shortages of inputs such as fuel and electricity became endemic. Inflation soon morphed into hyperinflation that became the highest in the world at the time. Capacity utilisation in companies plummeted as a consequence of the combination of input shortages and collapse in consumer demand. The disruption induced by land reform resulted in a steep decline in production in the short and medium term. Exports shrank. Deindustrialisation set in. Almost 50 per cent of GDP was wiped out between 2000 and 2008. The resort to quasi-fiscal measures by the Reserve Bank of Zimbabwe under Gideon Gono did not resuscitate the economy.[3]

---

2   Kanyenze, 2004; UNDP, 2008.
3   Gono, 2008.

The confluence of crisis and grievances amongst consumers and voters dealt ZANU(PF) its most severe electoral blow in March 2008. It lost its parliamentary majority and the first round of the presidential election.

These twin economic and political crises had a direct impact on the state itself. There were tensions between different branches and levels of the state as it lurched from political to economic crises in the early 2000s. Competent management, integrity and the 'rule of law' came under assault during elections, land reform and routine bureaucratic state functions. For example, interventions by war veterans politicised all areas of the public sector and seriously undermined professionalism in the public service:

> Zanu PF used veterans' disruption to newly conflate party and state structures at district and provincial levels and to set up new channels of authority. In so doing, Zanu PF has gained more control over the local state.[4]

Furthermore, the disorder previously encouraged through veterans' occupation of commercial farms was extended to other sites, with invasion of companies, the independent press, the Supreme Court and local authorities. Interventions in these areas were cast in populist terms – as supporting workers' grievances against employers, supposedly popular complaints against a white-dominated and biased judicial authority, and inefficient and corrupt local authorities.[5]

The long-term consequences of party-state integration were regressive for democratic process, checks and balances between branches of state, and accountability. Although conflation between party and state began at independence, it was not as systematic and systemic as it became after 2000. At one level, it was an insurance policy against the possible collapse of the regime. At another level, it served as a vehicle for party-related medium- to long-term predation and accumulation.

Consequently, corruption and cynicism became pervasive, professionalism was undermined and various levels of state institutions were forced to respond to an authoritarian centre.[6] The centre variously used tools of patronage (dispensing of land and mineral resources) and coercion to alternatively reward and subdue the population. This modulated approach became pronounced in the post-2008 period. While it would purchase electoral support, it would also exacerbate corruption, undermine the economy and demobilise the population.

---

4   McGregor, 2002.
5   Ibid.
6   Ibid.; Bratton and Masunungure, 2010.

Effects of the crises on labour, and its response

To state that the crises in the 2000s did not leave the labour movement unscathed would be a serious understatement. Economically, the crisis had profound effects on the number of jobs and the size and viability of unions. There was a severe contraction of the formal sector as GDP plummeted. Consequently, thousands of jobs were lost, and many livelihoods adversely affected. It was observed, for instance, that:

> ... the ZCTU lost much of its impetus after 2000 owing to state harassment, employment shrinkage and declining union membership (down from 16 per cent in 1990 to 12 per cent in 2000). The Zimbabwe Federation of Trade Unions (ZFTU) established by Zanu PF also weakened the ZCTU by creating splinter unions in nine sectors of the economy: furniture and timber, engineering, catering, leather, clothing, commerce, agriculture, sugar plantations and construction. The general informalisation of the economy made it extremely difficult for the labour movement to organize as informal sector workers turned to various methods in the 'kukiya-kiya' economy.[7]

As job lay-offs became routine in the 2000s, union membership declined even further. While potential union membership was above 800,000, actual membership was about 170,000 according to the General Council report to the ZCTU Silver Jubilee Congress of 2006.

A study on the relationship between deindustrialisation, informalisation and contraction of the working class marshaled evidence to show that the ZCTU was adversely affected by the deindustrialisation and economic crisis.[8] This contributed to the 'partial disintegration' of the working class in a number of ways:

> ... first, the depletion in the numbers of formal sector employment resulted in a drop in the rate of unionization and subscriptions, thus undermining the capacity of unions to carry out various organizational and educational activities of their working class members. Secondly, as a result of the shrinkage of the working class ... the labour movement was debilitated in terms of its organizational and mobilization activities. Thus the ZCTU was less able and willing to lead broad civic alliances as it did from the late 1980s.[9]

---

7   Raftopoulos, 2009.
8   Chagonda, 2011, p.139.
9   Ibid.

Thirdly, the informalisation of the labour force moved workers away from formalised labour practices and protest actions in the public sphere into more individualised and survivalist modes. Consequently, at the ideological level, the sense of working class consciousness that could have encouraged members of this class to unite in protest against hyperinflation, retrenchments, falling incomes and the political crisis was weaker during the peak of the Zimbabwean crisis.[10]

Specific examples of the contraction of the working class include the diminished size of the permanent agricultural workforce by almost two-thirds after 2000. There was a noticeable decline in the number of teachers from a peak of 100,000 as some of them migrated to other countries. Indeed, the period from 2000 witnessed almost every sector downscaling levels of employment with the exception of a few such as financial services and real estate.[11]

The number of formal sector workers shrank by about half from 1.4 million in 1998 to about 700,000 in 2008,[12] of whom about half are employed in the uniformed forces, the civil service and parastatals. The private sector now has a much-diminished workforce, with direct consequences for union membership. The twin processes of deindustrialisation and de-proletarianisation were perhaps the deepest and most rapid ever experienced in Africa or in any developing country in contemporary times. This had a direct impact not only on union membership levels but also on collective class-consciousness and civic participation.

Let us explore how unions have been affected by contraction of the formal sector working class. Fewer formal sector workers meant fewer members of unions. For instance, the teaching and catering sectors witnessed a steep decline in union membership, and the Zimbabwe Catering and Hotel Workers Union saw its union membership contract by half between 1998 and 2008 to about 6,000. The membership of the ZCTU's 36 affiliates declined during this period; estimates of the decline vary from about 155,000 to 210,000.[13] An exception to this general trend was the Zimbabwe Banking and Allied Workers Union, which maintained its level of membership during this period.

Between 2011 and 2014, deindustrialisation saw some 4,610 firms

---

10 Ibid.
11 Ibid.
12 UNDP, 2008.
13 Chagonda, 2011, p. 141; ZCTU, 2006, p. 21

closing, resulting in an estimated 55,000 jobs being lost.[14] Informalisation deepened such that the level of informal employment increased from 80 per cent in 2004 to about 94 per cent by 2014.

A more sobering effect of the economic downturn was the non-payment or irregular payment of wages to employees. This has been particularly prevalent in local authorities such as town councils but also occurred in parastatals. Sometimes described as 'wage theft', it is a phenomenon that dramatises the social reproduction crisis that results when workers cannot depend on their wages, but have to scrounge or seek informal sources for survival.

Finally, the size and orientation of the working class and unions would not be immune to deep qualitative and quantitative changes. An additional dimension to the decline in size of the working class was the substantial migration during the post-2000 decade. The numbers vary between two and three million. The outmigration included some of the most skilled and highly qualified workers and professionals from both the public and private sectors. The impact of this brain drain has undoubtedly been considerable.

The effects of the political crisis on the labour movement should not be underestimated. As we will see in greater detail in the next section, the crisis made the environment hostile to union activities and civic participation. There was hostility towards the ZCTU, and particularly its links with the MDC. A concerted strategy of the party-state was to isolate and cripple the movement, and 'demonise' its relationship with the MDC. This made it difficult and dangerous for the labour movement to carry out its mobilisation activities at workplaces. Legislation such as the Public Order and Security Act (POSA) was systematically used by the state to limit the number of meetings, forums and workshops that the labour movement could organise.

In spite of these constraints, in the early 2000s labour responded to the crises by organising strikes and participating in 'mass action'. These were often met with draconian force by the state, such as in the 2003 'mass final push'. As the decade wore on, participation in them waned as the working class base weakened in numbers. The most sweeping military-style measure against labour and the urban population was Operation Murambatsvina in 2005 which displaced up to 700,000 people. Such overwhelming force deployed by a joint police, army and intelligence operation was a new phenomenon. There was a retreat into individualist

---

14 Ibid.

survivalist strategies as the civic and political spaces shrank considerably by the mid-2000s. However, this did not mean that labour's political muscle could be written off. In the March 2008 campaign, the structures of the labour movement would still make a positive contribution to the parliamentary election performance of the opposition movement.

Authoritarian repression of labour

The labour movement represented the most formidable force in civil society against assaults on living standards and democratic rights during the decade after 2000. By and large, its political weight was still undiminished, which was why the Mugabe government waged a systematic and relentless attack against it. The repression of unions was probably even more concerted than that by the colonial state in the 1960s and 1970s. They were viewed as a possible vehicle for political change, as in Zambia under Frederick Chiluba in the early 1990s, and the stage from 2000 was set for a systematic suppression of them. There are few or no parallels of such state repression in post-colonial southern Africa. The state directed its repressive resources from the law and courts to police and intelligence forces, and from war veterans and the media to local state structures.

The unions were a major target for several reasons.[15] First, they were viewed as bedfellows of the MDC and were accused of having provided infrastructure and other forms of support to it. For example, the ZCTU's national presence through offices and branches in cities, towns and regions was an asset viewed as playing a facilitative role. In particular, union infrastructure and organisers were seen by the governing party as a major political threat, and therefore an object of attack. Examples include the murder of union activists such as Talent Chiminya, arson attacks on union offices in Bulawayo in 2000, and repeated raids on the ZCTU head office.

As we observed above, laws such as POSA in 2002, and the Access to Information and Protection of Privacy Act in 2003 facilitated the state campaign of harassment and coercion. In sum, unions were viewed as incubators for a new breed of opposition politicians with strong roots both at workplaces and in communities. The ZCTU was required to apply for police permission to hold public meetings. The police insisted on deploying POSA, insisting that 'speakers at meetings or conferences should spread messages of peace and not instigate violence or demonise

---

15 Sachikonye and Matombo, 2010.

the head of state, and that any member of law enforcement agencies would have access to the gathering'.[16] When the courts ruled that POSA contradicted the basic right to 'freedom of assembly', the government crafted the Criminal Codification Act (2006) to tighten repression, thus making it a serial offender against basic freedoms and civil liberties.

A number of key events illustrate the pattern of repression between 2001 and 2008. The first was a strike at ZISCO in Redcliff in 2001 that witnessed the shooting of 4 miners and the injuring of another 22. The second was in November 2003 when unions gathered to protest against basic commodity price increases. This resulted in the detention of a number of ZCTU leaders and officials. The third episode was in November 2005 when 37 unionists in Mutare and 119 in Harare were arrested in a bid to prevent a nationwide demonstration. In a fourth event, in April 2007, ZCTU officials and members were arrested and their campaign materials confiscated. In December 2008, there was a public protest against cash withdrawal limits, leading to the detention of union officials and members.

Perhaps the most comprehensive source of the impact of authoritarianism on the union movement in this period was a report compiled by the International Labour Organization.[17] Drawing on testimonies from unionists, business leaders and state officials, it paints a grim picture of how the state organs hounded unions. It observed:

- Routine infringements of workers' right to strike and demonstrate;

- Widespread arrests, detentions, assaults and torture of union officials and members;

- Intimidation and harassment of unions and their members, including teachers and farm workers;

- Patterns of interference in union affairs and anti-union discrimination;

- Obstructions to collective bargaining and social dialogue processes; and

- Failure in institutional protection of union rights.[18]

The report also observed that:

---

16 Ibid.
17 ILO, 2009.
18 Ibid., p. 75.

...often unionists were arrested and detained to be released some time afterwards without being charged. No one had been convicted of any crime despite the many detentions, thus evidencing a campaign against the ZCTU that was not based on criminal actions but aimed at penalizing union membership and activism.[19]

In this politicised environment, the machinery of repression was directed from the centre by the political leadership. Unionists believed that the police 'was controlled from outside the police force, and that the Central Intelligence Organisation (CIO) was everywhere.'[20] Members of the public service Apex Council stated that the CIO, police and army were politicised and consequently they believed 'that there was no one to protect you'.[21]

Perhaps no episode in the annals of repression was as emblematic as the torture of the ZCTU leadership in September 2006. This was perpetrated by the state to punish the leadership for its participation in a nationwide demonstration against government economic policies (see Box 1 below).

Box 1: Torture of unionists during the 13 September 2006 demonstration

The ILO Commission was informed of the particular violence by security forces associated with the ZCTU-organised demonstration of 13 September 2006. In Harare, 14 trade union officials were arrested and transported in a truck that was so overcrowded that many suffered injuries on the way to the Matapi holding cell. Once there, the unionists were taken into cells to be beaten by 5 police officers for up to 45 minutes.

Many unionists mentioned that they had seen the ZCTU President come out bleeding and weeping. He had stated that 'I never thought that I was going to survive'. The ZCTU President described the incident as 'excruciatingly painful for him', and a medical report listed bruising, a fractured finger and anaemia secondary to injury.

The Commission then heard a harrowing statement of the assault of the ZCTU Secretary General. He lost consciousness after he had been beaten until the next morning when he woke up to find himself soaked in blood. He was only admitted to hospital with the rest of the group 24 hours after the beatings. A medical report listed fractures to his wrist and hand, a laceration to his scalp and bruising. Injury to his wrist and hand had resulted in permanent damage.

Many unionists indicated that, as they had received medical treatment

---

19 Ibid., p. 73.
20 Ibid.
21 Ibid.

late, they had experienced permanent problems. One stated that he had been beaten on the soles of his feet and since then had not been able to wear closed shoes. He stated that he needed painkillers with him at all times and was disabled for life.[22]

Source: ILO, 2009, p. 73.

The ILO Commission was provided with 14 medical and psychological reports on an estimated 83 workers arrested and detained on that date in Chegutu, Chinhoyi, Chitungwiza, Gweru, Harare, Hwange, Kwekwe, Rusape and Victoria Falls. Reports detailed injuries such as fractures, lacerations, bruises, swelling and blood loss leading to anaemia.

The relentless onslaught on the leadership and membership of unions had profound consequences for their capacity to regroup and sustain pressure on the state. The media chose to focus on the assaults on MDC leadership in March 2007, and largely ignored that of September 2006 on unionists. By the end of the decade, some unionists spoke of a strong sense of fear and insecurity, and of an overriding threat of harassment and violence.[23] As the ILO Commission recalled:

> … the ZCTU stated that it had been 'brought to its knees' by the huge numbers of arrests and detentions of its members. Its resources had been 'depleted' by the cost of legal fees, bail fines, provision of food for detained unionists, transport for lawyers and officials searching for those detained in police cells around the country, and medical costs.[24]

The Reserve Bank of Zimbabwe controlled ZCTU funds accruing from overseas donations. Access to the account was controlled by the RBZ, and sometimes payment was withheld leading to delays in payment of its staff salaries and other costs.

The decade-long struggle yielded no material gains to unionists, although the opposition MDC parties received benefits from entering the Government of National Unity in 2009.[25] It was unfortunate that the ZCTU would not use the respite of the GNU to regroup and re-strategise.

---

22 Sachikonye, 2011.
23 Ibid., p. 97.
24 Ibid., p. 127.
25 Raftopoulos, 2013.

Box 2: ZCTU's Emergency Support Project (ESP)

The Emergency Support Project (ESP) was established in 2003 by the ZCTU to build its capacity to respond to urgent needs and issues of the working people and the entire nation in the face of the political, social and economic crisis that the country was facing. It sought to build its operational capacity, increase its visibility and respond quickly to national needs. It sought to:

- find an effective information dissemination strategy that will ensure swift response to urgent issues;
- campaign for repeal of draconian laws and to meet litigation costs; and
- revamp the ZCTU regional and district structures and establish the remaining regional offices.

The establishment of the ZCTU regions has made the organisation visible throughout the country. Some of the successes noted by the regions include a protest against high taxation, and the organising of stayaways, protests, labour forums, and Workers' Day events.

Source: ZCTU, 2006, pp. 27-28

The Minister of Labour was a former unionist who had sympathy for the labour movement, and the Prime Minister had been a former ZCTU Secretary General. Infighting amongst the leadership was so damaging at the 2011 ZCTU congress that a splinter federation was created. This resulted in some unions breaking away from the ZCTU, dealing it a huge blow from which it has yet to fully recover.

Long-term impact of deindustrialisation and fragmentation

In the late 1990s, the decline and closure of companies had already commenced as a consequence of structural adjustment. One sector that was significantly affected was textiles and clothing.[26] In the post-2000 period, there was an acceleration of this process in manufacturing, including agro-industry. The disruption of agriculture and industry linkages on the back of the land reform reverberated throughout the economy. That dislocation was reflected in the more than 50 per cent decline in GDP in the first decade of the 2000s. For instance, the formerly vibrant agroindustry shrank, as imports of fertilisers and tractors from China increased. The decline of manufacturing ensured the shrinkage of employment in the sector.

The process of deindustrialisation not only weakened the economy but abetted the expansion of the informal economy as thousands of workers were laid off. As one analyst observed, the departure of workers from Zimbabwe's formal sector left it severely depleted to such an extent that

---

26 Sachikonye, 1999.

in 2008 the ZCTU estimated that only 6 per cent of the population was in formal employment.[27]

The combination of economic contraction and hyperinflation contributed to the 'disintegration of the working class at various levels'.[28] Even those workers who remained in the formal sector had footholds in the informal economy to supplement their livelihoods. The shift to investing most of their energies in coping with the economic crisis left little time for civic and political activism. One strand of opinion argued that 'workerist' forms of responses such as protests and food riots were no longer viable, and that low levels of class-consciousness prevented the workers from rallying together against the crisis.[29] However, the militancy of the unionists remained undiminished, as evidenced by the ferocity of state repression.

As we observed above, 'survivalism', and straddling the formal and informal economies, became a coping strategy for most workers. This had an effect on class-consciousness but perhaps not to the degree claimed by some analysts. However, the more the numbers grew in the informal economy, the harder it became to organise demonstrations and mass stayaways. As a disparate constituency, informal economy operators were difficult to organise around a single agenda, and the state took advantage of this in subsequent years.

Broadly speaking, the shrinking of the political and civil space contributed to an increase in individualism as 'almost each worker was now looking at ways and means of sustaining one's family, due to the fact that confronting the regime as a collective was proving to be difficult, if not dangerous.[30] Large numbers of workers were now engaged in informal sector activities such as cross-border trading, moonlighting, forex and fuel dealing, mining and petty commodity production and marketing. The period between 2009 and 2017 saw a replication, if not intensification, of this process of informalisation.

The trend of fragmentation was a major setback to the labour movement after 2011. While previous attempts at fragmentation fomented by the state had been feeble, and were largely contained by the ZCTU, this changed in the aftermath of the 2011 Congress. The split within the

---

27 Chagonda, 2011, p. 189.
28 Ibid.
29 Ibid., p. 193.
30 Ibid., p. 187.

labour centre had a debilitating effect on the ZCTU and its constituent affiliates. The factors behind the split were complex, but the competition for leadership was a major one; refusal to abide by the election results was the immediate background to the split. A legal contest ensued in which the rump that refused to accept the results lost their case in the court. The reverberations of the split were still being felt some seven years later. Internal fragmentation weakened the labour movement in a way, and to an extent, that state authoritarianism had not.

Why did the interregnum of the GNU fail to provide respite to the labour movement? First, the coercive apparatus remained in the hands of ZANU(PF). The anti-labour tendencies of that apparatus were not curbed despite the presence of MDC ministers within the Cabinet. Second, in an act of commission or omission, the MDC parties did not actively cultivate ties with the labour movement, still less did they encourage mediation between the feuding sides. The organic ties between labour and the MDC became moribund, to the disadvantage of both sides. The electoral weight of labour was consequently much weaker in the 2013 election than in previous ones. Third, the 2015 Supreme Court judgment in the Zuwa case resulted in the retrenchment of up to 20,000 workers within a month. The Supreme Court had ruled in July 2015 that Zuva Petroluum could use the Common Law to terminate an employee's contract on notice without giving reasons (see Chapter 9 for background to this judgement). Many employers had taken advantage of this judgement to fire workers. This development became emblematic of a weakened and fragmented labour movement operating in a context in which the influence of business interests on the state had increased considerably. For its part, through the Labour Amendment Act No. 5 of 2015, the government subsequently sought to reverse the judgement and to slow down widespread retrenchments.

Sectoral responses to the crises: Agriculture

The shifts in the economy and state policies were keenly felt at sectoral levels. The nuances in the initiatives of the state and responses of labour are captured in developments in agriculture and mining during the period under review. Elsewhere, it has been shown how land reform diminished the numbers of permanent workers and displaced many casual workers, inducing profound changes within the agricultural proletariat.[31] The

---

31 Sachikonye, 2016; Hartnack, 2016.

national economic crisis was reflected at the sectoral level by a decline in the production of both cash and food crops for about 12 years before recovery to pre-2000 levels. This reflected the dispersal of skills, and capital, and the breakdown of order during the land reform. Labour was a major casualty in that decline but was also an active participant in resistance to the manner of the reform, and the struggles for better working conditions under the new black farmers. Displaced farm workers accounted for more than half of the original agricultural workforce, and they did not acquiesce passively to the new regime on farms.

Until 2000, farm workers had been dependent on a 'conditional mode of belonging', sometimes termed 'domestic government', that determined what claims they could make, and the terms of their struggles for access to resources and livelihoods.[32] The changes in ownership of farms and type of employer caused shifts in the labour regime, and two positions have emerged on the depth of the impact of those changes. The first is that there were overwhelmingly progressive changes for labour arising from land reform. It was claimed that some 170,000 farm households were beneficiaries of a land reform that went on to create 355,000 permanent posts in addition to a million casual jobs.[33] According to this perspective, the old relations of exploitation on farms were superseded by a freer labour regime.

The second position contends that while specific forms of power associated with domestic government and bio-political maternalism might have diminished, land reform had not done away with problematic power relations. Instead, the reform had provided a different set of power relations and challenges that farm workers must continue to negotiate to meet their short- and long-term needs.[34] Indeed, most evidence suggests that new modes of belonging often forced farm workers to rely on their own ingenuity as resources and welfare offered prior to 2000 became more insecure. In the post-land reform period:

> ... while still dependent on farms for cash and shelter, farm workers began to hedge their bets and to look elsewhere to meet the balance of their needs and long-term strategies.[35]

Not only was the labour regime far from settled, but also the above-

---

32 Hartnack, 2016.
33 Chambati, 2013.
34 Hartnack, 2016, p. 114.
35 Ibid., p. 118.

cited figures of new farm jobs were exaggerated.

Farm workers were embroiled in the violence and politics that accompanied land reform. They were often victims of state-sanctioned violence as bands of land occupiers, war veterans and ZANU(PF) party youth, with collusion of the CIO, 'invaded' the farms. In some instances, a number of farm workers also participated in the occupations with the hope of acquiring land. In other instances, farm workers joined farm owners to resist the occupations, and this resulted in defensive violence. In both scenarios, the long-term impact of that violence included trauma and displacement, as a number of surveys have shown.[36]

Early empirical studies on the redistributed farms referred to a fluid situation in the emergent labour regime.[37] However, by 2015 distinct outlines of that regime could be identified. On some of the researched farms, workers were dependent on small but reliable salaries that allowed them to invest in a range of off-farm projects to further their family interests.[38] Workers saw advantages in free accommodation, electricity and water, vegetable gardens and plots for crops. This was a benign regime of weakened 'domestic government' whose operators did not enforce strict rules on what the workers did with their free time. Most households survived on such crops, and piecework on more productive neighbouring farms, while others engaged in brick moulding and gold panning.

Thus the straddling of the formal sector and informal sector activities by agricultural workers replicated what was happening in other economic sectors. In both cases, precarious wage conditions compelled workers to engage in multiple income earning activities in the informal economy. There were certainly instances in which the emergent labour regime was much worse. As one interviewee put it graphically:

> ... with the old slavery, we used to get shelter, salary, food, clothes, but with this new slavery, we only got houses – no pay, no food, no clothes – and we are told we had to work for him in order to stay. It is modern day slavery.[39]

This is the broad context in which the farm labour unions have operated since the land reform. The most prominent has been GAPWUZ, whose fortunes have waned since the early 2000s for a variety of reasons.

36 Research and Advocacy Unit, 2009.
37 Sachikonye, 2003.
38 Hartnack, op. cit., p. 131.
39 Quoted in Hartnack, 2016, p. 133.

Displacement and decline in production resulted in membership dropping from an estimated 100,000 around 1999 to below 50,000 after 2000. The authoritarian repression of national level unions was replicated in the conscious suppression of GAPWUZ activities at the sectoral level. Unionists became targets of harassment and violence. For instance, electoral violence on farms served as retribution for commercial farmers' support for the MDC in the referendum and parliamentary elections, and as a deterrent to GAPWUZ activists and members. As an analyst observed:

> ... farm workers and former farm workers had to attach themselves to territorialized forms of power that were even more conditional as they operated through the extremely precarious landscapes of *jambanja*. Electoral politics began to reshape the grounds of everyday life throughout Zimbabwe, but nowhere as dramatically and effectively as the lands and social landscapes of commercial farmers.[40]

Thus farm workers and their main union, GAPWUZ, were in a much more vulnerable position in the post-reform period. Their labour rights were largely trampled on, and precariously low wages forced them to engage in supplementary informal activities. The Secretary General of GAPWUZ was summoned by the Joint Operations Command and harassed, before being hounded into exile. The state supported the formation of splinter unions in the sector, further weakening the presence of GAPWUZ. Examples of such unions included the Horticultural and General Agricultural and Plantation Workers' Union of Zimbabwe, the Zimbabwe Horticulture Agro-industries and General Workers' Union, and the Kapenta Workers' Union of Zimbabwe. These splinter unions were affiliated to the state-sponsored ZFTU. It is due to its resilience under adverse conditions that GAPWUZ did not disband.

Sectoral developments: Mining

Mining was no exception to the broad trends of patronage, fragmentation, informalisation and decline in formal sector employment. Risky though commodity dependence has often been, it was now touted by the authorities as a pathway to economic recovery and development. Yet the first half of the 2000s witnessed a contraction in mining: 14 mines closed, and employment in the sector slumped to about 45,000.

---

40 Rutherford, 2017, p. 192.

With the exception of platinum, gold and diamonds, there was a general decline in mining employment during the decade. It was observed that:

> ... those that left employment were hardly ever replaced unless their work could not be shared by those already employed. The loss of skills to the region and beyond had a telling effect on production and safety performance. Many supervisory positions in the industry are currently filled by young people who would ordinarily have been under supervision themselves.[41]

In the copper sub-sector, the closure of a major mine in Mhangura resulted in major job losses. Similarly, retrenchments followed cutbacks in coal production at Hwange and the cessation of iron and steel manufacture at ZISCO.

As the decade progressed, diamond discoveries at Marange renewed interest in the sector. Incentives for small miners encouraged delivery of gold to the RBZ. Platinum production expanded on the back of higher commodity prices.

Following the introduction of dollarisation in 2009, confidence was created in both the formal and informal sectors leading to a major rise in output in most mineral sub-sectors, and the mining contribution to GDP reached 37 per cent in 2011 before coming down to about 11 per cent in 2013. The improved macroeconomic stability and the global commodity boom prior to 2015 contributed to the good performance of the sector. It was a performance that fuelled employment growth of about 6 percent in 2010 and 16 per cent in 2011, before falling to 5 per cent in 2014.[42]

Significantly, there has been phenomenal growth in artisanal mining since the early 2000s. Fuelled by activities of small-scale gold and diamond miners, the informal sector has experienced unparalleled growth.[43] Artisanal gold mining saved the gold sub-sector from possible collapse in the mid-2000s, as production by small miners doubled in value between 2003 and 2004 due to price incentives introduced by the RBZ.

One assessment of the artisanal gold sub-sector observed that this period was a high point in the proliferation of mining by *'makorokoza'* (small-scale miners) in many regions of country, from Kwekwe and Kadoma to Mazowe.[44] Indeed, while official gold output was declining

---

41 Matyanga, 2011, p. 171.
42 LEDRIZ, 2016, p. 18.
43 Mawowa, 2013; Nyamunda and Mukwambo, 2012.
44 Mawowa, 2013.

due to 'the scaling down and closure of formal mining operations, artisanal small-scale mining output was rising. It is thus safe to say that formal figures portray an exaggerated picture of receding gold output; rather, most gold was channeled into the parallel market. By 2008, some two million Zimbabweans were dependent on ASM gold mining.[45] Of those, some 500,000 were estimated to be employed informally in the sector, compared with an estimated 700,000 in the formal sector.

Informalisation in mining has taken the form of proliferation of small miners who employ a few other miners often in difficult conditions. Occupational safety and health standards are low in this sector, and wage conditions are often unregulated, and below the gazetted levels. At the same time, the proportion of self-employed small miners is high. The precarious conditions of survivalism, individualism and contested ownership of mining claims make it difficult to encourage union membership. There does not appear to be a working relationship between formal sector mineworkers and small miners. This could well be a lost opportunity, given their common grievances and needs.

As in the lands sector, state patronage is a major factor in the distribution of access to mines. Mining claims have often been allocated or hoarded for explicitly political purposes. In such gold-rich districts as Kwekwe, Chegutu and Mazowe, landlords with strong political connections control access to mines. An elaborate system of patronage has developed in which the ruling party and the state exercise immense control.[46] Party membership and loyalties are requisites to access to the mining claims just as they are to rural land. Patronage has been deeply embedded in the accumulation and informalisation processes. In the short term, this might have been to the electoral advantage of the ruling party, as the 2013 outcome seemed to suggest.

Violence has also been a feature in the small-scale mining sector as well as in the large-scale diamond sub-sector. Contested access to mining claims has generated violence resulting in deaths and injuries in such areas as Kwekwe and Mazowe. In Marange, the most serious clash between state authorities and small miners was in 2008 when an estimated 200 of the latter were killed.[47] The army was directly involved .

The fragmentation of unions in mining has been acute as in agriculture. There are six mineworkers' unions: the National Mineworkers' Union of

45 Ibid.
46 Ibid.
47 Human Rights Watch, 2009.

Zimbabwe, the Mining Workers' Union of Zimbabwe, the National Union of Mine Engineers and Quarrying Workers, based at ZISCO, the Black Granite and Quarrying Workers Union, the Diamond Workers' Union of Zimbabwe, and the Associated Mineworkers Union of Zimbabwe. Although the latter remains the largest, it has lost members to the newer unions. Some of the splinter unions are affiliated to the ZCTU, others to the state-sponsored ZFTU.

Towards renewal of the labour movement?

By 2017, the labour movement had been through such formidable 'thick and thin' that it was remarkable that it still survived. This is not to underestimate the damage inflicted upon it by the state, the negative effect of decline in donor support, and the debilitating consequences of fragmentation. Yet some analysts might have exaggerated the overall effect of these developments.[48] For instance, the assertion that it was its adoption of a 'regime change' agenda and a misreading of Zimbabwe's social structure that contributed to the purported decline of the ZCTU was a misleading exaggeration. While some limitations in analysis and practice had occurred, there still existed room for self-criticism within the labour movement. For instance, the 2016 Congress provided a forum to ventilate views and criticism of what had gone wrong in the previous decade.

The Congress adopted a number of resolutions:

Expanded recruitment strategy

- Intensify membership recruitment, retention and renewal to bring back workers and unions who have fallen out of the ZCTU.

- Organise in areas that are not organised like the Kombi drivers, conductors and non-governmental organisations.

- Embark on recruitment in areas that are outside the realm of the ZCTU like the pensions sector.

- Speed up the affiliation of the Zimbabwe Chamber of Informal Economy Association (ZCIEA).

- Speed up the processing of applications by unions that have applied for affiliation.

- Minimise union fragmentation and splits and work towards union mergers.

---

48 Yeros, 2013.

Seeking of self-reliance

- Allow affiliates to hire some services they may need from ZCTU departments at a cost, e.g accounting services, as an option to employment or consultancy hiring.

- Live within the organisational financial means in the short term.

- Diversify sources and embark on income generation in the long term.

Pursuit of Renewal

- Rebrand the ZCTU operations to attain its former glory and attract members.

- Clarify the role and position of ZCTU in the political environment.

- Redefine how to deal with the politics of the country without losing identity as a labour movement.[49]

These resolutions sum up the aspirations of unions that had faced enormous difficulties on the economic, social and political fronts in the past decade. There was a new pragmatism in this labour movement that sought renewal in a challenging environment of low, jobless growth. Despite the euphoria associated with the coming of a 'new dispensation' in November 2017, neither the economy nor employment creation will improve immediately or automatically. The same caution will apply to political reform that leads to a democratic transition. The 2018 election outcome will give indicators on the direction of political sentiment but will not necessarily guarantee that a democratic transition follows.

Conclusion

Conventional wisdom tends to date the high point of the strength and popular reach of the labour movement as 1999, while from 2000 onward its fortunes were mainly downhill.[50] This chapter has sought to question that wisdom. It has argued that the toughest tests that the movement endured were during the 2000s, under relentless onslaught from a regime that was fighting for its survival. The ferocity of state's repression of labour was unprecedented; indeed, it could be argued that it was even fiercer than before 1980. This reflected the fear and apprehension of the incumbent government that it might be dislodged by a mass political

49 ZCTU, 2016.
50 Yeros, P., 2013

movement in which labour was the key player. The Zambian precedent of the ascendancy of the Movement for Multiparty Democracy (MMD) was anathema to the Mugabe regime.

However, the chapter began by setting the wider context of the contest between state and labour. Deepening political and economic crises constituted that context. The state itself was riven in crisis as policy coherence and competence levels collapsed. The economic crisis dealt a huge blow to production conditions in industry and agriculture, leading to company closures and job lay-offs. Not only did thousands of firms and farms close, but unions lost many members and subscriptions. Deindustrialisation led to spread of informalisation in which union organising was more difficult.

When labour responded through strikes to slow down the erosion of their wage conditions, and participated in civic and political struggles against authoritarianism, it was met with a ferocious state response. The scope and depth of that repression has not been given sufficient weight in analyses of the subsequent weakening and fragmentation of the labour movement after 2009.

The chapter then explored the crises and responses of labour at sectoral levels. Disruption of production conditions in agriculture following land reform, and trends towards informalisation in mining, have generated conditions of emergent labour regimes that remain fluid. Conditions of work and livelihoods have become more precarious for thousands of agricultural workers who have to pursue multiple activities inside and outside farms to survive. State patronage remains a major feature in the allocation of land and mining claims, and ensures an electoral base for the ruling party in both sectors. Labour unions in these sectors have splintered under the weight of state repression, and they will need to overcome that fragmentation to renew themselves.

If there are any lessons from labour's experiences in the post-2000 period, they include that the struggles for improved economic conditions and democratic space are not separable. State authoritarianism remains a formidable obstacle to labour's emancipation. Furthermore, the struggles are marathons, not short-term sprints. The labour movement needs to have medium- and long-term strategies to renew itself for those protracted economic and democratic struggles.

Chapter 6

Changes in Trade Unions and Trade Union Influences

Brian Raftopoulos, Godfrey Kanyenze and Lloyd Sachikonye

Introduction

The massive changes in employment patterns discussed in previous chapters predictably had substantive effects on the structures and activities of the labour movement. The rapid informalisation of the economy with its concomitant depletion of formal sector employment eroded the membership, sustainability and effectiveness of the unions and raised questions amongst workers about their relevance as representative organisations. Along with the other challenges faced by trade unions, which will be discussed below, this once central pillar of alternative mobilisation and critical debate within Zimbabwe's public sphere has had to confront the challenges of growing marginalisation in a trajectory that two decades ago placed it at the heart of an alternative socio-economic and political vision. This chapter will seek to draw out these changes and their implications.

Economic crisis and decline in membership

Some of the debilitating challenges facing the labour movement today were highlighted during interviews with unions as follows:

> What is troubling in moving union business forward is the current economic challenges. We are not finding enough time to move out in pursuit of union affairs and some union education of members is deficient.[1]

---

1 Notes recorded during the interview with the Federation of Food and Allied Workers' Union of Zimbabwe (FFAWUZ), 19 November 2016.

145

The challenges we are facing relate to financial issues. You know that we do not have money even though we are managing with whatever we have. But if we had money we could be doing outreach programmes.... The whole year we did not have education programmes such as training workers committees because of lack of funding.[2]

Significantly, the strength of a trade union is dependent on the size of its membership, and the extent to which they participate in union activities and pay subscriptions. Table 1 (see Appendix ZCTU Membership 2006-17) shows the membership of trade unions affiliated to the Zimbabwe Congress of Trade Unions (ZCTU) for the period 2006-2017.

The challenges experienced since the late 1990s resulted in a growing loss of union membership. While union membership stood at 155,000 (19.1 per cent of contributors to the National Social Security Authority (NSSA)) in 2000,[3] it increased to 179,982 (22.7 per cent) in 2001, declined to 170,238 (22 per cent) in 2002, recovered to 210,738 (21 per cent) in 2003, 219,418 (22.2 per cent NSSA) in 2004, 244,622 (25.7 per cent) in 2006, 250,131 (26.3 per cent) in 2007, and declined 137,754 (12.2 per cent) in 2013, 96,434 (7.8 per cent) in 2016 and 89,818 (7.5 per cent) in 2017 (see Table 1).[4]

The decimation of union membership is clearly underscored with respect to the ZCTU's largest affiliates. For instance, the membership of the National Engineering Workers Union dropped from 15,000 to 3,200 during 2006-10. The General Agricultural and Plantation Workers Union (GAPWUZ)'s membership fell from 15,000 during 2006-10 to 1,428 by 2017. The National Union of the Clothing Industry saw its membership decline from 10,530 during 2006-10 to only 1,118 by 2017, while that

---

2 Interview with Unner Goremusunda, National Organising Secretary of the Commercial Workers' Union of Zimbabwe, 17 December 2016.

3 Given the integrity challenges associated with formal sector employment data and its inconsistencies, we use the total contributors to the obligatory National Social Security Authority (NSSA) as a proxy of the workforce.

4 NSSA data excludes domestic workers who are not covered by the scheme. In addition, civil servants joined NSSA on 1 June 2002. For the period 2009-14, where employment data are available on a consistent basis from Zimstat since the break in 2002, the NSSA contributors are very close to the Zimstat statistics on total employment. The latter gives formal employment levels of 969,000 (2009), 1,199,000 (2010), 1,136,000 (2011), 1,089,000 (2012), 1,035,000 (2013 and 1,108,000 (2014). [See National Accounts, 2009-2014 Report, Zimstat, August 2015, Table 7.7(a), p. 49].

of the Zimbabwe Textiles Workers Union fell from 11,500 in 2006 to 1,252 by 2017. Membership of the Iron and Steel Workers Union of Zimbabwe ended in 2007 because the union was company-based; when Ziscosteel ceased operating, membership stopped. The precipitous fall in the membership of the Commercial Workers Union of Zimbabwe from 41,000 during 2006-10 to only 2,017 by 2017 is due to the internal disputes that resulted in the union breaking into two separate unions, with the larger grouping disaffiliating from the ZCTU.

This loss of membership in turn affected the financial viability of the unions because of the decline of membership subscriptions. One union described the issue of non-payment of union dues as 'rendering us useless as a union';[5] another spoke of the challenges of 4,000 workers out of a total of 7,120 not paying their subscriptions.[6] The Construction Workers Union also noted that of a potential 7,000 workers in the sector, their membership was a small fraction of that because of contract work.[7] The Catering and Hotel Workers' Union criticised employers for deducting subscriptions but not remitting these to the union.[8]

The factors affecting trade union membership are varied and some are specific to developments in the economy. During the period of escalating inflation and hyperinflation, when workers' earnings became meaningless, this also affected the value of their subscriptions. During the hyperinflation period of 2007 and 2008 in particular, most enterprises started paying workers in kind, which rendered subscriptions redundant. In some sectors, especially parastatals, it became increasingly difficult for ZCTU affiliates to collect union dues. In fact, in certain areas such as the sugar estates in Chiredzi and Triangle, and the diamond mining areas of Marange, ZCTU affiliates were barred from unionising workers.

Some unions such as the Associated Mine Workers' Union of Zimbabwe, the Leather, Shoe and Allied Workers' Union, Zimbabwe Energy Workers' Union, National Air Workers' Union (NAWU), Zimbabwe Rural District

---

5   Interview with Philemon Nhema, General Secretary, Mr. Matare, President, Ratidzo Gasva, Regional Officer Harare, and Margaret Mukucha, Regional Organiser of the Zimbabwe Security Guards Union (ZIZEGU), 1 December 2016.

6   Interview with Shepherd Mashingaidze, General Secretary and Moses Garira, President of the National Engineering Workers' Union, 13 December 2016.

7   Interview with Nicholas Muzarura the General Secretary of the Zimbabwe Construction and Allied Trades Workers' Union, 19 December 2016.

8   Interview with Gift Chibatwa, Education Officer in the Zimbabwe Catering and Hotel Workers' Union of Zimbabwe, 14 December 2016.

Councils Workers' Union, the Communication and Allied Services Union, the Progressive Teachers Union of Zimbabwe disaffiliated for various reasons. The first two withdrew their affiliation to the ZCTU for political reasons, while the others left after their leaders boycotted the 2011 ZCTU Congress alleging irregularities in the membership verification process. As a result of this dispute, seven affiliates left and later formed their own federation, the Trade Union Congress of Zimbabwe which was registered by the Ministry of Public Service, Labour and Social Welfare.

On a positive note, new unions also affiliated with the ZCTU, especially from the public sector, including the Zimbabwe Teachers Association, the Public Service Association, Zimbabwe State Universities Association, National Mine Workers' Union of Zimbabwe, ZESA Technical Workers' Association, Zimbabwe Revenue Authority Trade Union, National Energy Workers' Union of Zimbabwe, Energy Sector Workers' Union of Zimbabwe, Professional Educators Union of Zimbabwe, Railways Yard Operations Union, National Union of Metal and Allied Industries in Zimbabwe, Trade Union for Music and Arts Industry, and the Ceramics and Associated Products Workers' Union. However, even with these new additions, the net effect has been a substantial loss of membership for the labour movement.

Invariably, declining membership adversely impacts the financial position of the affiliates and the ZCTU, which in turn affects operations.

The ZCTU's liquidity ratio – a measure of the liquidity assets of the organisation – initially improved from 1.89 in 2000 to 6.81 in 2001, before declining, with some annual variations, to 0.61 by 2006, and 0.21 by 2017. With the exception of 2001 and 2003, the liquidity ratio was way below the recommended level of 2:1, suggesting that for the greater part of the period under review, ZCTU struggled to finance its operations. As noted in the Management Audit Report of 31 December 2001, 'There are some unions which appear on the register but which do not honour their subscriptions obligations. Inclusion of such unions' income on the books will materially overstate our income'.[9]

The Treasurer's Report to the 6th ZCTU General Congress on 19-20 May 2006 pointed out that the period January 2000 to December 2005 was '...generally, difficult in terms of financing our operations'.[10] To address the challenges in funding, the applicable subscriptions were raised from

---

9 ZCTU Management Audit Report 31 December 2001, p. 7.
10 Treasurer's Report to the 6th ZCTU General Congress 19-20 May 2006, p. 1.

Z$2.50 per month per member between January 2000 and July 2001 to Z$5 (August-December 2001), Z$7 (January to December 2002), Z$13 (January to July 2003), and Z$22 (January to December 2003).

During 2003, the minimum subscription payable by an affiliate was set at Z$18,750 per month from January to July, and Z$42,750 from August to December 2003, as the level of subscriptions from some affiliates were of no material value. When it became clear that the quantum based method of determining subscriptions was being undermined by rapidly rising inflation, the General Council adopted a self-adjusting system set at 5 per cent of affiliates' income with effect from 1 January 2004. However, this was still inadequate to meet the ZCTU's obligations.

At the time of dollarisation in 2009, workers were awarded allowances pegged at US$100 per month up to August of that year, at a time when the Poverty Datum Line was US$552. In the public sector, these allowances were converted to salaries with a 55 per cent increase in August 2009, while in the private sector most companies continued with the allowances. This implied that most employers could not deduct union dues from the allowances, leaving unions with no subscription income. After dollarisation, the funding situation was particularly difficult, with current assets marginally exceeding current liabilities in 2013. As highlighted in the ZCTU Treasurer's Report to the 7th ZCTU Congress:

> While companies were effecting deductions of union dues, these were not being remitted to unions in full. Some companies have gone for up to six months without remittances to the unions. As a result unions are owed varying amounts by the employers in the sectors they represent. This has created cash flow challenges crippling the unions in their endeavor to service, organize and educate their membership.[11]

A similar indictment appears in the Treasurer's Report to the ZCTU 8th General Congress, when it was indicated that:

> The trade union situation in Zimbabwe remains precarious due to the economic situation which is affecting most companies and organisations, restraining some employers from remitting union dues to unions. Retrenchments continue unabated in most sectors'.[12]

---

11 Treasurer's Report to the 7th ZCTU General Congress 19-20 August 2011, p. 9.
12 Treasurer's Report to the 8th ZCTU General Congress 29 September- 1 October 2016, p. 1.

Furthermore, while the need to charge service fees to non-members was considered, affiliate unions were reluctant to pursue the matter owing to the associated legal implications, especially as it affected freedom of association.

The total accumulated deficit as at 31 December 2015 amounted to US$1,459,759. By then, the ZCTU was failing to meet its salary and statutory obligations. Since the inception of the multi-currency regime, it incurred debts as costs exceeded income. When it became clear that this trend would persist, a resolution to restructure its operations was adopted by the General Council in April 2012, resulting in the centre approaching its external partners to assist in financing the restructuring process and liquidate its debt.

Critically, over the period under review, ZCTU remained highly dependent on its external partners, which accounted for on average 86.8 per cent of total income during the period 2000-08 and 59.1 per cent during the multi-currency period 2009-17. The decline in the share of total income arising from external support since 2010 reflected the scaling down of support and the withdrawal of some key cooperating partners.

Table 2 indicates the impact of the deteriorating financial situation on the operations of the ZCTU between 2011 and 2015.

Table 2: Financial Challenges and the Operations of the ZCTU, 2011-2015

2011	2012	2013	2014	2015
Recurring deficits	Non-holding of Constitutional meetings	Non-declaration of membership by affiliates	Non-remittance of statutory deductions	Non-confirmation of accounts receivables (subscriptions)
Deterioration of the Centre's liqudity position	Recoverability of subscriptions and levies	Late remittance of statutory deductions	Long standing receivables (subscriptions)	Corporate governance issues (non-holding of constitutional meetings) Non-declaration of membership by affiliates.

Source: ZCTU 8th General Congress, 29 September to 1 October 2016: Treasurer's Report, p. 1.

The deteriorating liquidity position resulted in the ZCTU failing to hold constitutional meetings, with the centre having to focus more on existential challenges than on mobilising and servicing its members, thereby undermining its influence. The ZCTU had to rely increasingly on its declining subscription base and focus on a sustainability strategy adopted in 2015 that emphasised investing in assets.

Politicisation, factionalism, and fragmentation

The period under review was marked by worsening relations between the ZCTU and the state. Since the ZCTU had played a leading role in the formation of the MDC, the organisation became marked, and targeted for retribution. As the General Council Report to the ZCTU 6th Ordinary Congress noted, 'The ZCTU was viewed as an enemy of the State, which in the ensuing years would play a big role in attempts to render the labour body ineffective'.[13]

The active role played by the ZCTU in the formation of the MDC weakened the trade union movement; in some cases the whole ZCTU structure, especially at district level, turned into an MDC structure overnight, leaving the ZCTU with few cadres on the ground. This was exacerbated by the high turnover of trained cadres, as some left for the diaspora. Moreover, as the leadership of the ZCTU crossed over to lead the new party, all the office-bearers elected at the 2001 Congress, except for the President Lovemore Matombo, were taking up leadership positions at the ZCTU for the first time. They therefore had to grow and learn quickly in a very hostile environment.

The situation was worsened by the fact that parliamentary elections were due in June 2000, and the presidential elections in March 2002. As the General Council Report recalled,

> Unfortunately, the ZCTU was viewed as an appendage of the MDC and thus partisan. The Labour Centre could not therefore be spared from the mudslinging and political debauchery of that period. In fact it won't be an exaggeration to suggest that during the period 2001 to 2005, the ZCTU experienced very serious political hostility and high levels of political intolerance in Zimbabwe.[14]

---

13 General Council Report to the ZCTU 6th Ordinary Congress 19-20 May 2006, p. 1.

14 Ibid., p. 2.

As a result,

> Before 1999, the ZCTU was a darling of the media especially
> during the time it led a lot of popular protests in the 1997-1999 era.
> But things soon changed in 2000 as government's stranglehold on
> the public media firmed and the assault on the ZCTU intensified.
> From then the ZCTU no longer enjoyed favourable public media
> coverage, thus the ZCTU was left with a huge task to fight for its
> visibility and survival while at the same time fulfilling its mandate
> of representing workers.[15]

This crippled the ZCTU's structures, which as reported to the 2006
Congress in the General Council Report, '…had become virtually non-
functional and activities had to be carried out from the head office'.[16] As a
result of the political situation prevailing in the country, '…the ZCTU has
not been able to establish district structures in some areas of the country'.[17]
Further, as the General Council Report to the 7th ZCTU Congress of 2011
observes, district structures experienced the highest rate of turnover of
office-bearers, a development which '…left some of our district structures
with little or no manpower, where possible co-options were done to sustain
the structure'.[18]

The measures adopted by the government to undermine the ZCTU were
well summarised in the General Council Report to the 2006 Congress:

> In the period starting from 2001, the Government of Zimbabwe was
> very determined to do away with ZCTU completely. Apart from
> making public statements to that effect and using the state controlled
> media (print and electronic) to demonize the ZCTU, other measures
> included support of the ZFTU by Government, suppression of all
> ZCTU activities, harassment and unwarranted arrests and torture
> of trade union leaders and cadres; creation of what was called the
> 'Third Force' which was a group of few unions affiliated to ZCTU.[19]

At the beginning of 2005, the group of ZCTU affiliates which christened
itself the 'Disgruntled Affiliate Workers' Union' (or 'concerned affiliates
of the ZCTU') sought to oust the ZCTU leadership from power, accusing

15 Ibid., p. 30.
16 Ibid., p. 28.
17 Ibid., p. 36.
18 General Council Report to the 7th ZCTU Congress 2011, p. 18.
19 General Council Report to the 2006 Congress, p. 14.

it of '... disregarding the ZCTU constitution, corruption and negation of duty by turning to politics instead of representing workers'.[20] This group became particularly disruptive, attacking the ZCTU leadership through the press, using aggressive behaviour at ZCTU meetings, assaulting some members of the General Council, and using the ZCTU letterhead without authority.

As their behaviour became increasingly raucous, the General Council resolved to suspend the four affiliate leaders in their individual capacities from the General Council at its meeting of 13 August 2005. These four leaders were Nicholas Mazarura of the Zimbabwe Construction and Allied Trades Workers' Union; Farai Makanda of the Transport and General Workers' Union; Langton Mugeji of the Zimbabwe Leather Shoe and Allied Workers' Union; and Joseph Midzi of the Associated Mineworkers' Union of Zimbabwe.

For similar reasons, on the recommendation of the Women's Advisory Council, the General Council further suspended Enjula Mpofu of the Zimbabwe Construction and Allied Trades Workers' Union, Sizai Shava of the Associated Mineworkers' Union of Zimbabwe, and P. Mukumbi of the Radio and TV Union. In addition, on 3 September 2005, the General Council further suspended the ZCTU's third Vice-President, Edmund Ruzive, for attending the 93rd ILO conference without approval and speaking against the positions, policies and principles of the ZCTU, thereby bringing the name of the organisation into disrepute.[21]

Even the ZANU(PF)-affiliated Federation experienced problems with employers connected to the ruling party. As the Secretary General of the ZFTU said:

> If you go to Chiredzi you will find that politicians are involved in the making of ... squabbles.... When you see people do not have the implements to convert sugar cane into sugar. All they are interested in as war veterans is to say I now have all these hectares of sugar. But what next? Are you putting it into production? No, because there is no other crop that can thrive in the Lowveld other

---

20 Ibid., p. 39.
21 The suspension of Nicholas Mazarura and Enjula Mpofu, both of the Zimbabwe Construction and Allied Trades Workers' Union, was lifted at the 7th ZCTU Congress held on 19-20 August 2011 following appeal by the affected and their union with the proviso for strict monitoring by the General Council (See Minutes of the ZCTU 7th National Congress, 19-20 August 2011, Elite 400, Bulawayo, pp. 30-31).

than sugar. So if you take it as a war veteran you are a ZANU(PF) staunch supporter and then you redund almost 200 workers. What does that mean? So that is politics which is so cruel and amateurish. Lack of revolutionary zeal. Lack of ideological pathway.[22]

Fragmentation and precariousness of unions has been on the rise, resulting in the weakening of their institutional bargaining power. This process has also been reflected in the trade union federations, where the splintering of these structures has eroded their power to bargain and to mobilise workers. To consolidate its power and to counter the involvement of the ZCTU in politics, the ruling party deliberately fragmented the labour movement.

Signifying the new trade union dispensation that has accompanied the increasingly authoritarian character of the state since the early 2000s, a new rival union federation, the Zimbabwe Federation of Trade Unions was formed in 1998 and since then splinter unions have dominated the agricultural and mining sectors, both key sites of ruling party accumulation. To further strengthen the membership of these splinter unions, the ZCTU-affiliated unions were banned from recruiting members in the mining and farming sectors in order to close down any perceived opposition influences in these areas. As one unionist describes the process, most splinter organisations were 'born out of political differences':

> In actual fact most were born when ZCTU itself paved the way for the creation of the MDC. So that's how most of these were formed because ZANU(PF) wanted its own unions which must pay allegiance to ZANU(PF). So the way I see it is that the people who then came to lead these organisations themselves did not have a trade union background. And initially their approach to issues was based on threats... So they actually managed to woo workers to say now we have an organisation which can threaten our employers and our employers can do this and that.[23]

The General Council Report to the 2006 Congress notes that in 2003 alone, nine splinter unions were registered. One example was the Private Security Workers' Union (PSEWU), which was politically affiliated to the ruling party and opposed to the ZCTU-affiliated Zimbabwe Security

---

22 Op cit., interview with the Zimbabwe Federation of Trade Unions.
23 Interview with Gift Chibatwa, Education Officer in the Zimbabwe Catering and Hotel Workers' Union of Zimbabwe, 14 December 2016.

Guards Union (ZISEGU). The formation of the former was described in the following terms:

> So they formed this other union as they did not want ZISEGU to have an impact. It came into being just like that and we began to hear that there is another union…There was nothing we could do because they already had a certificate we had to accept the situation. But that one is our rival union which says that these things are not important each time we advocate for good things.[24]

The closeness of unions to the state also provided them with a measure of negotiating and political muscle. In the case of the ZFTU, the Secretary General openly declared his use of political connections to push the Federation's agenda. 'Some of us,' he stated, 'are also brought up in political families so there is no one who can challenge me not even using an iota of political power. Because some of us have got bigger political clout than them. So we assist in that order.'[25]

This problem is compounded by the fact that a growing number of new employers are also government and ruling party officials. Thus, the perception amongst unionists is that what these indigenous, ZANU(PF)-linked employers are saying, 'is the same things that is being said by the Government. This means they are walking together'.[26] Statements from other unions confirm this trend. In the construction sector, unions were faced with ministers who refused to pay the statutory wages, saying, 'I am a minister, why are you asking me to pay this one?'[27] As noted above, this is particularly true in the mining and agricultural sectors, in both of which a new breed of politically connected employers emerged, sometimes blocking union efforts to organise and recruit members. This was especially true in the diamond mines, where their reported bureaucracy involved applications to the ruling party for unions to get permission to enter mines. There were cases where employers meddled in union affairs by way of choosing who could address their employees. If unions did not subscribe to certain political preferences they were dismissed and denied

---

24 Op cit., Interview with ZISEGU.

25 Interview with K. Shamuyarira, Secretary General of the Zimbabwe Federation of Trade Unions and the General Secretary of the National Education Workers' Union, 21 December 2016.

26 Ibid.

27 Op cit., Interview with the Zimbabwe Construction and Allied Workers' Union.

a chance to speak to potential recruits.[28]

An interesting case of interference in trade union work is with respect to the agricultural sector. Ever since the onset of the land invasions and the Fast Track Land Reform Programme in 2000, GAPWUZ has operated in a hostile and perilous environment:

> Farm-worker communities have perhaps been the greatest casualties of the fast-track programme, as many had to endure accusations of being aliens, of being saboteurs supporting the white farmers, and of being members of opposition political parties.[29]

Rival unions emerged which used unconventional methods of recruitment and operating. One such rival, H-GAPWUZ, which is affiliated to the ZFTU, often creates confusion by misrepresenting itself as GAPWUZ.

Agreements reached with the bona fide collective bargaining structures of the National Employment Council for the Agricultural Sector were ignored on the premise that these did not represent the interests of the new black farmers, who had not been capacitated to implement the Collective Bargaining Agreements. Those who asked questions of the authorities or advocated for rights were seen as agitating against the state. For instance, in 2006, the ministry refused to register a Collective Bargaining Agreement for Agriculture, arguing that it did not reflect the new reality of many small black farmers where large farms used to exist. This resulted in the ministry issuing a variation order of 2006 which restructured the parties to the NEC and the seats they held.

Whereas in the past GAPWUZ represented worker interests while the Agricultural Labour Bureau (ALB) represented those of the Commercial Farmers Union (CFU), the new configuration imposed in 2006 resulted in three unions (GAPWUZ, H-GAPWUZ and the Kapenta Workers' Union of Zimbabwe (KWUZ)) on the workers' side, while the employers were represented by the Zimbabwe Agricultural Employers Organisation (ZAEO), the CFU, the Zimbabwe Farmers Union (ZFU) and the Zimbabwe Commercial Farmers Union (ZCFU). On the employer side, various other associations exist (e.g. the Kapenta Producers Association and the Indigenous Kapenta Producers Association) which are only invited when their sectors are under consideration. Each side has ten seats in the NEC,

28 LEDRIZ Trade Union Study Report by Tarisai Nyamucherera on the Mining and Agriculture sector 2000-2015, 24 May 2017.
29 Kanyenze et al., 2011, p. 107.

broken down such that on the workers' side, GAPWUZ has seven seats, H-GAPWUZ has two, and KWUZ has one. Radical changes occasioned by the variation order occurred on the employer side, where the ALB was left with only one seat, with the new farmers being given four, and horticulture, agro-processing, timber, ZFU and ZCFU each having a seat.

Sectarian interests also weighed in, with the timber industry agitating for the establishment of its own NEC since 2002.[30] Eventually, a separate NEC for the industry was established. The significance of these developments is that they hampered the collective bargaining process under the aegis of the NEC, implying that the governing Statutory Instrument 323 of 1993, which was now outdated, could only be amended in 2014.

Grievances amongst farm workers remained unresolved due to the hostile environment, the attitude of the new farmers, lack of transport, high staff turnover on account of poor working conditions, closure of some of its offices due to non-payment of rentals and lack of adequate communication facilities, all of which handicapped GAPWUZ operations. Even the NEC itself could not carry out its mandate, as it was perceived to be in favour of white employers due to the presence of the CFU in its structures. It was only after the variation order in 2006 that the NEC could do its business. Thus, until the coming in of the Inclusive Government in 2009, GAPWUZ could not fulfill its core mandate of representing its members and negotiating for favourable conditions of employment.

Challenges of mobilisation and networking and the spectre of irrelevance

The challenges affecting affiliate unions of the ZCTU were highlighted above. The import of weak affiliates was well articulated in the General Council Report to the 2006 Congress:

> There is now a big gap between the centre and its affiliates when an ideal situation would be that affiliates have to be stronger for them to support the centre. Thus the ZCTU structurally now resembles a human being with a strong upper body and very thin legs to support the body.... The General Council realizes that strong affiliate unions will influence the emergence of a stronger ZCTU.[31]

The rapid informalisation of the labour force since the late 1990s resulted in major challenges around mobilisation for unions formed in an

---

30 The NEC covers five sectors: general, horticulture, agro, timber and kapenta.
31 General Council Report to the 2006 Congress, p. 36.

environment of formal sector employment within a particular trajectory of a modernising economic project. The precariousness of informalisation, though always part of labour processes since the colonial period, has taken on a more acute sense of permanence without any sense of a movement towards a future of more formalised labour. In this conjuncture, the labour movement has had to consider the long-term implications of new forms of mobilisation in the dominant informal sector. As one informal sector worker, formerly employed in the formal sector, observed:

> We have a big problem because the workers in the informal sector are detached from the workers in the formal sector. In fact their problems are not the same. In the informal sector I have noticed that people employ their relatives. So I am your cousin it is very difficult for me to go against you at work especially the smaller entities like us.[32]

Moreover, organising workers in the informal sector faces serious resistance from ZANU(PF) structures. The following description provides a good sense of this problem in an area that was considered to 'belong' to Sithembiso Nyoni (former Minister of Small and Medium Enterprises) and the ruling party:

> If you go to Magaba today you would find out that most of those guys at Magaba were once upon a time welders from our sector, fabricators from our sector, lathe machine operators from our sector, instrumentors form our sector, you name it. If you go there tomorrow they will tell you that this is a no-go area.[33]

A major outcome of these processes has been a growing loss of faith in the efficacy and promise of trade unions. In the words of one worker,

> Zimbabweans seem just busy to participate in non-profitable political processes... workers want empowerment and programmes that bring food on their table and not to be used by charlatans who are failing to show their relevance in the society.[34]

As a result of the decline in membership, coupled with the withdrawal of some key external partners whose funding had helped mobilise structures, attendances at national calendar events organised by the ZCTU waned over time, reflecting weakening influence. Table 3 reports attendance at

---

32 Interview with Barnabas Chinoona in Buduriro, Harare, 24 December 2016.
33 Op cit., Interview with the National Engineering Workers' Union.
34 Op cit., interview with Tarisai Nyamucherera.

national ZCTU events during the period 2006-15. This declining influence is poignantly captured in the attendance at Workers' Day commemorations, where the numbers plummeted from 42,681 in 2006 to 11,890 in 2015.

Table 3: Participation at National Events Organised by the ZCTU, 2006-2015

Year	International Women's Day	Workers' Day	Health and Safety (June 6)	Sept. 13	World Day for Decent Work
2006	578	42,681	1,406		-
2007	515	26,166	1,204		-
2008	1,402	29,329	851		576
2009	2,423	33,577	1,100		1,020
2010	2,234	21,301	815		921
2011	1,651	15,232	1,179	702	992
2012	1,384	13,900	1,092	795	408
2013	1,401	15,680	1,002	577	581
2014	1,138	14,501	620	640	286
2015	765	11,890	548	396	1,093

Source: ZCTU 2011 and 2016 General Council reports to Congress

While the latter half of the 1990s witnessed heightened labour activism, the period under review is by contrast one of subdued activism. Table 4 captures the actions undertaken by the ZCTU during the period 2001-15. During this period, most demonstrations took place between 2000 and 2008 (including the well-known 13 September 2006 where 256 workers were arrested and the 3-4 April 2007 stayaway). After the signing of the GPA on 15 September 2008, the ZCTU did not call for any action for five years. Three demonstrations took place in 2015:

- 11 April 2015, against wage and salary freeze; and

- 8 August 2015 and 22 August 2015, against job losses after the 17 July 2015 Supreme Court ruling in the case of Don Nyamande and Kingstone Donga v Zuva Petroleum.

However, in September 2016, the government banned all forms of demonstrations in Harare, ostensibly because of inadequacies in the Public Order and Security Act (POSA). It is important also to mention the role of police in banning demonstrations, as well as police brutality, as factors that led to the falling participation in demonstrations. The weakening of the ZCTU also saw the rise of individual and social media social movements, in particular the #Tajamuka and #ThisFlag by Pastor Mawarire.

Table 4: Labour Activism During the Period 2001-2015

Year	Type of Action	Reason
2001 July	Stayaway	Reversal of Fuel Price
2003 March	Stayaway	Abuse of Human and Trade Union Rights
2003, 8 October	Demonstration	Against poverty
2003, 23-25 April	Stayaway	Demand the reversal of prices of fuel
2003, 18 November	Demonstration	Protest against high levels of tax and poverty
2003, 19-20 November	Stayaway	Demand for the release of detained ZCTU leaders
2004, 25 February	Stayaway	Calling for an investigation of NSSA funds, Dismissal of 41 Colcom workers and the dismissal of the ZCTU President from work
2005, 8 November	Demonstration	High taxation, low wages, high cost of living, unavailability of ARVs
2006, 13 September	Demonstration	Poverty, poverty datum line wages, free ARVs
2007, 3-4 April	Stayaway	High cost of living and deteriorating economy
2007, 19-20 September	Stayaway	Poverty
2008, 3 December	Demonstration	Cash withdrawal limits
2015, 4 November	Demonstration	Wage and salary Freeze
2015, 8 August	Demonstration	Job losses after the 17 July 2015 Supreme Court ruling

Source: 2006, 2011 and 2016 General Council Reports to Congress.

One effective strategy the ZCTU used to build social movement unionism beyond traditional bread and butter issues in the 1990s was reaching out to other civil society groups to create broader alliances for national impact. Through this networking thrust, the ZCTU helped to establish a number of civic organisations such as the National Constitutional Assembly, Zimrights, Community Working Group on Health, the Musasa Project and the Crisis Coalition of Zimbabwe in the 1990s, and the Zimbabwe Chamber of Informal Economy Associations in 2002.

However, as pointed out in the General Council Report to the 2006 Congress,

> While initially (before 2001) a lot of ground had been covered by ZCTU on this particular aspect, the reverse is now true for the period under review (2001 to 2005). During this period (2001 to 2005), most CSOs which were working hand in hand with the ZCTU in the past generally distanced themselves from ZCTU for fear of being labeled MDC allies, and therefore be subjected to state repression, harassment, arrest and torture of leadership and activists the ZCTU experienced over the referred period.[35]

The two main vehicles born out of this network, the Crisis Coalition of Zimbabwe and the National Constitutional Assembly, became pale shadows of their former selves, with the latter transforming itself into a political party, thereby depriving the civic movement of a powerful lobbying and advocacy group.

Notwithstanding this bleak view of the declining influence of unions, some workers still pointed to the advantages of belonging to trade unions. Firstly, the advantage of linkages to international trade union federations, such as funding for training and office equipment, and the solidarity that national unions continue to receive from these international federations. In addition, the work of the ZCTU in leading national campaigns, as well as negotiating at the Tripartite Negotiating Forum, was well appreciated.[36] Secondly, the continuing importance of standing together as workers still retains its importance. In a message that echoes the persistent resilience of a few unions, one union leader observed:

> We are very strong because we can stand in this environment by ourselves managing to bring together 60 people on the ground, give them food, accommodation and T-shirts for four days.... We are strong because we are managing to fulfil all our constitutional

---

35 General Council Report to the 2006 Congress, p. 15.
36 Interview with Gilbert Karikuimba in Harare, 4 December 2016. Also op cit., interviews with National Engineering Workers' Union and the Zimbabwe Construction Workers' Union.

obligations. The Harare branch sits every month for its meetings. We give them their allowances every month. We manage to conduct Women's Advisory Committee meetings when they are due. We are doing staff workshops annually since 2013. Our books are being audited every year and we present the results to the councillors.[37]

Conclusion

While the resilience and optimism of the above statement could still be found in a few unions, particularly in the public sector,[38] the more general picture is one of growing pessimism and a loss of faith in the relevance of trade unions. This mood was clearly expressed by a trade union Education Officer:

> You know if you are discussing with anyone you will find the only saying is '*tozvisiyira kuna Mwari*' (we wait for God's intervention), 'tirikurarama nenyasha' (we are surviving because of God's grace). It's an indicator that people have lost hope... In whatever is happening they are saying just leave it like that. That attitude is also affecting unions. There are a few people joining unions because they are always saying, 'what is it that you can do?' Cases are going to Labour Court; you win the case but enforcing the judgement, even if you are asked to recover some monies, it will take you years to recover that money. And at times you will not even recover it. You may go to the messenger of court, the messenger of court will tell you, my friend we have got piles and piles of goods we have collected in areas like Borrowdale. They are there at the auction floors. But there is no one buying. We are even tired of going out to collect these things.[39]

---

37 Op cit., interview with the Commercial Workers' Union of Zimbabwe.
38 Report by Lynette Ndlovu on the Public Sector Unions, Women and Youth, December 2016.
39 Op cit., interview with the Catering and Hotel Workers' Union of Zimbabwe.

Chapter 7

New Forms of Work Organisation
and Employment Patterns

Lloyd Sachikonye, Godfrey Kanyenze and Brian Raftopoulos

Introduction

In what ways have the economic and political developments in the post-2000 period shaped new forms of work organisation? What structural changes have occurred to shape the outlook and responses of employers and workers during this period? This chapter stresses the fluidity in the emerging labour regime with particular reference to agriculture, mining and manufacturing. It examines the new forms under which the work process is being organised, and the resultant employment patterns.

This assessment of new forms of work organisation takes into account the broad context of deep economic change as elaborated in Chapter 4. This wider context is the contraction of the formal sector, adversely reducing the size of the working class and unions. As earlier chapters have illustrated, the size and skill structure of the agricultural workforce changed significantly during the period under review. Significant changes have also occurred in mining, with a notable reduction in the size of the workforce, while the artisanal mining sub-sector has witnessed phenomenal growth of a self-employed but non-unionised workforce.

Similarly, the manufacturing sector has experienced a major reduction in the size of the workforce on the back of a significant contraction of its capacity utilisation. In 2017, the sector's capacity utilisation had shriveled to below 50 per cent. Symptomatic of an economy in the doldrums, the export capability of the sector has been declining over the years despite state legislation such as SI64 of 2016 to protect local industry. This is the context in which some firms resorted to a short working week, and others shut down for extended periods.

Broadly speaking, the new forms of organising the work process are occurring against a background of deindustrialisation. For instance, there is a trend towards labour-intensive forms of production in agriculture, while artisanal mining is characterised by hard labour in insecure environments. Manufacturing experiences some challenges in seeking to modernise its production operations. At the same time, the advent of new technology, especially information and communication technology, has influenced the organisation of work in these sectors. However, without detailed empirical work, it is difficult to assess the impact of this development on work in the post-2000 period. Impressionistic evidence will be drawn upon to explain such changes as are occurring.

Employment patterns: Formality and informality, 2004-14

In the past, employment was categorised according to the production unit (or enterprise) in which a person works, but this approach was criticised owing to its failure to 'capture all aspects of the increasing so-called "informalisation" of employment, which has led to a rise in various forms of informal (or non-standard, atypical, alternative, irregular, precarious, etc.) employment'.[1] Given the increased informalisation of work, it became necessary to capture the nature of an employment relationship in both the formal and informal sectors of the economy. This resulted in the adoption, at the 2003 International Conference of Labour Statisticians, of a job-based concept of informal employment which looks at the characteristics of a person's job and not just the enterprise that employs them.

This approach groups together those who are not in a formal employment relationship and generally suffer from inadequate social protection, a lack of rights at work, poor working conditions and insufficient incomes – regardless of whether they are employed by a formal enterprise, in the informal sector or in production for own consumption (including communal agriculture). The 2004 Labour Force Survey applied these two complementary concepts of informality: (i) the enterprise-based concept of informality, and (ii) the jobs-based concept of informality, in order to assess the quality of employment in Zimbabwe, a process which was repeated in 2011 and 2014. The results are reported in Table 1 below.

---

1   Hussmanns, 2004, p. 1.

Table 1: Employment in the Formal and Informal Sectors and Informality, 2001, 2011 & 2014

Enterprise-based concept of informality			
	2004	**2011**	**2014**
Formal sector enterprises	1,200,549		963 444
Informal sector enterprises	710,015	566,833	859,060
Households	3,152,590		4,442,718
Job-based concept of informality			
	2004	**2011**	**2014**
Formal employment	976,228	606,163	346,754
Informal employment	4,086,926	4,572,771	5,919,115
Not classified	-	252,093	-
Total	**5,063,154**	**5,431,027**	**6,265,869**
Job-based concept of informality (%)			
	2004	**2011**	**2014**
Formal employment	19.3	11.2	5.5
Informal employment	80.7	84.2	94.5

Source: Derived from 2004, 2011 & 2014 Labour Force Surveys, ZimStat.

Clearly, informality is higher when the job-based concept is used than under the enterprise-based concept. This arises because most workers in the informal sector are also included under the job-based definition of informality (i.e. are informally employed).[2] A number of workers in the formal sector who lack secure contracts with entitlements to social security and other employment benefits are also considered as informally employed. Figure 1 below indicates the extent of informality in Zimbabwe using the job-based definition. Informal employment has increased from 80.7 per cent of all the employed in 2004 to 84.2 per cent in 2011 and 94.5 per cent by 2014.

Whereas the formal sector accounted for 23.7 per cent of all employment in 2004, by 2014 it was down to 15.4 per cent. However, because of the increased informalisation of jobs, formal employment was much lower, at 19.3 per cent of total employment in 2004, 11.2 per cent in 2011 and 5.5 per cent in 2014.

---

2   The International Labour Conference of 2002 defined informal employment as 'all economic activities by workers and economic units that are – in law or in practice – not covered or insufficiently covered by formal arrangements'.

Figure 1: Informal Employment in Zimbabwe, 2004, 2011 & 2014 (%)

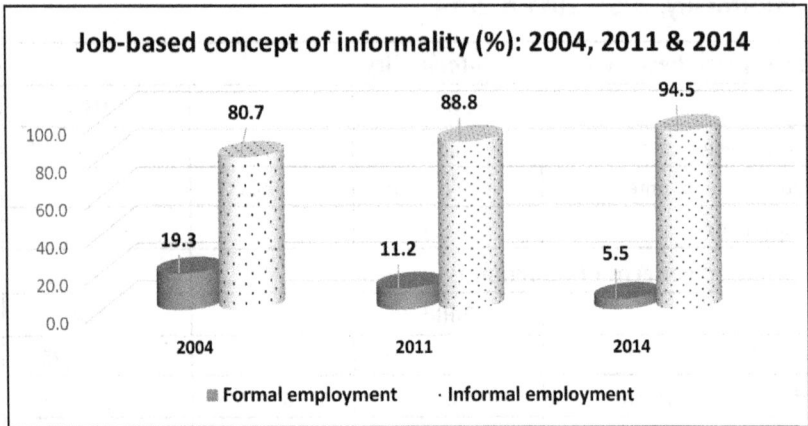

Source: Derived from the 2004, 2011 & 2014 Labour Force Surveys, ZimStat.

Employers, old and new

Any sectoral discussion of work changes needs to identify the patterns in ownership and control of the means of production. While some patterns of ownership have not changed substantially, in some sectors there have been significant shifts. Corporate interests in mining are still substantial, to which state enterprises and local firms have been added, and thousands of artisanal miners form a distinct group of local mining entrepreneurs. Manufacturing draws on both corporate and local interests, although the diversification of owners has been constrained by the weak performance of the sector since 2000. The most significant shift in ownership has been in the agrarian sector, with the white commercial farming class being dispossessed and replaced by 'new farmers' under the A1 and A2 categories after 2000.

How have these different patterns of ownership affected work organisation? The expulsion of 4,000 white farmers reshaped the 'domestic government' relations and patterns of work. The new farmers were a motley group but most operated from a low capital base, which limited their production capacity in most instances. As a consequence, the number of permanent workers retained on farms fell from about 150,000 prior to land reform to about 18,000 in 2016.[3]

The new breed of politically connected employers in agriculture has blocked union efforts to organise and recruit members. There were

---

3   Interview with GAPWUZ Secretary General, Harare, November 2016.

instances of employers meddling in union affairs by choosing who could have access to their properties to address their employees.[4] Where a union did not subscribe to certain political preferences, they were denied an opportunity of access to potential recruits. The casualisation of labour became more widespread. There were instances of some workers spending up to ten years as casual workers without receiving the benefits due to permanent workers.

The politically polarised operating environment made it very difficult for unions to carry out their recruitment and representation roles. There were many instances where new farmers who were ZANU(PF) members refused to allow ZCTU-affiliated unions to enter their farms. In addition, they threatened employees with termination if they continued to be associated with such unions. This hindered efforts to recruit members. Nor has the state been a disinterested actor: the Ministry of Labour deliberately registered multiple unions in agriculture to neutralise and fragment the unions in the sector:

> Coupled with the reduced number of workers, there have been challenges for unions, mainly lack of membership whose subscriptions can sustain viability of a union. Unions have fought each other over membership while fragmentation has fleeced unsuspecting workers of their hard earned money.... Moreover, the emergence of numerous unions all vying for the same membership has made collective bargaining negotiations difficult.[5]

In the same vein, intimidation and victimisation of workers has been on the rise. For instance, more than 1,600 contract workers were fired from Hippo Valley Estates after carrying out a crippling strike in 2016. Consequently, casual workers are afraid to defend their rights for fear of losing their jobs. Generally, levels of intimidation were higher on farms owned by the new farmers, most of whom are linked to the ruling party, and regard themselves as exempt from labour laws. Instances of intimidation against union activists at workplaces continue to be reported.[6]

Mining has also witnessed notable changes in production and labour conditions. After 2009, there was a pronounced recovery of the economy, and the sector grew by over 10 per cent over the next three years. However, there was a shift from the production of asbestos, iron ore

---

4   Field Notes by Tarisai Nyamucherera, May 2017.

5   Ibid. p.10.

6   *The Herald*, 29 April 2016.

and beryl to six key minerals, namely gold, platinum, diamonds, nickel, coal and palladium.[7] Unlike elsewhere in the economy, levels of capacity utilisation were relatively high at 71 per cent in 2014 before declining to 64 per cent in 2016.[8] However, capacity utilisation varies from commodity to commodity. For instance, while it declined in coal from 50 per cent to 30 per cent, and nickel from 55 per cent to 41 per cent, capacity utilisation increased from 77 per cent to 79 per cent in gold production. In addition, the contribution of small artisanal producers has been increasing significantly in the past few years.

Employment in the mining sector, which had peaked at 68,200 in 1981, declined (with annual variations) to 44,600 by 2000, before falling to 39,200 in 2014 as international commodity prices weakened. There was an 11 per cent decline in 2016. About 5 per cent of the workers were female, and some 15 per cent were drawn from neighbouring local communities.[9] The stagnation and decline in employment opportunities should be set against the background of challenges of high costs of capital and energy, and low commodity prices in the post-2014 period. Respondents in a mining industry report expressed concern about what they termed labour market rigidities, and argued for flexible labour laws that responded to the prevailing operating environment.[10]

Much mining production is concentrated in the gold and platinum sub-sectors. Employing in excess of 25 per cent of the labour force in the sector, gold accounted for 47 percent of mineral exports in 2016. Significantly about 40 per cent of the gold output originated from the artisanal sector, where about 300,000 small operators were active.

As in agriculture, there has been a diffusion of production amongst thousands of small producers whose productivity levels are not necessarily high but are just sufficient for them to maintain and marginally improve their livelihoods. It is inevitable that amongst the small operators are ex-miners, and entrepreneurs who employ several workers on each mining claim. Working conditions in the artisanal sector are often precarious due to hazardous working conditions.

The platinum sub-sector has expanded rapidly and operated at almost full capacity during the period under review. Productivity has

---

7   Chamber of Mines, 2015, p. 8.
8   Chamber of Mines, 2016, p. 7.
9   Ibid.
10 Ibid.

also increased, although the cost drivers in the sub-sector remain labour, power and royalties.[11] Although profitability improved in 2016, major challenges relate to depressed metal prices, high operating costs and a suboptimal fiscal regime. There have been trends towards 'labour rationalisation' through multi-skilling, negotiated wage reductions and retrenchments. Significantly, the platinum producers have installed concentrators for treating ore into concentrates. One of the firms owns a smelter that treats concentrates into matte.[12] In addition, there were plans for mine development projects over the next five years that would exceed US$300 million with a potentially positive impact on output and on beneficiation.

An overview of labour conditions in mining would be incomplete without reference to the growing footprint of Chinese firms, which are particularly prominent in chrome and diamond mining. Their labour conditions have generally been poor. As one study observed, 'hard labour, exposure to risky conditions, violation of labour laws, long working hours, non-payment of overtime and disregard of public holidays were among the difficult conditions faced by workers in Chinese-owned mines'.[13] Other allegations include the use of contract labour in ways that violate the Labour Relations Act.[14] Minimum wages were generally not observed. Communication barriers between the mine-owners and unions were reinforced by avoiding English as the main language at the workplace. Furthermore, even where there were Zimbabweans who spoke the English and Chinese languages, there were problems between the locals and the official interpreters. Skills transfer at small-scale Chinese companies was non-existent as they operated like big *Makorokoza* (large panners).

Child labour in mining was another growing feature in the sector, and a source of great concern. In Shurugwi, for example, scores of children worked in opencast mines, ferrying chrome ore in buckets and wheelbarrows, without formal contracts, protective clothing or medical benefits.[15] A child worker who had been bedridden three times from severe coughs and headaches from working at a chrome mine, stated that:

I get ten dollars for every ton I fetch and it takes me three days to

11 Chamber of Mines, 2015.
12 Ibid.
13 Shelton and Kabemba, 2012, p. 155.
14 Ibid. p. 156.
15 IRIN, 2010.

do so. We work from sunrise to sunset together with the adults and are treated the same, but the job is so hard.[16]

The poor labour conditions in chrome mining were replicated in the diamond sub-sector. During 2008-09, before the commercialisation of mining was formalised, the Zimbabwean army forcibly employed hundreds of children in the diamond fields at Marange. An estimated 300 child miners worked for the soldiers; one girl miner said that:

> ... every day I would carry ore and only rest for short periods. We always started work very early in the morning before 8, and finished when it was dark after 6.[17]

Employment conditions in the manufacturing sector have not been unaffected by the wider changes in the economy. Most firms have constraints of access to capital and power, forcing them to resort to a short working week. This explains the capacity underutilisation and lack of competitiveness that has long been a bane of the sector. These changes in working conditions were noted by interviewees in this study. Commenting on changes in the commercial sector, one informant observed:

> The pattern started changing around 2000. Employers began not replacing those people who resigned, retired, or were dismissed. They began encouraging multi-tasking.[18]

The effects of these changes could also be felt in the demise of permanent workers:

> They no longer want to employ people on a permanent basis because the conditions of employment for permanent employees are too many. They need medical aid and pensions. So fixed contracts are becoming the order of the day. They know that the Zimbabwean Government allows such things.[19]

The feelings of despair even drew out romanticised and nostalgic memories of the settler colonial period:

> It's surprising that the government says that they came from the war

---

16 Ibid.
17 Human Rights Watch, 2009.
18 Interview with Unner Goremusandu, National Organising Secretary of the Commercial Workers' Union of Zimbabwe, 17 December 2016.
19 Interview with Christopher Chizura, General Secretary of the Communication and Allied Services Workers' Union of Zimbabwe, 2 December 2016.

of liberation where they were fighting the colonial Smith regime. Smith had no casual workers.... They had permanent employees such that getting a job one becomes a permanent employee guaranteed a pension upon deciding to go back to the rural areas. Now there is nothing like that.[20]

The gender dimension in employment conditions in the manufacturing sector was explored in a 2017 survey that observed that:

- Female workers earned far less than their male counterparts;

- About 34 per cent of female workers were employed full-time in 2017, compared to more than 50 per cent of male workers; and

- Most female workers were employed in foodstuffs, textiles, clothing and footwear, and only a minority in the metal and chemical subsectors.[21]

> Unions contend with retrenchments as one of the consequences of deindustrialisation. In an assessment of the impact of the economic downturn since 2000, LEDRIZ found that in all sectors of the economy, employment levels were way below their historic levels with the exception of finance and insurance; real estate; public administration; health services and private domestic service. In 2014, the employment gap (the difference between the estimated historical trend and actual employment) was highest in manufacturing at 131,200, followed by other services (102,700), agriculture (72,800), construction (68,000), distribution, hotels and restaurants (57,700), education services (41,500), mining (23,300), transport and communications (12,200), and electricity and water (1,300).[22]

Reflecting on the crisis in the manufacturing sector, the main representative body in the industry, the Confederation of Zimbabwe Industries, observed that a third of firms were on the brink of collapse.[23] A significant number of large manufacturers were re-categorised as 'small' because their staff levels had declined below their original size. Some 30 per cent of firms in this group employed skeleton staff to take care of plants after scaling down or calling off production.

20 Ibid.
21 CZI, 2017.
22 LEDRIZ, 2016.
23 CZI, 2017.

The changes in forms of work were marked by several characteristics. Firstly, the casualisation of labour, as has been noted above. This was described by several interviewees as such:

> They (employers) do this to run away from legal obligations. To employ a person for a fixed three months period and then discharging them so as to employ another one. Employers do not have any statutory obligations and expense. This is because the casually hired employees do not have a right to gratuity and benefits which permanent workers deserve. So you are casually hired and paid for your duration of employment and discharged. The employer employs others in that fashion continuously.[24]

Secondly, workers had to face the challenge of deferred payments or payments in kind. In such cases employers staggered the wages of their employees pushing them to agree to accept piecemeal payments over a period of time.[25] Because of the precarity of work in both the formal and informal sectors, workers 'think that buying and selling may not be sustainable in the long run and so keep their jobs as security for the future',[26] in the hope that 'we will end up getting paid'.[27] In other cases the balance of workers' wages was paid in kind; they were told to accept property such as 'sofas, beds and stuff',[28] or workers labored for periods of ten hours but were told they would only be paid for eight hours of work.[29]

'Old' and 'new' workers, multiple livelihoods and dependencies

Just as the composition of ownership and control of land and mines has undergone change since 2000, so has that of the working class employed in those enterprises. In the new configuration, 'old' or former workers have diversified into other economic activities. While some have become owners of land, and received income from their farming activities, others

---

24 Interview with Philemon Nhema, General Secretary, ZISEGU (Zimbabwe Security Guards Union); Mr. Matare, President; Ratidzo Gasva, Regional Officer Harare; Margaret Mukuchu, Regional Organiser, 1 December 2016.
25 Interview with Gift Chibatwa, Education Officer, Zimbabwe Catering and Hotel Workers' Union of Zimbabwe, 14 December 2016.
26 Op cit., interview with ZISEGU members.
27 Interview with Barnabas Chinoona, Informal Sector worker, 24 December 2016.
28 Ibid.
29 Op cit., interview with Commercial Workers' Union.

have become part-time workers who supplement their wages with income from other pursuits.

There are now around 100,000 permanent workers on the farms and plantations, compared with 300,000 before 2000. The fate of the remainder is an issue that has been investigated by a number of scholars.[30] What is clear is that few farmworkers were integrated into the land redistribution programme; former farm workers constituted only 11.5 per cent of settler household heads in the A1 villagised scheme, and 5.3 per cent in the A2.[31]

Increasingly, the post-2000 developments relating to accumulation by dispossession, the worsening of working conditions and diversification of livelihoods, suggest that the categories of 'farmer' and 'worker' have to be revisited and refined. For example, some 'farmers' have a fluid identity:

> ... old categories do not work well with the new group of commercial farmers. Urban links are important but so is investment. Off-farm employment for A2 farmers is very common.[32]

Unlike their A2 counterparts, most farmers on A1 schemes are full-time and resident; they also have extensive off-farm activities to generate additional income. Both categories of farmers drew on farm workers but on different scales.

Most concentrations of farmworkers were on A2 farms, despite their variable record of production. For instance, some of the farms in the Mvurwi area have become major 'labour reserves' for surrounding farms, including A1 farms.[33] One such A2 farm had as many as 400 workers staying in its compound, leading to the observation that:

> ... the former farm workers have been vital in helping new tobacco farmers to prosper in their enterprise through past employment and knowledge skills.... Most former farm workers combine casual labour supply with micro-scale farming activities. But there are wide variations in the combination of these livelihood strategies.[34]

In one sample in Mvurwi, land ownership by such farm workers ranged

---

30 Chambati, 2013; Hartnack, 2016; Rutherford, 2017, and also the Introduction to this volume.

31 Scoones et al., 2010.

32 Sukume et al. 2010.

33 Ibid.

34 Ibid.

from 0.25 ha to 1.2 ha each. These variations in access to land by former farm workers were also reflected in the degree of dependency on their production relative to casual farm work. In addition, some workers rented land on which they grew crops for home consumption and sale, financed by their wages. Earnings from farm labour spawned growth in small retail activities owned and operated by the more entrepreneurial of the former farm workers within the compounds.[35]

A common strategy amongst workers was to combine farm work with other economic activities such as *maricho* (task work on adjacent farms), petty trading of meat, clothes and vegetables or making and selling beer.[36] However, as workers, renters or occupiers, they were wary of the rules of the farm owner in this new context of 'conditional belonging', in which they were expected to do certain tasks as a form of labour tenancy.

Research carried out some 15 years after land reform undermines previously optimistic claims that there has been substantial progress in the fortunes of former and present farm workers. Some of the findings:

- While the specific forms of power associated with domestic government and bio-political maternalism may have diminished, land reform had not done away with problematic power relations, but has provided a different set of power relations and challenges that farmworkers must continue to negotiate to meet their needs; and while the racialised master-servant relationship had been replaced, social patronage and coercive domestic relations had taken its place, and were as fraught and coercive as those that had existed previously.

- The new modes of 'conditional belonging' of farm workers often left them to rely on their own ingenuity, as resources and forms of welfare offered prior to 2000 were more insecure.

- Farm worker beneficiaries incorporated themselves into different systems of dependence and performance of loyalty in order to broaden their livelihood options; many farm workers had goals and ambitions for themselves and their families which they sought strategically to achieve.

- In sum, previous modes of belonging were displaced after 2000 when many farm workers sought to find alternative dependencies in which

35 Ibid.
36 Rutherford, 2017, p. 199.

to incorporate themselves. Those farm workers who were successful in this respect have tried to build multiple dependencies, skillfully building their livelihoods and future prospects in combination.[37]

While a category of part-time workers and part-time small entrepreneurs who combine their identities and livelihoods has emerged, there was still a category of farm workers that did not have access to land for its own production. Conditions of work for this category appeared to have steadily worsened during the post-2000 period. As one study observed:

> Cases of compulsory overtime work and overburdening of work are rampant in all subsectors.... Some workers indicated lack of specific working hours as the work is task-based.[38]

Underpayment and irregular wages were also widespread. It was not uncommon for workers to go for several months without wages.

In mid-2017, the average wage for a farm worker was USD75 a month.[39] A newspaper report carried vivid details about the poor working conditions, quoting one worker who stated that:

> Getting wages is a real struggle. We are paid in groceries most of the time. We get the groceries at the farm shop but there are no prices and we will be told that for what we have taken, we have spent our wage, yet one would have taken a few items. Imagine two bars of soap, a packet of matemba, 2 litres cooking oil, a bucket of maize and few other items taking the whole salary.[40]

Additional concerns of farm workers relate to the collective bargaining agreement for the agricultural industry. Statutory Instrument 67 of 2017 stipulates that labour contracts of nine months can be renewable six times. This ensures that a worker can be treated and paid as a casual or contract worker for up to four years despite continuous service.

There have also been notable changes in employment conditions in mining, especially in informal artisanal sector. As we observed, there has been growth in the proliferation of unregistered small miners, also known as *makorokoza*, in the post-2000 period. As employment in the formal mining sector shrank, the number of *makorokozas* was swelled by workers retrenched from the formal sector. By 2015, the they ranged between

---

37 This section draws from the work of Hartnack, 2016.
38 Chakanya, 2016.
39 The Standard, 17 September 2017.
40 Ibid.

300,000 and 500,000, with the wide estimation underlining the difficulty of establishing a precise figure.[41]

An example of such expansion of mining was presented in a study of Torotoro in the Kwekwe area. The growth of artisanal mining in Torotoro dated to the closure of the Empress and Venice Mines.[42] The *makorokoza* were mainly drawn from former mine workers who had continued to stay at the mines' townships, eking out a living from farming and informal vending. As it was observed:

> The semi-arid climate and poor geological conditions of the area means that seasonal crop cultivation alone can never be a reliable and adequate means of subsistence.... With rising unemployment, artisanal mining became a means of supporting collapsing livelihoods.[43]

The spread of artisanal mining has become a major source of living for hundreds of thousands families. However, hazardous working conditions remained a challenge. Conflicts that spill over into violence tended to be endemic in artisanal mining. It was a sub-sector in which local politicians and businessmen and women got entangled and created conditions for patronage networks that thrive on corruption.[44] Police officers and local political leaders tapped into this political economy of accumulation by regulating access, mediating connections between elites and grassroots extractors, and widening the set of beneficiaries.[45]

A number of artisanal miners' organisations, including the Zimbabwe Miners Federation, existed to represent the interests of small miners. However, there were no organisations representing workers who were employed by the artisanal owner-operators. The informal working conditions were the most precarious in this sector. It was unclear whether any of the mine workers' unions had attempted to collaborate or represent the interests of these informal workers. This is an important lacuna that needs to be addressed.

---

41 Mawowa, 2014.
42 Ibid., p. 928.
43 Ibid.
44 Transparency International, 2012.
45 Mawowa, 2014, p. 935

Living with informality and precarity

All the self-employed workers interviewed in this study reported that they once worked in the formal sector. They also stated that they entered the informal sector either because they were laid off and could not find alternative employment in the formal sector, or were not receiving payment for their labour. Of the respondents interviewed, 54 per cent had no access to electricity, water or sanitation facilities. On average they laboured for nine hours per day, six days per week. All indicated that there is stiff competition amongst vendors who sell more or less the same products. Some workers, such as security guards, often straddle both the formal and informal sector. As described by one unionist:

> During the day they sell juice cards and they go to work during the night. Others work as touts (*vanahwindi*). Some do all sorts of things to generate income but during the night work as security guards. If you go to Epworth now, a guard comes from work; he goes to dig the field after the rains have fallen. They work in the fields of other people ... to get money for the children to survive and to get some money to go to his job, but at the end of the month you get nothing. We cannot talk about women. Most of them are now calling *zvikomba* (male clients) at their work station to get money because there is no other way they can survive.[46]

With the loss of a certain level of predictability in employment, we observed once again a romanticisation and nostalgia for a past work culture and discipline:

> If anyone wants to be honest everyone will tell you that we have got the ideas ... even the knowledge we have. Like I told you I have been to training and I have been in industry for almost 20 years. So you would appreciate the experience I have in my own area of work. If I am given the chance to do it I will do it quite diligently. Unfortunately, industry is closed. Customers are few.[47]

Technology and work

No assessment of new forms of work organisation and employment trends would be complete without an explicit reference to the role of technological change. This is an area where there has been little in-depth research.

---

46 Op. cit., Interview with ZISEGU.
47 Op cit., interview with Chinoona.

While the proliferation of information communication technology (ICT) has been commonly experienced at a personal level through access to the mobile phone and Internet, its wider impact on the economy has not been systematically explored.

Impressionistic evidence suggests that there has been no wholesale adoption of new technologies in agriculture, partly due to the disruption of the land reform process. The technological inputs (from seed to fertilisers and agrichemicals to ploughs) in small-scale agriculture have been easier to access than the more sophisticated technology such as combine harvesters, curing barns and irrigation. This explains the relatively poor performance of large-scale farmers on A2 farms: capital constraints have been more acute, resulting in the under-utilisation of farms.

Some analysts believe that there exist opportunities to create more employment in agriculture by making it more productive through shifting from low-value grain production to higher value-added horticulture and biofuel crops.[48] More employment and diffusion of technology would be accomplished through the development of downstream agro-processing industries such as food and beverage manufacturing and textiles. Value chains and contract farming arrangements in such diverse areas as horticulture, livestock, legumes and oilseeds, tree crops, forestry, timber, grains, tobacco and cotton would have an impact on technological diffusion and employment growth.[49] Technological upgrading in agriculture will require the provision of skills training to the old and new workforce in the sector.

Mining has traditionally required more sophisticated technology than other sectors, particularly heavy capital equipment. The formal mining sector requires huge capital investments, and this has been the trend in gold, chrome, platinum and diamond production. Gold mining companies defined their key challenges as the shortage and high cost of capital, and the high price and availability of energy; those in engaged in platinum production cited similar challenges.[50] The formal sector mining companies in that same survey often cited high labour costs as a major factor.

As stated above, retrenchments of 11 per cent of the mining workforce occurred in 2016. The main factors were viability challenges and the

48 LEDRIZ, 2016.
49 Ibid.
50 Chamber of Mines, 2015.

Table 2: Sectoral Analysis of Capacity Utilisation (CU), Output Growth and Investment in Equipment, 2017

Subsector	Average CU (%)		Output growth	Respondents who invested in technology
	2016	2017	2017	2017
Chemical & petroleum products	43.6	36.1	8%	36%
Textile, clothing & footwear	46	50	20%	17%
Drinks, tobacco & beverages	52.4	51.2	3%	56%
Foodstuffs	56.1	56.3	7%	88%
Metal & metal products	37.5	37.1	14%	25%
Non-metallic mineral products	57.5	33.2	16%	67%
Paper, printing & publishing	52.9	52.2	13%	75%
Plastics & packaging	52.9	53	-1%	29%
Transport, equipment	45	39.3	8%	38%
Wood & furniture	57.8	45.2	1%	50%
Other manufacturing	43	45.8	-28%	33%

Source: Confederation of Zimbabwe Industries (CZI) 2017 State of the Manufacturing Sector Survey.

transition to more capital-intensive technology.[51] As in agriculture, technological upgrading in the mining sector will require improved skills training. While low-cost technology appears to be the trend in small-scale artisanal mining, the challenges of occupational safety and health and the need to raise ore yields will compel the miners to seek improved technologies.

In manufacturing and services sectors, the link between technology and work processes has also not been systematically explored. In manufacturing, capacity challenges have a bearing on constraints of access to suitable technologies. Table 2 reports the capacity utilisation levels by manufacturing sub-sector as well as investments in technology in 2016 and 2017.

Forty-seven per cent of the respondents made new capital investment in 2014, up from 41 per cent in 2013. Most of the investment (97 per cent) was for replacement of machinery and equipment (60 per cent) and expansion (40 per cent). These investments were mainly financed by ploughed back profit, with 71 per cent of respondents indicating so. The 2015 CZI State of the Manufacturing Sector Survey acknowledges that since Zimbabwe is not highly mechanised, labour remains a key input in production. Because of the international isolation and prolonged economic crisis, industry has had to make do with unreliable, antiquated machinery.

However, the penetration of the mobile phone and Internet is relatively advanced, and this has contributed to the boom in mobile banking and ICTs generally. For instance, Zimbabwe's Internet penetration was nearly 50 per cent, well above the regional average of 20-30 per cent, while mobile penetration is pegged at about 96 per cent.[52] Whether the finance, banking, education and other service sectors have adapted the new technologies to enhance labour conditions and employment remains to be explored.

In the banking sector, the main union has observed the mixed effects of technology:

> Now we have a machine doing that work formally done by humans
> ... although to a certain extent we now have a significant portion of
> the jobs requiring someone to have some skills in ICT. Buts it's not
> as much as the traditional kinds of jobs that were there.[53]

In the security sector many companies either downsized or folded due

---

51 Ibid.
52 Lewanika, 2016.
53 Op cit., interview with ZIBAWU.

to technological innovations in the industry. The impact of technology diffusion is likely to increase, with the government planning to migrate from sub-contracted security services to ICT-based security systems such as biometric access systems, and the use of cameras and sensors to secure premises and facilities.[54] Commenting on the effects of technological changes on some indigenous security companies, ZISEGU observed:

> I think they were beaten because of technology. They continued to send guards to work with the baton stick yet companies such as SafeGuard had begun to use electronic systems and alarms in the industry. Consequently, clients ran to companies that were advanced in their understanding of security. Companies are also saying their clients are downsizing their operations such that where they used to deploy 50 guards they are now deploying 20.[55]

The Emergence of labour broking in Zimbabwe

The phenomenon of 'labour broking' has caught up with Zimbabwe.[56] The matter has begun to receive a fair amount of coverage in the local press.[57] Addressing the annual congress of the Employers' Confederation of Zimbabwe (EMCOZ) in Victoria Falls in 2016, the director of Industrial Psychology Consultants, Memory Nguwi, noted that 'Labour broking is new but the take-up rate especially by those workers on contract is rising.'[58] According to IPC's 'State of Human Resources in Zimbabwe Survey', covering 51 companies from different sectors of the economy, 14 per cent of the respondents used labour broking services.[59]

This practice, which is also referred to as 'labour hire,' entails labour intermediation or subcontracting whereby labour brokers make workers

---

54 2018 National Budget Statement presented to Parliament by the Minister of Finance and Economic Development on 7 December 2017.

55 Op cit., interview with ZISEGU.

56 'Mutare-Based Labour Broking Firm Spreads its Wings to Harare', *Financial Gazette*, 24 February 2005. This reported that Clive Bruce and Charles Consultancy, a labour broking firm formed in 1999, planned to expand its operations into Harare.

57 See, for instance, 'Mutare-Based Labour Broking Firm Spreads its Wings to Harare', *NewsDay*, 18 April 2012; 'Labour broking: To ban or to regulate?', as well as Matthias Ruziwa's article (HR issues) in the *Business Herald* of 8 December 2016.

58 'Businesses advised to adopt labour broking', *Business Chronicle*, 29 November 2016.

59 'HR Perspectives: State of recruitment in Zimbabwe', *Financial Gazette*, 8 September 2016.

available to third-party clients who assign duties and supervise their work.[60] In most cases, the labour broker has a contract of employment with the worker, manages the payroll of all the employees placed with clients and is responsible for deducting tax liabilities and other obligations. The practice thus externalises the employer-employee relationship into a triangular labour broker nexus.

The contract of employment is often tied to the continued requirement of the services offered to the client. In this case the labour broker enters into a commercial agreement with the client, invoices for the services being rendered, and pays the worker's wages. This implies that there is no contractual relationship between the client and the worker, providing the flexibility the client requires as well as the transfer of risk, as the client is exonerated of responsibility for issues such as unfair dismissal, termination benefits, time spent on recruitment, grievance handling, and performance management.

One such organisation, FC Platinum Holdings, commenced labour broking operations in July 2014, and specialises in supplying skilled and unskilled labour to clients. Its clients include some of the largest mining companies in Zimbabwe. It describes its attractiveness thus:

> We have in place mechanisms and working systems that allow our clients to reduce their labour demands as and when the need arises; thus ensuring that the clients do not have to go through the lengthy and cumbersome process of employee separations.[61]

However, for the worker, this flexibility is often associated with job insecurity, low wages, exclusion from collective bargaining agreements, and quite often violation of labour rights. In Namibia and South Africa, where this practice has been widespread, much debate and contestation has emerged around its practice. Although the Congress of South African Trade Unions has been calling for a complete ban of labour broking, it is permissible – under strict regulation – through section 198 and 198A of the Labour Relations Act, 66 of 1995. Under the Labour Relations Amendment No 6 of 2014, labour broker staff are deemed permanent after three months, when they are to be treated like permanent employees of the client.

In Namibia, labour brokers are regulated by the Labour Act, 2007

---

60 The most affected workers by the practice are in the food industry and beverage manufacturing (see *The Herald*, 13 December 2012).

61 http://www.platinumholdings.co.zw/services/labour-broking/

(Section 128 & 128A) and the Employment Services Act. Under Section 128, those employees placed by a labour broker are deemed to be employed by the client, and cannot be treated less favourably than existing employees.

In Zimbabwe, there is no express provision for labour broking in the Labour Act [Chapter 28:01]. While the relationship between a labour broker and their employees may be regarded as valid in terms of the law, the former director of labour administration, Paul Dzviti, declared the practice illegal.[62] Courts have started to interpret the phenomenon as reflected in the case of Schweppes Zimbabwe v Stanley Takaendesa, judgement No. LC/107/2014 where the latter was reinstated through an arbitral award after having his employment terminated when he had been transferred to a labour broker, Lorimak. The arbitrator, Rodgers Matsikidze, ruled that:

> What is clear from the two contracts is that on the switch from Schweppes to Lorimark, there was no break. The employee only changed the employer but his duties remained the same.... What is clear is that Lorimark is not the employer, but Schweppes. To allow employers to use middlemen in order to avoid statutory regulations will be to put to ransom the workforce.

Be that as it may, others insist that labour broking is legal. Addressing the annual congress of EMCOZ in Victoria Falls, IPC's Memory Nguwi advised that:

> In the past few months a lot of businesses have been taking this route. Currently, there is no law which prohibits labour broking and so, until someone decides to go to court, companies can pursue this route. It helps employers manage cost of labour and companies would adopt this just like insurance, you will just be passing risk to a third party.[63]

The ILO's Private Employment Agencies Convention, 1997 (C181) recognises and regulates 'private employment agencies' as long as workers working under these are protected in terms of collective bargaining, freedom of association, minimum wages, working conditions, statutory and social benefits, and occupational health and safety.

---

62 'Labour broking illegal, warns Govt', *The Herald*, 13 December 2012.
63 'Businesses advised to adopt labour broking', *Business Chronicle*, 29 November 2016.

Conclusion

This chapter has explored new forms of work organisation and the related issue of emerging patterns of employment in the post-2000 period. Such a focus required detailed empirical research over extended periods of time, a resource we were unable to secure. Despite this shortcoming, the broad features of the work process were explored. Empirical evidence was mainly drawn from agriculture, mining and manufacturing sectors. Shifts in ownership in these sectors had a bearing on labour policies. Production relations in agriculture were characterised by more intense exploitation of both permanent and casual or seasonal workers. Generally, the conditions of these workers had become more precarious than before, and similar crude levels of exploitation existed in mining operations of Chinese firms. The difficult environment in which unions in these sectors operated was highlighted.

The chapter also observed the fluidity in identities and diversification of livelihoods by 'new' farmers and 'former' workers, and the adjustments made by small-scale farmers and 'new' workers in the new environment. There was a general trend toward multiple livelihoods and dependencies based on a diversity of economic activities rather than on specialisation and monoculture. There was an overlap between formal employment and production on A2 farms, and between farm work and participation in informal activities as well as production on land. Informalisation in economic activities in agriculture and small-scale mining by the *makorokoza* were key features of this 'new economy'.

Finally, the chapter briefly examined trends in manufacturing, observing the production constraints that resulted in utilisation of less than half of the capacity in that sector. This was a reflection of the persistent crisis in the wider economy and a source of its malaise. While there was a substantial penetration of information communication technologies, the impact of these technologies had not been systematically studied. This gap should be addressed in order to explore how new technologies are shaping the work processes in the manufacturing and services sectors.

Chapter 8

Gender, Youths and Disability in the Changing Industrial Landscape

Naome Chakanya

Introduction

This chapter provides an analysis of the impact of the structural changes in the economy and the labour market on the vulnerable groups, of women, youths and people with disabilities (PWDs). It provides the gender, generational and disability perspectives of the structural changes in the labour market. The point of departure is that economic crises and structural changes in the economy have differential impacts on these vulnerable groups, which, however, largely remain excluded from the dominant narratives. Hence, the majority of the populace remains excluded from developmental and, in particular, labour market policies. For instance, women and youths, who constitute a numerically significant group in the population, suffer disproportionately in the labour market in times of economic crisis and persistent deindustrialisation, and they risk being more trapped in un- and underemployment or the informal economy which is characterised by low productivity jobs and indecent working conditions. Additionally, youths and PWDs are essentially at the receiving end of economic crises and structural changes in the economy which further exacerbates their vulnerabilities and social exclusion.

Conceptual framework: The dual and enclave structure of the economy

The structure of the Zimbabwean economy that the government inherited at independence is critical in understanding the historical gender imbalances in both the economy and the labour market. At independence, the government inherited a dual and enclave economy (Figure 1) which was the foundation of the economic superstructure that continues to marginalise economic sectors and activities dominated by women, youths and those living with disability.

The economy was dual in that a well-developed, modern and male-dominated formal sector co-existed with the underdeveloped and backward non-formal sectors where the majority of women were found. Enclavity was explained by the fact that the male-dominated formal economy had a growth momentum of its own due to its linkage with the global economy, and was isolated from the activities that took place in the non-formal sector.

After independence, the government failed to address this dual and enclave nature of the economy. Instead, its economic policies, programmes and support were mainly targeting the formal economy, which had been in decline for several years. Even during the years of structural adjustments, female-dominated sectors such as clothing and textiles were more affected by the liberalisation policies than other sectors, thus further entrenching women in the informal and rural economies. For instance,

Figure 1: The dual and enclave structure of the Zimbabwean economy

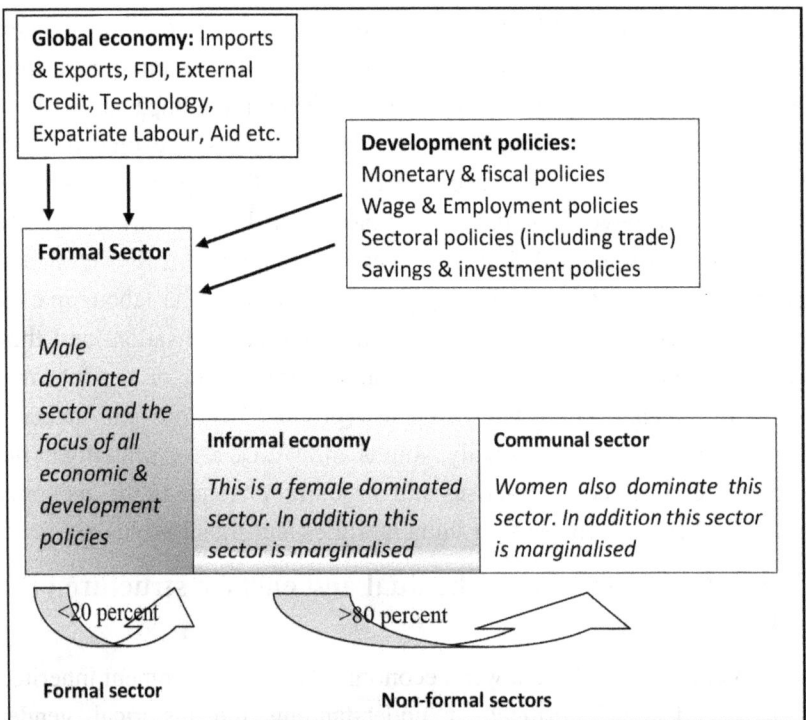

Source: Kanyenze et al., 2011

12,478 jobs were lost in the textiles sector between 1990 and 2005, whilst the clothing sector lost 10,000 jobs in the same period. After the onset of the economic crisis in 2007, the country lost its high degree of industrialisation which was largely unmatched on the continent, leading to the subsequent exponential growth of the informal economy.

Over the years, the majority of women, youths and PWDs became trapped in the underdeveloped non-formal sectors. Thus, the informal economy exhibits three faces: a 'woman's face', and more recently a 'youth face' (as fewer school-leavers and graduates are absorbed in the formal sector) and a 'disability face', as those living with disability continue to be marginalised, with most policies and strategies remaining disability-blind. In addition, the colonial legacy of treating activities that are informal as 'illegal' persists, and further entrenches the feminisation of poverty. For instance, the government's policy towards the informal economy has been ambivalent, vacillating between tacit support and open revulsion, as clearly seen by the Operation Murambatsvina in May 2005, which targeted the urban informal economy. The UN envoy reported that the operation '…was carried out in an indiscriminate and unjustified manner, with indifference to human suffering, and, in repeated cases, with disregard to several provisions of national and international legal frameworks'; she also referred to it as a '…humanitarian crisis of immense proportions'.[1] The UN report estimated that 700,000 people across the cities in Zimbabwe lost either their homes or source of livelihood or both, with a further 2.4 million people indirectly affected. Women bore the brunt of this action in two ways: as informal economy players and as mothers having the extra caring responsibilities on their shoulders.

This marginalisation and neglect of the informal economy explains the persisting gender-based barriers and structural challenges for women-owned enterprises, youth-owned enterprises, and PWD-owned enterprises. Their lack of access to resources (credit, skills training, markets and a conducive policy environment) has had negative implications for the success of initiatives intended to support these marginalised groups in society. Overall, the informal economy suffers from decent work deficits, lack of collateral, poverty and earnings risks due to irregular and low incomes, financial exclusion, unfavourable working conditions and lack of representation.

---

1   Tibaijuka, 2005.

Gender dynamics in the informal economy

The structural changes in the economy and the associated challenges explained in Chapter 4 resulted in the exponential growth of the informal economy. Figure 2 shows the gender dynamics in the informal economy.

Figure 2: Percentage Share of Currently Employed Population in the Informal Economy by Sex, 2001, 2011 & 2014

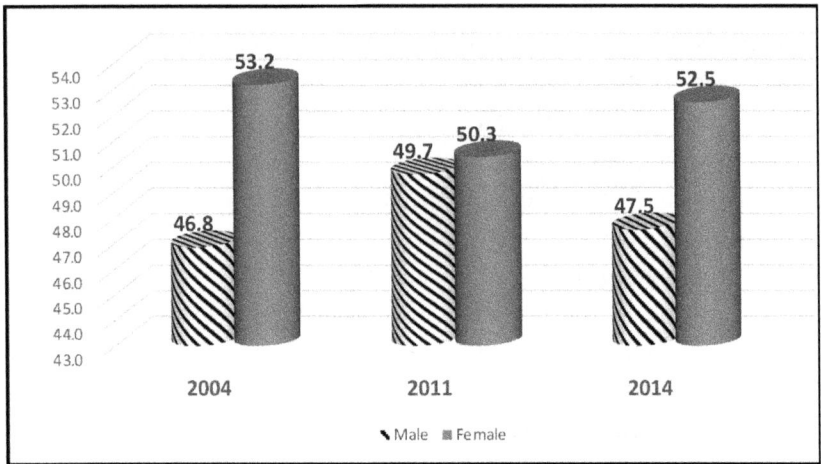

Source: Calculated from 2004, 2011 & 2014 Labour Force Surveys, ZimStat.

Figure 2 confirms that females have been over-represented in the informal economy in the three periods. These statistics are in line with the 2012 FinScope Survey which concluded that 53 per cent of the 2 million individual entrepreneurs in the informal economy were females, while 54 per cent of the 800,000 business owners with employees were females. The growth of women in the informal economy over the years was explained by the fact that as thousands of men lost jobs in the formal economy and could not find any alternative employment, while others migrated out in search of employment, women took up the role of breadwinners in the households by engaging or working in the informal economy. Thus, since the economic downturn, women have been valued as important economic agents.

Being outside the regulatory framework implies that the majority of the women in the informal economy remain less productive, as they are locked out of markets for finance, technology, and other resources that would enable them to grow their businesses.[2]

---

2   Ndlela and Kanyenze, 2017.

More recently, new gender dynamics have emerged in the informal economy; due to the continuing deindustrialisation, more men are entering the informal economy with better resources and networks, increasing competition in a once 'female-dominated' economy. As a result, there is a tendency for women to be elbowed out of workspaces, opportunities and deals.[3]

Youths and disability dynamics in the informal economy

> With the ongoing social, political and economic unrest unfolding in Zimbabwe, the youths were mostly at the receiving end.[4]

Zimbabwe's population is youthful, as reflected in the average age of 21.7 years for males and 22.7 years for females,[5] which gives the country an opportunity to leverage the youth bulge. As clearly articulated by Katie Raymond in 2017:

> Youth are risk takers. They offer the world fresh perspectives to complex problems, yet the world rarely talks about them this way.[6]

The contraction of the formal economy and its failure to absorb the new entrants into the labour market has left youths (school-leavers, college and university students) with no option but to find employment and eke out a living in the informal economy, also commonly referred to in ChiShona as the *kukiya-kiya* or *zig-zag* economy[7] especially by most youths. *Kukiya-kiya* means resorting to strenuous or difficult activity with an eye to fulfilling basic needs, thus indicating a survivalist economy, an adjunct to 'bare life' and a search for opportunity in the hardened face of reality with no prospects of decent livelihoods.[8]

Thus, the informal economy has become the largest employer for most youths, trapping them in low productivity jobs, precarious employment, or under-employment, all of which are at odds with the principles of decent work. For example,

> Youths are found in the vending, street type activities such as car washing and car watching, making and selling simple crafts and in menial forms of housework or other forms of service activities for

---

3 LEDRIZ, 2017, p. 6.
4 '90% of Zim youths unemployed', *NewsDay*, 10 August 2016.
5 Zimbabwe National Employment Policy Framework (ZiNEPF), 2013.
6 Raymond, 2017.
7 Scoones, 2014.
8 Jones, 2010.

which their being viewed as children is used as a pretext for paying them low wages or treating them paternalistically by embracing them as part of the family.[9]

As a result, the country is significantly losing the capacity to realise the demographic dividend which investment in a substantial youth cohort can achieve. This unsustainable situation led the unemployed youth graduates to form the Zimbabwe Coalition for the Unemployed Graduates who have since 2016 organised waves of protests expressing their discontent at the rate of unemployment in the country.

Similarly, people living with disability are also over-represented in the informal economy and gendered dimensions are prevalent. The 2003 National Poverty Assessment Study Surveys (PASS II) revealed that for people with disabilities, 46 per cent of all the employed females are in the informal economy compared to 36 per cent for males.[10] In line with this finding the ZIMSTAT census report of 2012 highlighted that only 2 per cent of those with disabilities were formally employed whilst about 64 per cent were said to be employed in the informal economy. Likewise, a study by UNICEF[11] revealed that individuals with disability are more often unemployed because of illness, and evidently because of disability, and fewer are in formal and paid employment. The limited opportunities for PWDs to participate economically are further compounded by their having less opportunity to acquire the qualifications, experience and social networks necessary to participate effectively in the labour market.[12] Thus, the structural changes in the economy, coupled with the disability-blind policies over the years and the failure by government to address the dual and enclave economy, has failed to uplift the status of people with disability and graduate more PWDs into formal labour market.

Informal employment by gender: enterprise-based and job-based concepts

Gender inequalities also feature in informal employment. Figure 3 shows the gender dynamics of the enterprise-based concept of informality.

---

9 Zimbabwe National Employment Policy Framework (ZiNEPF), 2009, p. 15.
10 Ibid.
11 UNICEF, 2013, p. 36.
12 Marcus and Gavrilovic, 2010, p. 17.

Figure 3: Gender distribution of employed persons by enterprise-based concept of informality (%), 2004 and 2014

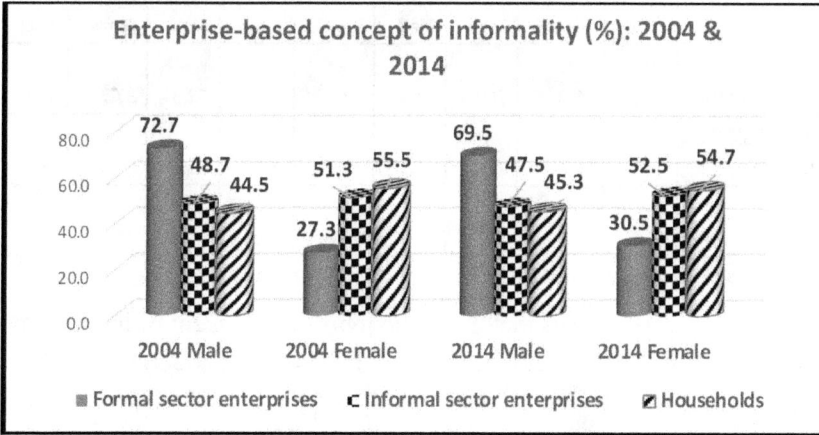

Source: Calculated from 2004 & 2014 Labour Force Surveys, ZimStat.

Using the enterprise definition of informality, Figure 3 indicates that there were more males in the formal sector enterprises, and that females are more concentrated in informal sector enterprises. For instance, in 2004 more males were in formal sector enterprises (72.7 per cent) than females (27.3 per cent). Similarly, in 2014 more males were in formal sector enterprises (69.5 per cent) than females (30.5 per cent).

Furthermore, Figure 3 stresses that more females than males were in insecure employment. For example, in 2004, 51.3 percent of those in informal sector enterprises were females compared to 48.7 percent males. A similar trend is exhibited in 2014 where 52.5 percent were females versus 47.5 percent males.

The percentage share of women in household enterprises was also higher for females than for males. In 2014, females constitute 54.7 per cent compared to males, 45.3 per cent. This trend was similar to that of 2004. Tellingly, the existence of more females operating in households is explained by the institutionalised gender roles where women are forced to balance mutiple family responsibilities, care work and economic activities in the labour market. Operating from households further reinforces the historic invisibility of women's participation and positive contribution in the economy and labour market, which in turn further excludes them from accessing the requisite resources necessary to grow their businesses. Table 1 shows the gender dynamics in the job-based concept of informality.

Table 1: Job-based concept of informality (%)

	2004			2011			2014		
	Male	Female	Total	Male	Female	Total	Male	Female	Total
Formal employment	73.8	26.2	100	71.1	28.9	100	62.3	37.7	100
Informal employment	46.6	53.4	100	47.1	52.9	100	48.6	51.4	100
Total employment	51.8	48.2	100	49.8	50.2	100	49.3	50.7	100

Source: Calculated from 2004 & 2014 Labour Force Surveys, ZimStat.

Table 1 clearly shows that using the job-based concept of informality, more males were in secure employment than females across the three periods. For instance, males constituted 73.8 per cent, 71.1 per cent and 62.3 per cent of formal employment in 2004, 2011 and 2014 respectively. More females were in less secure and precarious employment than their male counterparts. For example, females in informal employment constituted 53.4 per cent in 2004, 52.9 per cent in 2011 and 51.4 per cent in 2014. In a nutshell, using both the enterprise-based and job-based concepts of informality, more females than males remained in insecure and precarious employment.

Status of employment by gender

Table 2 clearly indicates huge gender disparities in status of employment. The share of males in paid permanent employment and paid casual/ temporary/seasonal employment was higher than females. For example, in 2014, 66 per cent and 64.5 per cent of males were in paid employment compared to only 34 per cent and 35.5 per cent of females in the same category. Furthermore, three times more males than females were employers in 2014.

Women were over-represented in the categories of own account workers (communal, resettlement and peri-urban farmers), unpaid contributing family worker and those not stated. This clearly shows that females are disproportionately located in jobs with high insecurity compared to their male counterparts.

Furthermore, an analysis of the data for unpaid contributing family workers over the years reveals sharp differences between men and women. In 2011, the number of females (65.4 per cent) was almost double that of males (34.6 per cent). There is also a disproportionately higher share of

Table 2: Status of employment by gender (%)

Status of employment	2004			2011			2014		
	Male	Female	Total	Male	Female	Total	Male	Female	Total
Paid employee-permanent	70.8	29.2	100	70.1	29.9	100	66	34	100
Paid employee casual/temporary/seasonal	60.2	39.8	100	61.2	38.8	100	64.5	35.5	100
Employer	82.1	17.9	100	69.8	30.2	100	75	25	100
Own account worker (communal, resettlement & peri-urban farmer)	38	62	100	43.2	56.8	100	43.1	56.9	100
Own account worker (other)	47.9	52.1	100	48.3	51.7	100	47	53	100
Unpaid contributing family worker	51.9	48.1	100	34.6	65.4	100	39.8	60.2	100
Member of producer cooperative	0	0	0	0	0	0	83.5	16.5	100
Not stated	0	100	100	52.8	47.2	100	31.4	68.6	100
Total	51.4	48.6	100	49.8	50.2	100	49.3	50.7	100

Source: Calculated from 2004, 2011 & 2014 Labour Force Surveys, ZimStat.

males who are members of a producer cooperative than women, 83.5 per cent and 16.5 per cent respectively in 2014.

The 2013 National Budget Statement recognised the role of women in the labour market:

> Hence, Government recognises women as essential to the realisation of food security, as well as formal labour across various industries. As such, the 2013 National Budget will give priority to those policies and programmes which advance women in development as well as achieving gender balance in economic activity.

Despite this recognition, trends from 2004 to 2014 have shown that more females are found at the lower levels of the employment strata where work is irregular and low paying, coupled with job insecurity and higher exposure to poverty and earnings risk.

Gender dimensions in national decision making structures

Table 3 depicts women's participation in national decision making structures. There is wide recognition globally that women's full participation in such structures and institutions is critical in ensuring that women's issues, concerns and interests are addressed in order to set a country on a developmental trajectory path.

Table 3 indicates that in 2015 women's participation in the economy and labour market at decision making levels still remained very low and below the 50/50 gender parity stipulated in the National Gender Policy. Part of the challenge lies in the working culture in various state and non-state institutions that continue to be patriarchal and perpetuate overt and covert forms of gender-based violence such as sexual harassment, bullying, and verbal and psychological violence against women.

The youth dimensions of status of employment

Table 4 shows that most youths, both male and female, were in insecure employment as they were more concentrated in the category of own account worker (communal, resettlement & peri-urban farmer). This is a clear sign of the failure to absorb youths into paid employment due to deindustrialisation and the challenge to young people of the school-to-work transition. Interestingly, females had the larger share in this category, 63 per cent versus 53.3 per cent for males. In addition, more female youths than men were own account worker (other) and unpaid contributing family worker. This clearly indicates that without paid permanent employment

Table 3: The state of women leadership in the economy, 2015

Office	(%)	Office	(%)
Cabinet Ministers	15.4	Boards of Parastatals / State Enterprises	29
Ambassadors	24.4	Chief Executive Officers of Parastatals/State Enterprises	23
Permanent Secretaries	29.2	Consulars	0
Principal Directors	23.5	Vice Chancellors of State Universities	27.3
Directors	27.6	Parliament – Lower House	31.9
Deputy Directors	25.5	Parliament – Upper House	47.5
Provincial Ministers	40		

Source: ZIMSTAT, 2016

Table 4: Status of employment of the youths by gender, 15-34 years, 2014 (%)

Status in employment	Male	Female	Total
Paid employee (permanent)	16.3	10.5	13.5
Paid employee (casual/temporary/ contract/seasonal	14.0	8.3	11.3
Employer	0.4	0.2	0.3
Own account worker (communal, resettlement & peri-urban farmer)	54.3	63.0	58.5
Own account worker (other)	12.4	15.2	13.8
Unpaid contributing family worker	2.1	2.7	2.4
Member of producer cooperative	0.4	0.1	0.3
Not stated	0.0	0.1	0.0
Total per cent	100	100	100

Source: Calculated from 2014 Labour Force Surveys, ZimStat.

and social security, the youths in Zimbabwe are becoming stereotyped as the 'lost generation'.

In trying to address the challenge of youth unemployment, various initiatives have been implemented by the government, UN agencies and NGOs. For instance, the International Labour Organization (ILO) has been supporting the government, employers and workers organisations, the private sector, CSOs and other partners through its flagship programmes, the Training for Rural Economic Empowerment (TREE) and the Quality Improvements in Informal Apprenticeships (QIA). According to the 2015 Assessment Report of the ILO,[13] more than 6,500 youths in rural areas were reached under the TREE programme and were engaged in diverse economic ventures after receiving skills development training and access to microfinance institutions. The QIA reached over 3,300 urban youths who were informal apprentices and were attached to more than 2,300 Master Craftspersons in order to learn various trades. However, the assessment report highlighted some of the challenges faced in the implementation of the programme, notably the lack of access to finance, scarce assets and production equipment, marketing of products and gaps in methods of value addition.[14] Other non-state actors also cited the exclusion of key stakeholders when the ILO hands over the programme to the government towards the end of the programme, thus undermining effective participation and monitoring. Addressing these challenges would lead to better outcomes.

Sectoral distribution of employed by gender

Whilst it is applauded that paid employment opportunities for women in the labour market has been rising over the given periods, the statistics clearly indicate that female workers are highly over-represented in sectors commonly stereotyped as 'female domains', or regarded as an extension of women's traditional and maternal role (care, preparation and serving of meals, training and education of children, cleaning and decorating). The trend from 2004 to 2014 shows that feminisation of sectoral employment increased in agriculture, distribution, restaurants and hotels, education, health and private domestic work. Sadly, these sectors often have atypical jobs (casual, contract and part-time) which lack social security and are more poorly remunerated than those sectors where males are more dominant.

13 ILO, 2015.
14 Ibid.

Table 5: Sectoral distribution of employed persons aged 15 years and above by gender, 2004, 2011 and 2014 (%)

Status of employment	2004			2011			2014		
	Male	Female	Total	Male	Female	Total	Male	Female	Total
Paid employee-permanent	70.8	29.2	100	70.1	29.9	100	66	34	100
Paid employee casual/temporary/seasonal	60.2	39.8	100	61.2	38.8	100	64.5	35.5	100
Employer	82.1	17.9	100	69.8	30.2	100	75	25	100
Own account worker (communal, resettlement & peri-urban farmer)	38	62	100	43.2	56.8	100	43.1	56.9	100
Own account worker (other)	47.9	52.1	100	48.3	51.7	100	47	53	100
Unpaid contributing family worker	51.9	48.1	100	34.6	65.4	100	39.8	60.2	100
Member of producer cooperative	0	0	0	0	0	0	83.5	16.5	100
Not stated	0	100	100	52.8	47.2	100	31.4	68.6	100
Total	51.4	48.6	100	49.8	50.2	100	49.3	50.7	100

Source: Calculated from 2004, 2011 and 2014 Labour Force Surveys, ZimStat

The choices and opportunities available to women and men in terms of their education and training also result in differentials in representation in industries. The sectors dominated by women are generally seen as being less important, requiring lower skills, and, thus, deserving lower earnings than the sectors dominated by men.[15]

By contrast a larger and increasing percentage share of males is found in mining and quarrying, manufacturing, construction, transport and communications, finance, insurance and real estate, and public administration, which are regarded as technical in nature.

The 2004, 2011 and 2014 LFSs also provides statistics on employment by institution and by gender. The statistics clearly shows that the share of males has remained disproportionly higher in the private sector, central government, parastatals and cooperatives. For example, in 2004, men in the private sector constituted 50.2 per cent increasing further to 56.1 per cent by 2014. In 2004, men's share in the central government was 58.1 per cent which increased to 59.5 per cent by 2014. Similarly, the share of men in NGOs increased from 57.2 in 2004, to 58.4 per cent in 2011 and further to 65.6 per cent in 2014. Although the proportion of females in the local government and parastatals remained lower than males, the share of females was increasing over time in these institutions, an indication of women breaking ground as a result of better education.

In terms of the gender wage gap, the Global Gender Gap Index (GGGI) improved between 2006 and 2016, from 0.646 to 0.710.[16] In the same period, the GGGI rank improved from 76/115 to 56/144. However, these figures indicate that there still exist gender gaps. Furthermore, the Interim Poverty Reduction Strategy Paper (2016-18) concluded that women in Zimbabwe earn on average about two-thirds of men's income, largely because women dominate low remunerating sectors and occupations with high level of precarious work in both the formal and informal economy. The gender pay gap was also explained by gender differences in education and experience and the numbers of hours worked either in the formal or informal economy.

15 ILO, 2009, p. 17.
16 World Economic Forum, 2016.

Distribution of employed by gender, education and skills level

Table 6: Percentage distribution of currently employed persons aged 15 years and above by level of education and gender, 2004, 2011 & 2014

Level of education	2004			2011			2014		
	M	F	Total %	M	F	Total %	M	F	Total %
No primary education	29.7	70.3	100	25.3	74.7	100	23.2	76.8	100
Primary	46.2	53.8	100	44.0	56.0	100	44.9	55.1	100
Secondary	57.2	42.8	100	53.8	46.2	100	53.0	47.0	100
Tertiary	61.0	39.0	100	62.0	38.0	100	57.9	42.1	100
Not stated	30.4	69.6	100	28.0	72.0	100	28.3	71.7	100
Total	**51.4**	**48.6**	**100**	**49.8**	**50.2**	**100**	**49.3**	**50.7**	**100**

Source: Calculated from 2004, 2011 & 2014 Labour Force Surveys, ZimStat.

Table 6 demonstrates that:

i.   The percentage share of females with no primary education was significantly higher than males and has been increasing over the years.

ii. Gender disparities exist at primary level, where the percentage share of females is higher than males, but this trend shifts dramatically in both the secondary and tertiary levels.

iii. Gender disparities continued to further widen at tertiary level in favour of males, a clear indication that there is a lower transition rate for female than male students from primary to secondary and from secondary to tertiary levels.

Over the years, there have been huge gender differentials in skilled and semi-skilled work, with the percentage share being higher for males than females. For instance, in 2004, 73.5 per cent of skilled workers were males, and 26.5 per cent were females, a trend which was maintained up to 2014. The percentage share of females, although lower, exhibited an increasing trend between 2001 and 2014 in the professional and semi-skilled categories. Women are over-represented in the unskilled and not

Table 7: Percentage distribution of currently employed persons aged 15 years and above by skill level and gender, 2004, 2011 & 2014

Skill Level	2004			2011			2014		
	M	F	Total (%)	M	F	Total (%)	M	F	Total (%)
Professional	59.7	40.3	100	59.3	40.7	100	57.3	42.7	100
Skilled	73.5	26.5	100	74.7	25.3	100	73	27	100
Semi-Skilled	73.5	26.5	100	69.1	30.9	100	69.1	30.9	100
Unskilled	46.4	53.6	100	46.4	53.6	100	45.9	54.1	100
Not Known	61.1	38.9	100	46.4	53.6	100	55.3	44.7	100
Not Stated	38.8	61.2	100	45.9	54.1	100	31.1	68.9	100
Total	51.4	48.6	100	49.8	50.2	100	49.3	50.7	100

Source: Calculated from 2004, 2011 & 2014 Labour Force Surveys, ZimStat.

stated categories in all the years, and are more concentrated in sectors such as agriculture and private domestic work. Jobs that are unskilled have high chances of decent work deficits such as low pay, less social security, and long and unpaid work hours.[17] This was echoed by Katie Raymond:

> There is also a gender dimension to the formal economy, as women occupy a smaller piece of the pie – and a piece that pays less.[18]

Care and unpaid work and the labour market

> People being well cared for is as much a contribution to society as the production of goods.[19]

The time spent on care and unpaid work has a bearing on the time spent participating in the labour market and economic activities. This is often due to the gendered social norms that view unpaid care work as a female duty. Research conducted in five main parastatals in Zimbabwe in 2012 revealed that the most prevalent challenges which hindered women in so far as recruitment, transfers and promotion were concerned included but were not limited to:

i. attending to care work and other family responsibilities;

---

17 ILO, 2009, p. 20.

18 Raymond, 2017.

19 Professor Susan Himmelweit, UK Women's Budget Group, 'Transforming the Care Economy' webinar, 8 June 2016.

ii. direct and indirect discrimination as a result of gender stereotyping in the workplace; and,

iii. the failure of the government to domesticate and enforce legal instruments to enable them to enforce certain critical internationally recognised labour rights (e.g. access to child care facilities at the workplace and leave to attend to sick family members).[20]

Over the years, the deterioration of the socio-economic environment has in turn increased time spent in care and unpaid work by women and girls. This, coupled with the rollback in the state's provision for social services, has resulted in the disproportionate burden of care and unpaid work on women and girls. As clearly articulated by Ranchod-Nilsson in 2006:

> As the economy moved into a state of crisis after the introduction of the ESAP, women's unpaid labour was essential to meet subsistence and health care needs with decreasing levels of state support. In this climate, the state's rhetoric shifted from women's rights, to women's responsibilities, and controlling the activities of women became more important than ever.[21]

Care and unpaid work are essential in sustaining and reproducing the market economy, but unfortunately they remain under-recognised and undervalued by the government and society, and take up a significant amount of women's and girls' time and effort, leaving them with less time for engagement in socio-economic activities. Figure 4 underscores this dilemma.

It is clear that more time is spent by women than men on care and unpaid work. In fact, women spend twice as much time in caring for children, housekeeping and home duties. A study by Oxfam in three districts revealed that:

> Many women and girls carry the heavy, unequal and seemingly natural burden of care work, which is rarely appreciated, not financially beneficial and deeply rooted in culture. Women do three to six times more hours of care work than men.[22]

---

20 Mutangi, 2016.
21 Ranchod-Nilsson, 2006, p. 66.
22 '16-hour days for Zim's women', NewsDay, 10 March 2017.

Figure 4: Average time spent in unpaid activities (hours/week) in own household by gender (%)

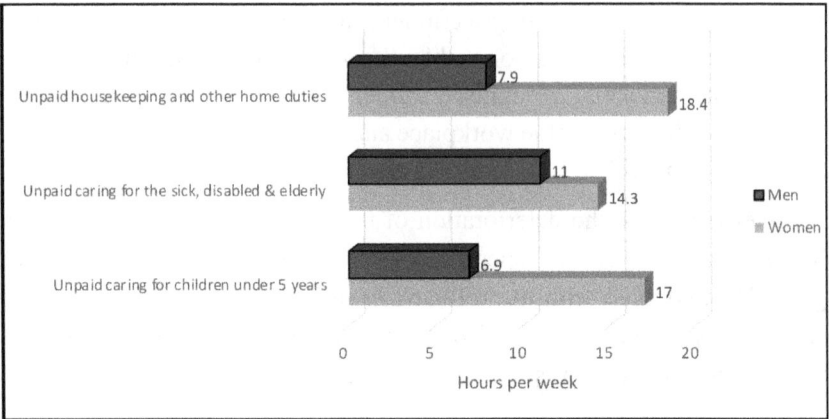

Source: ZIMSTAT, 2016

Another study revealed that the burden of care work prevents most women workers from actively participating in trade union activities, especially if they are done outside working hours when, according to gendered social norms, women are expected to be at home caring for the family.[23]

Over the years, the increasing burden of care work has pushed women to participate in industrial strike actions in support of their spouses, thus radically transforming the industrial landscape and the social norms and gender roles. The economic crisis, poverty wages and 'wage theft' (non-payment of wages and salaries) compounded the gender roles of women as caregivers. As a result, women were forced to stand by their husbands when they went on strike. Three noteworthy cases can be cited:

i. The nationwide strike over outstanding salaries by National Railways of Zimbabwe workers in 2006 which lasted for about two months. Women and children joined the strike and camped at the NRZ offices. One woman stated:

Life has become difficult at home so we have decided to camp here with our husbands until they get their outstanding salaries.[24]

Other women cited failure to pay exam and school fees for their children, rentals and other basic needs.[25]

---

23 Shindondola-Mote et al., 2011.
24 ZBC News Online, 5 April 2016.
25 'Spouses, children join NRZ strike', The Zimbabwean, 20 April 2016.

ii. The 2008 Shabanie Mine strike where the women and their children demonstrated by beating pots and pans in solidarity with their husbands who had gone for months without salary payments. The Police fired live ammunition on the demonstrating women and children.[26]

iii. The 2018 Hwange Colliery Company case where over 1,000 women joined their striking spouses over non-payment of salaries for close to five years. The women and young children camped at the firm's premises for more than 100 days resulting in seven NGOs launching a coalition to offer moral and humanitarian support.

All these cases prove women's capacities and capabilities to organise themselves to fight for socio-economic justice even within a challenging political context. The government's militant and aggressive response to the plight of these workers, women and children clearly emphasised its shallow commitments to the upholding of women's and children's rights and improving their livelihoods, as summarised by Ranchod-Nilsson:

> As the government of Zimbabwe becomes increasingly weak in terms of domestic legitimacy and financial capacity, and increasingly repressive toward those who voice any opposition to the ruling party, women's organisations have been able to carve out important spaces from which to operate. Organisations such as the Women's Action Group (WAG), the Zimbabwe Women's Resource Centre and Network (ZWRCN), and the Musasa Project have strong domestic constituencies as well as strong linkages to international NGO networks. ...despite the dramatic decline in economic circumstances, political participation and state support for women's rights, and the mixed legacy of the liberation war, women are carving out spaces from which they are working on meaningful political and social transformation. However, such transformations will only be possible within a broader context of economic stability and meaningful political participation.[27]

Gender dynamics in the trade unions

Since its establishment in 1981, the Zimbabwe Congress of Trade Unions (ZCTU) has been making efforts to increase the participation of women,

26 Zimbabwe Congress of Trade Union reports, 2018.
27 Ranchod-Nilsson, 2006, p. 67.

who historically were deprived from participating due to engendered social norms and the patriarchal system. The first initiative by the ZCTU was the establishment of the Women's Department in 1985 in order to make it easier for women to organise other women to participate in trade unions.[28] The Department's strategy then was to:

i. Facilitate the formation of women's committees in the ZCTU.

ii. Organise the establishment of branches of women's committees in all areas with women workers.

iii. Formulate and implement educational programmes for women workers.

By 1987, the ZCTU had established 16 women's committees. The Women's Advisory Committee (WAC) was also established, as the highest decision making body. To complement this development, Regional Women Advisory Councils (RWACs) were also established in the six ZCTU regions. Later on, the Women's Department was renamed the Women and Gender Department and has been headed by a woman ever since.

Gender dimensions at ZCTU Leadership Levels

Table 8: Gender dimensions at ZCTU leadership level

Position	2012				2017			
	No. of wmn	No. of men	Total	% of wmn	No. of wmn	No. of men	Total	% of wmn
President	0	1	1	0	0	1	1	0
Vice-President	1	2	3	33	1	2	3	33
Secretary General	0	1	1	0	0	1	1	0
Deputy Sec. General	0	2	2	0	0	2	2	0
Treasurer	0	1	1	0	0	1	1	0
Exec. Comm. Members	4	11	16	25	8	13	21	38
General Council Members	6	35	45	13	8	34	42	19

Source: ZCTU Women and Gender Department, 2018

28 Chakanya and Siwela, 2011, p. 262.

Table 8 indicates that notable improvements in women's participation were realised in the Executive Committee and General Council structures. The number of females in the former increased from 25 per cent in 2012 to 38 per cent in 2017, and in the latter from 13 per cent to 19 per cent. In order to enhance women's participation in the decision making level of the ZCTU, it was resolved that three members of the WAC should sit in the ZCTU's General Council. However, whilst these improvements are applauded, there is need to further increase the share of females in all ZCTU and affiliate structures in line with the 2016 ZCTU's Congress resolution of 50/50 representation.

Gender dimensions at ZCTU affiliate level and membership

Table 9 shows the gender dynamics in ZCTU's affiliate unions in 2012. The table indicates that the proportion of women at affiliate leadership level was higher in the Executive Committees (44.4 per cent), followed by Presidents (28.6 per cent), Deputy General Secretaries (25.7 per cent), Vice-Presidents (14.3 per cent) and Treasurers (11.4 per cent). The lowest share of women was found in the General Secretary positions (8.6 per cent) .

Table 9: Gender dimensions in the ZCTU affiliates' structures, including the ZCIEA,[29] by gender, 2012

Position	No. of wmn	No. of men	Total	% wmn
President	10	25	35	28.6
V. President	8	48	56	14.3
General Secretaries	3	32	35	8.6
Deputy General Secretaries	9	26	35	25.7
Treasurers	4	31	35	11.4
Executive Committee Members	233	292	525	44.4
Grand Total	**267**	**454**	**721**	**37.0**

Source: ZCTU Women and Gender Department, 2018

The proportion of females in leadership positions at affiliate level was generally low at 37 per cent, meaning that more efforts are required to ensure 50/50 gender parity in line with the ZCTU's Constitution and Gender Policy.

29 The Zimbabwe Chamber of Informal Economy Associations.

Other initiatives by ZCTU to increase women's participation

i. Development of the ZCTU Gender Policy in 2013.

ii. Development of ZCTU's Affiliate Unions Gender Policies in the following unions:

   a) Cement and Lime Workers Union of Zimbabwe

   b) Commercial Workers Union of Zimbabwe

   c) General Agriculture and Plantation Workers Union of Zimbabwe

   d) Zimbabwe Banks and Allied Workers Union

   e) Zimbabwe Teachers Association

   f) Zimbabwe Amalgamated Railway Workers Union

   g) Zimbabwe Catering and Hotel Workers Union

   h) Zimbabwe Chamber of Informal Economy Associations.

iii. Implementation of the Decisions for Life (DFL) Campaign by the ZCTU's Women and Gender Department (2009-11) which focused on empowering young women to actively participate in trade unions. The initiative resulted in:

   • The inclusion of the Young Workers structure in the ZCTU Constitution which has the same powers and functions as the Women Committee.

   • Lobbying for the increase in the breastfeeding time allocated under maternity leave and inclusion of a family responsibility holiday in the Labour Act (process still underway).

Challenges inhibiting the full participation of women in trade unions

Whilst the ZCTU has undertaken several steps to promote women's participation in trade unions, there still exist barriers.

Box 1: Voices of young women empowered through the DFL Campaign

'I have been taught about my rights, and I learnt how to organise new young members and now have skills to lobby for women's rights. I now know that the union is there to protect our rights and to give us information and knowledge to participate in the community where we live. The union allowed us as the young to participate in our own special way and new slogans that interest us as young women were invented. We enjoyed the programme.' Immaculate Chingwere, Railway Artisan Union.

'The DFL Campaign has taught me to be confident and I know my rights now. The campaign has changed my attitude towards the trade union and I appreciate the union more. We need to engage our employer to stop victimising workers and allow casual workers to be trade union members.' Solomy Mandizvidza, Chemicals Union.

Source: Adapted from the ZCTU's DFL Report, 2011

i. Patriarchal system and stereotypes in the Zimbabwe society

The low levels of women's participation in decision making in trade unions is embedded in the patriarchal system and gendered social norms that historically stereotype trade unionism and leadership in trade unions as a male domain. Those active in trade unionism are sometimes regarded as 'barbaric'.

> Some women raised the concern that trade unionism is regarded by some people as 'barbaric'. Such labelling instils stigma in some women hence they avoid participating in trade union activities because they would not like to be referred to as 'barbaric women' by the rest of society.[30]

> There is a myth that only single women without anyone to report to at home can undertake trade union work.[31]

ii. Women's multiple roles

Women's dual roles at home and at the workplace limit them from fully participating in trade union activities.

> ...the collapse of social service delivery in Zimbabwe during the time of the crisis has increased the burden on women in that they have to take extra responsibilities at home in terms of searching for water and firewood, among others. In such a situation more women tend to

---

30 Chakanya and Siwela, 2011.
31 Interview with female trade unionist, 3 May 2018.

prioritise taking care of the family than attending union activities.[32]

The multiple roles of women hinder them from rising up in trade union structures as fast as their male counterparts.[33]

Some of the trade union women we assign trade union responsibilities end up being forced by their husbands to choose between undertaking trade union work or marriage. Many women end up choosing marriage so as to keep peace in the family.[34]

We have a chairlady in our structure but the problem is that most of the times she will be chairing the meeting, the husband comes and demands that she comes home. So the chairlady ends up leaving the meetings even without finishing discussions.[35]

iii. Lack of prioritisation of women structures and programmes

One of the key challenges cited by women trade unionists is that most of the trade union leadership and trade unions do not prioritise women programmes and activities in their budgets and policies. Some of the affiliates have structures at national, regional and district level but these are not supported by financial resources. As a result, they remain dormant, stifling capacity development and empowerment programmes, and women's full participation in trade union activities.

Sometimes budgets and funds meant for women's activities are side-tracked to other activities without consultation with the women structures. This seriously undermines women's programmes and derails capacity development of women activists.[36]

Youths in trade unions

Ignoring youth is catastrophe.[37]

The ZCTU has made commendable efforts to increase the participation of youths in trade unions, but more efforts are still required.[38]

Historically, trade unions in Zimbabwe did not prioritise the participation

---

32 Ibid.
33 Interview with a female trade unionist, 7 May 2018.
34 Interview with a female trade union activist, 9 May 2018.
35 Ibid.
36 Interview with a female trade unionist based in Harare, 7 May 2018.
37 2017 ZCTU's Youth Council Statement.
38 ZCTU young worker.

of youths. More recently, the integration and inclusion of younger workers in trade unions has gained momentum internationally. In Zimbabwe, the formation of young workers committees started in the 1990s. The ZCTU defines youth as those aged 15- 35 years, in line with the National Youth Policy and the African Youth Charter. By 2016, the ZCTU recorded about 35,000 youths, representing about 20% of total membership.

The following are some of the trade union initiatives to promote the active participation of youths:

i.   Resolution by the 6th ZCTU Congress in 2006 to formulate young workers structures.

ii. Formulation of the ZCTU National Interim young workers structure in 2008.

iii. Formulation of Young Workers Committees in affiliate trade unions. Eight out of 34 ZCTU affiliates have established these Committees. The sectors include: commercial, urban councils, banking, security, agriculture, chemical, hotel and catering and science and education.

iv. Participation of young workers as observers at 7th ZCTU Congress in 2011.

The ZCTU Constitution and youths

The ZCTU formally adopted the young workers structure as a constitutional structure in 2013 following the proposal by young workers from the affiliate unions. The following are the constitutional provisions:

i.   Inclusion of the Young Workers Council in the ZCTU Constitution.

ii. Establishment of young workers structures up to the districts level.

iii. Provision of three mandatory meetings of the National Young Workers Committee.

iv. Provision that the Young Workers National Council shall attend Congress with full voting rights.

v.   Participation of three representatives from the National Council, namely: Youth Chairperson and Vice Chairperson and a Youth Committee member.

A number of successes have been realised:

    i.   One of the ZCTU Presidents is a younger worker.

    ii.   Development of the ZCTU Youth Policy in 2015.

    iii.   Nomination of one of the ZCTU's Youth Council members to be the Chairperson of the Southern African Trade Union Coordination Council's Interim Committee.

    iv.   Selection of one of the ZCTU's Youth Council members as a titular member of the ILO Governing Body.

Challenges faced by youths in trade unions

There still exist barriers to full participation of young workers in trade unions.

The structural changes in the labour market and the changing world of work has resulted in the rise in the number of youths entering the formal economy holding casual or precarious jobs. As a result, they do not join trade unions as they feel it is a preserve of permanent workers who are largely in the older age groups.

> With the precarious jobs and the growing trade union bashing by management, many youths are forced not to join the trade union or participate in related activities as they fear job loss, name calling, discrimination or non-renewal of contracts.[39]

> Most young workers with precarious contracts and who are trade union members are highly vulnerable to victimisation by employers.[40]

Many of the trade union policies, constitutions, programmes and structures disregard the youth. This makes the trade union less attractive to the youths and causes them to be disengaged. In addition, most trade union affiliates do not have youth structures or youth officers or youth focal persons.

> The ZCTU has made strides at national level to integrate the youths in its national structures… but the challenge remains with the affiliate unions who are slow in establishing youth structures and implementing youth programmes at their regional and district levels.[41]

---

39 Interview with a member of the ZCTU Youth Council, Harare, 9 May 2018.
40 Ibid.
41 Interview with a member of the ZCTU Youth Council, Harare, 8 May 2018.

Most of the trade union activities are not tailor-made to attract and retain young people's interests.[42]

Lack of appreciation of the positive role of youths in trade unions by older age groups remains a challenge. Hence, most youths are marginalised from decision making bodies and structures.

Most of the older trade union leaders are unwilling and not keen to have youths in their structures especially in decision making structures for fear of losing their positions, whilst some feel that the youths have nothing substantive to contribute to the development of trade union – generational gap. This demotivates us the youths.[43]

The lack of dedicated financial resources for youth-related activities lowers the participation of youths in trade unions. Without financial resources, capacity development programmes for youths are stifled. Sadly, most trade unions are suffering from dwindling membership and a corresponding reduction in membership fees.

The lack of investment in youth-disaggregated data in trade unions remain a challenge.

Most of the stop order forms of trade unions do not specify age and other related data. This make it difficult for trade unions to enumerate their membership by age.[44]

Persons with disability at national level

According to the 2013 National Survey on Disability and Health, the prevalence of disability in Zimbabwe was estimated to be 7 per cent, translating to approximately 914,300 persons.[45] The same survey concluded the following (as reflected in Table 10):

i.   That while males seemed to be more exposed to disability in the younger age groups, the results indicated a strong association between increasing age and disability among women as compared to men.

ii. Persons with disability were often marginalised in the labour market and belonged to the poorest segments of society.

iii. Fewer individuals with disability were in formal, paid employment.

42 Interview with a young worker based in Bulawayo, 9 May 2018.
43 Interview with a member of the ZCTU Youth Council, Harare, 9 May 2018.
44 Young trade union activist, Harare, 9 May 2018.
45 UNICEF, 2013.

    iv. Six times more individuals with disability (14.8 per cent) than without disability (2.2 per cent) reported that they are retired, sick or too old to work.

    v. Individuals with disability are less involved in formal employment (16.05 per cent) and higher education as compared to individuals without disability.

    vi. Individuals with disability are more often unemployed because of illness, and evidently because of disability, whilst individuals without disability are more often unemployed due to being retired, retrenched or discharged.

Table 10: Selected indicators on persons with disability (%)

Indicator	Case	Control	Average
Persons aged 15 - 65 years in employment	16.05	26.15	21.1
Persons aged 15 - 65 years not working but previously employed	22.15	15.05	18.6
Persons aged 15 - 65 years who have never been employed	49.85	46.05	47.95
Housewife/homemaker	9.25	11.45	10.35
Disability –related as a reason for current unemployment (those not in employment)	12.2	0.3	6.25
Disability-related reason for not attending school	12.2	0.3	6.25
Retired/sick/too old	14.8	2.2	-

Source: UNICEF, 2013

Persons with disability in trade unions

More recently, there has been a conscious decision by the ZCTU to integrate persons with disability in its policies and programmes. In 2018, it was in the process of developing a Disability Policy as well as integrating disability in one of its departments. Given the prevalence of persons in the informal economy, ZCIEA already has existing structures for persons with disability at national level and the structures have been decentralised to grassroot levels. ZCIEA also undertakes capacity development programmes for these structures.

Conclusion

The analysis in this chapter clearly indicates that the government of Zimbabwe failed to address the dual and enclave structure of the economy that it inherited at independence. Rather, the formal economy has shrunk, whilst non-formal sectors have expanded, further entrenching the marginalised groups in the informal economy. In fact, the structural regression of the economy has worsened the situation of these marginalised groups as the jobs are characterised by serious decent work deficits which include low-quality long working hours, very low and irregular earnings, limited opportunities to acquire skills and financial resources to expand businesses and absence of social protection. All of these deficits have long-term adverse implications for the marginalised groups which narrows their capacity to escape poverty.

The analysis also indicated that even in the formal sector, women are over-represented in casual, contract and part-time work, where again decent work deficits abound. It was also clear that structural regression of the economy further increased the high concentration of females in sectors of the economy commonly stereotyped as 'female domains' or regarded an extension of women's traditional and maternal roles. These sectors are often more poorly remunerated than those sectors where males are more dominant which is also attributed to the choices and opportunities available to women and men in terms of their education and training. There is a lower transition rate for female students from primary to secondary and from secondary to tertiary levels as compared to males, compounding the persistent gender differentials in representation in industries.

Within trade unions, whilst there have been efforts to increase the participation of women, their share in decision making structures continues to lag behind the ZCTU's 50/50 parity policy. In addressing the challenges of gender inequalities, trade unions need to dedicate financial resources at ZCTU and affiliate levels to implement capacity development programmes, develop demand-driven gender-based programmes, implement mentoring programmes for women, invest in provision of gender disaggregated data at affiliate level and eliminate gender-based violence in trade unions. Women, on the other hand need to continue fighting for and demanding their space in trade union structures, especially decision making ones.

Critically, even where buy-in and commitment at national and senior levels of institutions (both government and non-state institutions) is achieved, and gender policies developed, real transformation in favour of women's empowerment, women's rights, and gender justice cannot occur without subsequent changes in the working culture of government institutions, political parties, trade unions and CSOs. This requires the elimination of sexual harassment, violence and bullying against women. On the other hand, women who have managed to find themselves in decision making spaces and structures and those who are on the journey to do so have to increase their levels of resilience, assertiveness and perseverance as gender equality implies to many the loss of male privilege and male hegemony and a change in internal power dynamics and hierarchies.

In the context of the crisis and structural regression, the potential developmental gains from harnessing the demographic dividend means that the economic crisis undermines young people's current well-being and future opportunities. With the challenge of the school-to-work transition, the youths continue to be trapped in un- and underemployment, and in low productivity jobs which are extremely fragile. Due to the economic crisis and the fragmentation of the labour market, youths are disproportionately vulnerable to precarious jobs and lay-offs. Furthermore, they also face the already extensive barriers to first employment compared to older workers.

Whilst it is clear that ZCTU has made strides in integrating the youths in trade unions, especially in national structures, the low level of unionisation among young people persists for reasons including their limited presence in affiliate level structures, the lack of tailor-made programmes to attract the young workers, marginalisation in decision making structures, victimisation by employers due to casualisation of labour, lack of dedicated funding for youth programmes and limited capacity. Hence, at the affiliate level, there is a need to establish and adequately resource youth structures in order to overcome the age representation gap, and structures for people with disability; to implement youth-friendly programmes including marketing such programmes using modern ICTs; to change attitudes in older workers regarding the positive role and energy that youths can bring to positively transform the unions; and to implement trade union organising strategies around precarious work including programmes focused on a life-cycle approach rather than a job-centred one. Furthermore, trade unions should integrate youth issues in their constitutions, policies, and collective bargaining agreements.

Chapter 9

Political, Judicial and Legislative Responses to Labour and the Changing Regime of Industrial Relations

Zakeyo Mtimtema

Introduction

Zimbabwe's political landscape has over the years shaped the industrial relations system in the country. Soon after attaining independence in 1980, the government introduced progressive labour laws which were set to protect the black workers from exploitation by the white employer. These progressive laws were reversed in fundamental areas through the adoption of economic reforms of 1990s. The formation of the Movement for Democratic Change (MDC) in 1999 and its contest of the 2000 elections resulted in a reformed labour law regime through the Labour Amendment Act No. 17 of 2002. The amendment saw workers gaining a plethora of rights they had lost during the structural adjustment programme of the 1990s. For the first time in the history of the country, a unified Labour Act brought into its realm public service employees. However, the joy was short-lived as the Labour Amendment Act No. 5 of 2005 removed the public service from the scope of the Labour Act. The fragmentation of legislation remained in place in 2017.

The enactment of a new constitution in 2013, with a strong bill of rights that included labour rights, was welcomed by workers and trade unions. However, enforcement of the labour rights remained a challenge with the judiciary's interpretation in some fundamental areas becoming a cause of concern.

The country's political landscape remained negative and was viewed largely as being undemocratic. The government was in a quandary regarding how to balance the interest of the working people, who are also their political springboard, against the demand of market forces. The quest for labour market flexibility in a context of competition in the global market has over the years tilted the bargaining power towards capital. The International Monetary Fund (IMF) has also pushed for labour law reforms to remove protective legislation and encourage decentralised collective bargaining. During its re-engagement process with the IMF in June 2013, through the Staff Monitored Programme and Article 1V Consultation, the Government of Zimbabwe pronounced in its National Budget the need for labour market flexibility and a policy of linking wages to productivity.[1]

In 2015, the judiciary interpreted the labour laws to give effect to labour market flexibility dictates. In the case of Don Nyamande and Kingstone Donga v Zuva Petroleum (Pvt) Ltd, the Supreme Court ruled that an employer had a common law right to terminate a contract of employment without any reason, provided notice was given.[2] Whereas the Labour Amendment Act No. 5 of 2015 was said to have been enacted to protect the workers, it worsened the situation as it introduced relaxed regulations in the retrenchment process. The Act imposed a retrenchment package of one month's salary for each two years of service.[3] The employers seized the opportunity provided by these legal relaxations to terminate contracts of employment en masse.

This chapter provides an analysis of judicial activism in the labour market in its attempt to both protect vulnerable workers and at the same time support the politics of the day and the economic policy to liberalise the economy. The judiciary also created principles that in some respects curtailed union power and limited compensation of employees who have been unfairly dismissed. The chapter also examines the changing of work patterns; strike and retrenchment regulation in law and in judicial interpretation; the fragmentation of labour laws; and the challenges of trade unions in responding to the onslaught. The chapter concludes by noting the piecemeal upholding of labour rights by government and the judiciary that gave power to capital.

---

1   Ministry of Finance and Economic Development, 2014 National Budget statement.
2   Case No. SC 43/15.
3   Section 12C (2).

Labour legislative framework, 1990 to 2017

Zimbabwe's labour legislation is divided into several segments depending on the nature of employment and institution. The majority of the employees in the country fall under the ambit of the Labour Act Chapter 28:01, the Public Service Act Chapter 16:04 and the Public Service Regulations Statutory Instrument 1 of 2000. The public sector is further fragmented into: the Health Services Act Chapter 15:16; the Police Act Chapter 11:10; the Defence Act Chapter 11:02; the Prisons Act Chapter 7:11; and, the Judicial Service Act Chapter 7:18. What is significant to note is that legislation in the public service combines both administrative functions and labour relations. The fragmentation of labour laws indicates a diversionist approach in Zimbabwe's industrial relations system.

The Labour Act Chapter 28:01

The Labour Act Chapter 28:01 is the current legislation covering employees and employers in the private sector and quasi government companies and local authorities. Prior to its enactment, industrial relations were regulated by the Labour Relations Act No. 16 of 1985. This Act recognised trade union rights and attempted to redress the shortcomings of the colonial legislation that had limited rights to freedom of association and collective bargaining. The 1985 Act recognised the notion of one union in one industry, strengthened collective bargaining and banned unilateral dismissal of employees. All dismissals required ministerial approval before being effected, save for mutual termination of the contract employment.[4]

In 1992, the Act was amended to facilitate the new economic policy, the adoption of the Economic Structural Adjustment Programme (ESAP). The amended law allowed for multiple unions and employers' organisations in one industry. Government argued that the opening of space was to give workers and employers their constitutional right to freedom of association, and the the monopoly of one union in one industry was against freedom of association principles. The amended law also allowed employers and employees to regulate themselves through adopting codes of conduct to discipline workers.

Most codes of conduct were badly drafted and workers' representatives at the workplace level were not legally equipped to draft them. As a result, management codes of conduct were used to dismiss workers. In one of the

---

4   Labour Relations (Termination of Employment Regulations) SI371 of 1985.

cases heard by the Supreme Court, ZFC Limited v Malayani,[5] the Court noted that:

> We have often remarked that codes of conduct are badly drafted... This one is particularly so. It would seem imperative to us that a great deal more care should be taken by the Registrar of Labour Relations before he agrees in terms of section 101(2) of the Act to register a Code of Conduct. This code in particular needs redrafting.

Another example is the case of Olivine Industries (Pvt) Ltd v Patrick Jack and 3 others.[6] The code of conduct did not provide for an appeal to the Labour Court. The employees' appeal was dismissed. The Court held that parties governed under a code of conduct did not have an inherent right to appeal to the court because a code was an agreement of the parties. The Court remarked that:

> It would be difficult to deal with complaints if parties entering into a binding agreement to regulate their industrial relations were to be readily allowed to turn against their agreement when they so wished.

The ZCTU opposed ESAP and the amendment to the Labour Relations Act. It engaged in protest actions that were not tolerated by the government. The government unleashed the police on the demonstrators, and disrupted the demonstration and arrested some of the participants. Those arrested were charged with violating provisions of the Law and Order Maintenance Act of 1960. The Supreme Court rescued the demonstrators by dismissing the charges against them in the case of In re Munhumeso.[7] The Court ruled that the protesters were exercising their right to freedom of expression. The Supreme Court, quoting the European Court of Human Rights, remarked as follows:

> The importance attaching to the exercise of the right to freedom of expression and freedom of assembly must never be underestimated. They lie at the foundation of a democratic society and are one of the basic conditions for its progress and for the development of every man.

Despite the protests, the government still went on to liberalise and

---

5   Case No. SC 34 of 1999.
6   Case No. SC 138/04.
7   1994 (1) ZLR 49 (S).

commercialise some economic sectors. In 1996, it enacted the Export Processing Zones Act Chapter 14:06 of 1996. The Act ousted the application of the Labour Act in Export Processing Zones.[8] Investors in EPZs were given the following incentives:

i. Corporate Tax holiday of 5 years and a low flat rate of 15 per cent thereafter.

ii. Duty-free importation of capital equipment and machinery for EPZ operations, duty-free importation of all raw materials and intermediate goods required in the production process and in construction.

iii. Exemption from withholding tax on dividends.

iv. Exemption from fringe benefits tax on EPZ employees; exemption from withholding taxes on interest-earned fees, remittances and royalties.

v. Exemption from branch profit tax for a branch of a foreign registered company operating in EPZs, sales taxes refund on goods or services purchased from customs territory and exemption from capital gains tax.[9]

The objectives of enacting the Export Processing Zones Act were to facilitate investment, to make it easy for investors not to be burdened with a plethora of rights provided in the Labour Relations Act, and to fast-track the resolution of disputes. A new dispute resolution system was created for employers and employees in EPZs, separating them from those under the Labour Relations Act. Separate regulations governing employment were enacted through Statutory Instrument 372 of 1998. The regulations prohibited discrimination in employment and provided the right of membership in trade unions and the right to bargain collectively in export processing zones. Employees hired for three consecutive months were to be considered permanent employees.

The Export Processing Zones Act was repealed by the Zimbabwe Investment Authority Act Chapter 14:30, Act No. 4 of 2006 together with the Zimbabwe Investment Centre Act Chapter 24:16. The two bodies that managed investments, the Export Processing Zones Authority and the Zimbabwe Investment Centre, were merged to form the Zimbabwe

8   Section 56 (1).

9   ZCTU, 2013, 'Study on the Level of Unionisation in EPZ'.

Investment Authority (ZIA) and all assets of the two bodies were transferred to the latter with all contractual and regulatory powers.[10]

However, the results of investments in EPZ did not amount to much. The government did not manage it well and the expected results of economic growth, foreign investment and creation of jobs were very limited. The Labour Relations Act was amended in 2002 to cover employees and employers in EPZs.

Following the formation of the MDC, there were significant changes in governance as, after 20 years of ZANU(PF) dominance, the 150-seat parliament had 58 opposition party members. The Parliamentary Portfolio Committee on Labour and Public Service contained former trade unionists belonging to the MDC, and the tone of debate on labour law reform changed from antagonism to accommodation. In 2002, for the first time in the history of the Zimbabwe, the Labour Relations Act and the Public Service Act were harmonised, bringing Public Service employees under the scope of the Labour Act No. 17 of 2002.

The aim of harmonisation was to broaden equality of workers' rights in the public and private sectors. Public service employees for the first time enjoyed the right to collective bargaining, the right to strike and other fundamental and basic rights which had not been provided in the Public Service Act, including the right to 98 days of maternity leave for pregnant female employees. In addition, Section 2A (3) of the Act made it clear that it would prevail over any other enactment inconsistent with it.

However, the harmonisation was short-lived. In 2005, ZANU(PF) used its parliamentary majority to amend the Labour Relations Act to remove public service employees from the scope of the Labour Act and reverted to the Public Service Act. This was effected by the adoption of the Labour Relations Amendment Act No. 5 of 2005. The reasons for the amendment were clear: the government wanted to maintain its tight grip on collective bargaining in the public sector and weaken trade union unity and strength.

In 2015, a Court ruling worsened job security in the country. The Supreme Court decision in the case of Don Nyamande and Kingstone Donga v Zuva Petroleum (Pvt) Ltd[11] allowed the termination of employment on notice and without reason as long as notice was given. The Court reasoned that employers had a common law right to terminate a contract of employment and the current Labour Act had no provision

---

10 Section 34 and 35 of the Zimbabwe Investment Authority Act Chapter 14:30.
11 Case No. 43/2015.

that bars an employer from resorting to common law in terminating an employment contract. The judgement received a lot of criticisms for failing to interpret using international labour jurisprudence, in particular the International Labour Organization's convention on Termination of Employment that required termination to be for a valid reason and for operational requirements.[12]

As a result of the miscarriage of justice, over 20,000 workers were dismissed in a period of less than two months.[13] The figures were disputed by the Employers' Confederation of Zimbabwe, which put the figure at about 4,800 without any justification.[14]

The commotion that followed the ruling and sacking of workers led to the ZCTU demanding the amendment of the Labour Act Chapter 28:01 to stop termination on notice. As a result, the Labour Amendment Act No. 15 of 2015 was enacted banning termination on notice and providing for one month's salary for each two years of service or the equivalent lesser proportion of one month's salary or wages for a lesser period of service as compensation to the affected employees.

The government took advantage of the reforms by giving itself the power to remove trade union leaders and employment council administrators, and impose its own administrators if it believed there was mismanagement of the organisation. Government could also interfere in collective bargaining by amending an agreement voluntarily entered by the parties if the agreement was contrary to public policy.

The Amendment Act's provision on compensation[15] in retrospect spilled into the courts in the case of Greatermans Stores and anor v Minister of Public Service, Labour and Social Welfare.[16] The employer challenged Section 18 of the Labour Amendment Act that obliged it to pay compensation in retrospect stating that it was unconstitutional. The Constitutional Court ruled in favour of the dismissed employees by upholding that

> There is no doubt that the welfare of employees upon termination on notice is a matter of public interest deserving of legislative protection.

The Court ruled that compensating employees in retrospect was

---

12 ILO Termination of Employment Convention, 1982 (No.158) Article 4.
13 'Tens of thousands lose jobs in Zimbabwe', allafrica.com, 8 November 2015.
14 'Job dismissal figures fake: EMCOZ', Financial Gazette, 2015.
15 Section 18 as read with section 12C (2).
16 Case No. CCZ2/18.

constitutional and ordered the employer to pay the employees concerned.

In 2016, the government enacted the Special Economic Zones Act Chapter 14.34. As if nothing had been learned from the EPZ experience, it provided as follows, in Section 56 (2):

> The Authority must in consultation with the Minister responsible for the administration of the Labour Act [Chapter 28:01], provide rules for conditions of service, termination of service, dismissal from service and disciplinary proceedings that apply within every special economic zone.

The regulation was not yet in place in 2017. However, of paramount importance is the alienation of trade unions in the crafting of such regulations. The Act only gives power to the SEZ Authority to make regulations in consultation with the minister. The room for collective bargaining in crafting the regulations is at the discretion of the minister. This is another attempt to deny employees the broad labour rights provided in the Labour Act in order to lure investors.

Prior to the enactment of the Act, the Special Economic Zones Bill had repeated the same provision that was in the Export Processing Zones Act, removing the application of the Labour Act in Special Economic Zones. The ZCTU was instrumental in opposing this provision. The ZCTU engaged the then President Mugabe who refused to sign the bill into law and ordered a revision as demanded by the ZCTU.[17] This was a notable achievement for the labour federation.

The right to strike

The right to strike has remained restricted since 1985. Employees who intend to embark on a strike are required to give 14 days' written notice to the employer,[18] the employment council and the trade union registered in the industry. They are also required to conduct a ballot and vote in favour of the strike. The issue in dispute must first have been conciliated and a certificate of no settlement must have been obtained from the Labour Officer or Designated Agent of an Employment Council. In addition, the issue in dispute is restricted to a dispute of interest only. Employees in essential services did not enjoy the right to strike. A failure to comply with the requirements render the strike illegal and there are criminal and civil

---

17 'President rejects Special Economic Zones Bill', The Herald, 27 September 2016.

18 Section 104 of the Labour Act Chapter 28:01.

sanctions for failing to comply with the law.[19] The employer can dismiss the striking workers in terms of its code of conduct or upon proving the illegality in the Labour Court.[20]

However, Section 104 (4) of the Labour Act exempts employees from following procedures if: (i) the intention is to avoid an occupational hazard which is reasonably feared to pose an immediate threat to health or safety of the persons concerned; or, (ii) in defence of an immediate threat to the existence of a workers' committee or a registered trade union. In National Railways of Zimbabwe vs Zimbabwe Amalgamated Railways Workers Union and others,[21] the Labour Court ordered the employer to produce proof that it had provided safety equipment to the employees and remitted union dues to the trade unions for it to determine the illegality of the strike as alleged. The employer failed to provide proof hence the strike was deemed legal.

The Right to strike in terms of the new constitution

The right to strike is now recognised in the new constitution that was adopted on 22 May 2013.[22] The new constitution only excluded the security services and essential services employees from embarking on strike. Section 65 (2) provides for the following fundamental rights:

- Except for members of the security services, every person has the right to form and join trade unions and employee or employers' organizations of their choice, and to participate in the lawful activities of those unions and organizations.

- Except for members of the security services, every employee has the right to participate in collective job action, including the right to strike, sit in, and withdraw their labour and to take other similar concerted action, but a law may restrict the exercise of this right in order to maintain essential services.

- Every employee is entitled to just, equitable and satisfactory conditions of work.

- Except for members of the security services, every employee, employer, trade union, and employee or employer's organisation has

---

19 Labour Act section s109.
20 TelOne (Pvt) Ltd v Communications and Allied Services Workers Union of Zimbabwe Sc 26/06.
21 Case No.LC/JDT/MT/99/12.
22 Constitution of Zimbabwe Amendment (No. 20) Act, 2013.

the right to engage in collective bargaining, to organise and to form and to join federations of such unions and organisations.

The new constitution marks a departure from the old, which did not directly provide for the right to collective bargaining and to strike. However, the enjoyment of the right remains theoretical, as the Labour Act and the Public Service Act have not yet been harmonised under the constitution. In National Railways of Zimbabwe v Jeremiah Muzangwa and 1357 others,[23] the Labour Court ruled that the strike by the employees was unlawful as it did not comply with the procedures set out in the Labour Act, despite the non-limitation of the right to strike in the constitution. This was a deliberate refusal by the Court to enforce a constitutional right.

In a related constitutional matter of Farai Katsande v Infrastructure Development Bank of Zimbabwe,[24] the Constitutional Court did not make a ruling on the constitutionality of Section 45 (1) (b) (i) of the Labour Act. The said provision was alleged to have violated Section 65 (2) of the constitution in that it prohibited a managerial employee from enjoying the right to freedom of association.

The Constitutional Court, after sitting on the case for four years, made a ruling that the matter was not properly before it as it was capable of being heard by the Labour Court. Justice Gwaunza JC remarked as follows:

> I find in the circumstances of this case, and based on the authorities cited above, that the doctrine of avoidance can properly be invoked against the applicants. A remedy was clearly available to them in the Labour Court, had they chosen to pursue the matters pending in that court, to their logical conclusion. In other words, they could have secured a determination of the issue in question in the lower court, without having to 'reach' the Constitutional Court in the manner they did.

This was another glaring attempt by the Court to protect the employer. The Court could not delay justice for four years only to make a technical judgement. The Court had the power to hear the matter on its own and make a decision. This was an important matter that deserved an exemption to the rule because it dealt with a fundamental right that was violated by the employer. Section 85 of the constitution makes it clear that any person whose fundamental right has been violated has the right to approach the

23 Case No. LC/MT/66/16.
24 Case No. CCZ9/17.

Court on the basis that a fundamental right or freedom enshrined in the constitution has been infringed and the Court will therefore have to grant an appropriate relief.

The High Court was also not helpful in the matter of Zimbabwe Banks and Allied Workers Union v Officer Commanding Police, Harare and others and Econet Wireless Pvt Ltd.[25] In this matter the union sought an order to allow its members to demonstrate at Econet Wireless as its subsidiary Steward Bank Limited was refusing to pay compensation to employees it dismissed following the Supreme Court ruling that allowed termination on notice. The demonstration was banned by police. Justice Foroma ruled that the union had not properly consulted its members before approaching the court. The judge reasoned that:

> Having found that the applicant has not established that it had authority of its members to institute this application the resolution on p17 of the application cannot therefore be considered as *intra vires*. I accordingly find that the applicant has no *locus standi* to institute or prosecute this application or demonstrate at Econet Wireless Zimbabwe Limited Registered Offices on behalf of its Steward Bank Ltd membership.

The Court's reasoning was to stifle the employees' right to demonstrate as provided in Section 59 of the Constitution of Zimbabwe. The Court refused to recognise a resolution passed by the union executive to embark on such action and wanted ZIBAWU to obtain direct authority from the employees neglecting the fact that some of the employees were still in employment and may have been victimised for challenging the employer. The union had the authority to act on behalf of its members and there was no need to consult individual members. This was another onslaught on labour rights aimed at weakening the representative status of trade unions.

Industrial relations in the Public Service

The Public Service Act Chapter 16:04

Public sector employees are governed by the Public Service Act No. 21 of 1995, now referred to as the Public Service Act Chapter 28:04. The Public Service Act refers to employees as 'members'. The Act covers those who render direct services to government except the security services,

---

25 Case No. HC 387/16.

the judiciary, parliament and intelligence services and established commissions. It established the Public Service Commission, now referred to as the Civil Service Commission,[26] as the employer on behalf of government. The Commission acts in consultation with the Minister of Public Service, Labour and Social Welfare. The Act provides for the recognition of employees' freedom of association,[27] but the Minister has the power to revoke such recognition.[28] The Commission is compelled to engage in regular consultations with recognised associations and organisations in regard to the conditions of service of public servants. However, notwithstanding this obligation, the conditions of service so fixed or determined by the Commission shall not be invalid solely on the ground that they were not subject to prior consultations or were not agreed to by all the parties to a prior consultation.[29]

The conditions of service of public servants, including their remuneration, benefits, leave of absence, hours of work and discipline, are determined by the Public Service Commission in consultation with the Minister as well as the Minister responsible for Finance. Such conditions may be fixed by means of service regulations, notices, and circulars or in such other manner as the Commission considers appropriate.[30]

Contrary to the established principle of freedom of association, the Public Service Act does not recognise the right to strike. However, employees who embark on a strike can be disciplined in terms of the service regulations which provides that engaging in a collective job action is misconduct.[31] Furthermore, there is no collective bargaining in the civil service except consultations through the Joint Negotiating Council.

Although the constitution recognises collective bargaining,[32] there are restrictions with regards to the civil service. In terms of Section 203 of the constitution, the Commission has the power:

> to fix and regulate conditions of service, including salaries, allowances and other benefits, of members of the Civil Service and to exercise control and disciplinary powers over members of the

---

26 Constitution of Zimbabwe s202.
27 Section 24.
28 Section 24 (2).
29 Section 20.
30 Section 19 (1) and (2).
31 1st Schedule Public service regulations SI1/2000.
32 Section 65 (5).

Civil Service. In fixing the salaries, allowances and other benefits of members of the Civil Service, the Civil Service Commission must act with the approval of the President given on the recommendation of the Minister responsible for finance and after consultation with the Minister responsible for the Civil Service. These provisions demonstrate the restrictions imposed by law on collective bargaining in the civil service.

The International Labour Organization has critised such provisions but the government has refused to amend its laws to comply with ILO standards, in particular Convention 154. The ILO remarked that 'measures which unilaterally fix conditions of employment should be of an exceptional nature, be limited in time and include safeguards for the workers who are the most affected.'[33]

The Health Services Act Chapter 15:16

The Health Services Act covers employees in the health sector only. It established the Health Service Board as the employer. The Board acts in consultation with the Minister responsible for Health and Child Care. The Act recognises the right of employees to form associations or organisations which can engage in consultations with the Board if so recognised by the Minister. The Board in consultation with the Minister has the power to fix conditions of service for the health service employees (s13). The right to strike is not recognised in terms of this Act or service regulations since the health sector is classified as an essential service.

Critically, there is no material difference between the Health Services Act and the Public Service Act, except that the former only deals with health workers. There is no right to collective bargaining, except for consultations in the Health Service Bipartite Negotiating Panel. The failure to provide for collective bargaining is a violation of Section 65 (5) of the constitution.[34]

The Judicial Service Act Chapter 7:18

This Act applies to members in the administration of justice. It established the Judicial Service Commission which is responsible for fixing conditions of service for its members.[35] The Commission derives its power from the constitution, which provides that:

33 ILO, 2010. 'Harmonisation of the Public Service and Labour laws', Issues Paper, International Labour Standards Department (unpublished).
34 Section 203 (4) of the Constitution.
35 Section 5 (1) (a).

An Act of Parliament may confer on the Judicial Service Commission functions in connection with the employment, discipline and conditions of service of persons employed in the Constitutional Court, the Supreme Court, the High Court, the Labour Court, the Administrative Court and other courts.[36]

The Act recognises members' rights to freedom of association (S13) and to consultations regarding conditions of service (S11). The Act does not recognise the right to strike; however, members can use their constitutional right in order to do so.

The Defence Act, the Prison Service Act and the Police Act

Members of the defence forces, prison service and police service do not have the right to form trade unions or staff associations. Their conditions of service are determined by the Defence Force Service Commission, Prison and Correctional Service Commission and Police Service Commission in consultation with the Minister responsible for Defence, Justice and Home Affairs respectively. The constitution prohibits these groups from enjoying the right to freedom of association and to strike.[37]

Strikes in the public service in practice

Despite the denial of the right to strike in the public service, employees in particular in the education and health sector have been embarking on strikes to enforce their demands. In Zimbabwe Teachers Association and others v Minister of Education and Culture,[38] the government was ordered to reinstate striking teachers who defied its order to return to work, after the government breached their right to be heard before a decision was taken (the *audi alteram partem* rule*)*. The teachers went on strike after the government unilaterally withdrew their annual bonus. Although the employees lost the case in the Supreme Court the government reinstated the benefit. The Supreme Court had ruled that a bonus was a privilege and not a right. This was another attack on labour rights by the Supreme Court as the Court failed to recognise that a bonus had become a custom in the public service and therefore constituted a right that could not be withdrawn without agreement of the parties.

In a related matter, Jiah and Others v Public Service Commission and

---

36 Section 190 (4)
37 Section 65 (2).
38 1990 (2) ZLR 48 (HC).

another,[39] the government was ordered to reinstate the striking doctors' leaders it had dismissed for embarking on an illegal strike. The Supreme Court ruled that the Commission had breached the parity principle by disciplining only the strike leaders and not all of those who participated in the strike action. In this case the Court was alive to the protection of labour rights.

Industrial relations in the informal sector

Zimbabwe's informal economy accounts for 94.5 per cent of the country's total employment in 2014 compared to 84 per cent in 2011.[40] The informal economy is dominated by female and unskilled workers. Despite being the largest employing sector it remains unregulated in terms of industrial relations with the workers being subjected to precarious forms of employment. The informal economy workers face challenges of police harassment and confiscation of their wares. The government remains ambivalent in its support to the sector, with some supporting (e.g. the Ministry of Small and Medium Enterprises and Cooperative Development) whilst others are against (e.g. security agencies and the Ministry of Local Government). Furthermore, the workers are not unionised. However, there are associations representing the sector such as the Zimbabwe Chamber of Informal Economy Associations, the National Vendors Union Zimbabwe and Zimbabwe Informal Sector's Organization.

Judiciary intervention in termination of employment and compensation

In law, the procedures for retrenchment are separate from those for other disputes. Since the 1990s, retrenchment was governed by the Labour Relations (Retrenchment) Regulations, 1990 published in Statutory Instrument 404 of 1990. The regulations required consultations with the employees. The Statutory Instrument empowered the Retrenchment Committee to redress disputes arising from retrenchments and the minister responsible could approve or disapprove the retrenchment acting on the recommendation of the Retrenchment Committee. As from 2002 the Labour Act provided for the retrenchment process for five or more employees while those cases with less than five were covered by the Labour Relations (Retrenchment) Regulations of 2003.[41] The end result was either an agreement by the parties or, if in dispute, redress by the

39 1999 (1) ZLR 17 (SC).
40 ZimStat. 2014.
41 Statutory Instrument 186 of 2003.

Retrenchment Committee with the Minister having final authority.

As disputes escalated in the process of retrenchments, the courts were active in attempts to redress them. In some instances, the court's decisions were controversial. In Continental Fashions (Pvt) Ltd v Mupfuriri and others, Justice McNally remarked that in deciding the retrenchment package to be paid to the retrenched employees, the 'ability of the company to pay the retrenchment package is the ultimate criterion – the bottom line', and that the duty to negotiate in good faith provided in Section 76 of the Labour Act did not apply in retrenchment cases.[42] This reasoning took the approach that all retrenchments were a result of economic and financial difficulties whereas there were cases related to the need to downsize the labour force to maximise profits. Furthermore, if the duty of good faith was taken away then employers would not take the negotiations seriously, leaving workers without protection against unfair labour practices. The Court's decision created fertile ground for employers to deny a reasonable package, citing an inability to pay.

In Chidziva v ZISCO[43] an argument arose as to whether a package negotiated by a workers' committee and agreed to in the works council bound every person to be retrenched and that an employee who took a package waived his right to appeal if not satisfied. The majority of the Supreme Court judges ruled that once an employee accepted the package, he or she waived the right to appeal. However, Justice Muchechetere JA, in the same matter, disagreed and remarked that 'I am of the view that the appellants did not, by accepting the retrenchment packages, waive their rights. In the first instance an allegation of waiver should be specially pleaded.'

In Nyangoni and Others v Zimbabwe Development Corporation and others,[44] the High Court remarked that:

> The decision of the works council does not bind the employer or the employees concerned even if they were represented on the works council, unless they had given their prior consent to be bound by the council's decision.

In the absence of such prior consent, the works council had to endeavour to obtain the parties' agreement.

---

42 1997 (2) ZLR 405.

43 1997 (2) ZLR 368 (S).

44 Case No. HH34-98.

In Fungura and Anor v Zimnat Insurance Co Ltd,[45] Justice Gillespie made a different interpretation. After protracted negotiations for a retrenchment package, the applicants objected to the package agreed by the majority of the employees. They argued that they deserved a better package and alleged that an agreement reached by the retrenchment committee was not binding to them because they did not ratify it. The court held that:

> An agreement reached in works council by workers representatives about a retrenchment package is binding on the workers, provided that the formal requirements of the regulations are complied with and provided that the representatives have the authority of the workers for whom they act to give consent. Individuals amongst the body of workers who dissent from the package properly agreed by authorised representatives will nevertheless be bound by the will of the majority so represented.[46]

In circumstances where retrenchment regulations were violated, the judiciary would order compliance despite the employer having paid the package without agreement with the employee. In Stanbic Bank Zimbabwe Limited v Arthur T. M. Charamba,[47] in which the bank was restructuring and abolished the employee's post and offered a retrenchment package that was approved by the retrenchment committee and the Minister, the employee declined the package alleging non-compliance with retrenchment regulations. The Court held that the retrenchment committee which approved the retrenchment and the package did not comply with the timeframes set in the regulations and did not play a role in securing an agreement between the parties. It failed to keep minutes of its other proceedings and no measures were considered to avoid the retrenchment. The Court nullified the retrenchment and ordered reinstatement of the employee.

Since 2002, if retrenchment processes started at the works council level or company level and if no agreement was reached, the dispute would be heard by the employment council in that industry. A failure to agree would result in the dispute being heard by the Retrenchment Board with the Minister making the final decision.

---

45 2000 (1) ZLR 379(H).
46 2000(1) ZLR 379 (H).
47 Case No. SC 77/05.

In 2015, advocates of labour market flexibility, championed by the Ministry of Finance and Economic Development, influenced changes to the retrenchment law. They argued that the Labour Act procedures were too long, making it difficult for companies to downsize. The retrenchment provisions were against the 'ease of doing business' mantra adopted by government. As a result, the Labour Amendment Act No. 5 of 2015 was introduced. It stipulated a minimum package of one month's salary or wages per each two years of service or a share thereof.[48] Negotiations were no longer mandatory and the works councils, employment councils and the Retrenchment Board were rendered redundant. These bodies' functions were limited to only considering applications for exemptions from paying the stipulated package. The bodies were also required to respond to an application within 14 days and a failure to do so made the application successful.[49] This was the death penalty to workers' rights to negotiate a better retrenchment package.

The 2015 Labour Amendment Act left workers at the mercy of the employer. It gave an employer power to indirectly victimise workers' representatives or trade union activists under the guise of retrenchment. It changed the dispute resolution system by removing arbitrators except for voluntary arbitration. The Labour Officer and a Designated Agent of an Employment Council are now only required to make a draft order that is subject to confirmation by the Labour Court.[50] The Act gives power to the Labour Officer or Designated Agent to appear in the Labour Court. An employee who has lost a matter before the Labour Officer or Designated Agent has no right of appeal in the Labour Court. In the case of Patrick Muchovo vs. N Matenda and 22 others and SteelMakers Zimbabwe Pvt Ltd,[51] the Labour Court held that once an employee losses a matter before a Designated Agent there was no need to register the Agent's draft order. The legislature was only concerned about an employee who was successful and not otherwise. The Labour Amendment Act of 2015, though it attempted to stop massive dismissal of employees on notice, went on to destroy workers' fundamental rights by taking away collective bargaining in retrenchment matters and denied the employees the right of representation in the Labour Court.

---

48 Section 12C.
49 Section 12C.
50 Section 93 (5a).
51 Judgement No. LC/MD/26/2017.

Casualisation of labour

One of the negative consequences of the structural adjustment programmes was the casualisation of labour. As protective legislation was amended, casualisation increased. According to the Zimbabwe Statistics Agency's 2014 Labour Force Survey, of the 6.3 million people currently employed, 13 per cent were in precarious employment.

The Labour Amendment Act of 2002 did not ban casualisation but set out the period after which the employee could be deemed permanent. The Act defined casual work as 'work for which an employee is engaged by an employer for not more than a total of six weeks in any four consecutive months'.[52] This meant an employee who exceeded six weeks in four consecutive months would be deemed to be under a contract of unlimited duration. In practice, some employers placed their employees on perpetual fixed term contracts for long periods. In the event of termination other than by mutual agreement, the employer was not obliged to follow the termination process but simply had to give the required notice period of 24 hours in terms of Section 12 (4) (e) of the Labour Act.

Judicial interpretation in labour disputes

The Labour Court tried to stop the practice of continuous renewal of fixed term contracts, arguing that it was a clear attempt by the employer to circumvent the law. In Rachel Kadzinga and 20 others v Eastern Textiles (Pvt) Ltd t/a Devstar Clothing,[53] the Labour Court declared illegal the dismissal of employees whom the employer claimed were on fixed term contracts. The employees were engaged for periods that ranged from three years to 16 years. At the end of each month, or after every three months, the employees were ordered to sign new fixed term contracts. It was the employer's argument that each contract was independent of the other and terminated on the agreed date. The Labour Court's ruling was welcome to the workers, but the relief was short-lived.

In a similar case that was brought before the Supreme Court, Magodora v Care International Zimbabwe,[54] the employees signed contracts with the following wording:

> This contract shall in no way whatsoever lead to a legitimate expectation of further employment beyond the contract's date of termination.

---

52 Section 2.
53 Case No. LC/MC /02 2007.
54 Case No.SC 24/2014.

The employees approached the Court to confirm that they were on contract without limit of time. Justice Patel held that:

> Parties are bound by the express terms that they had agreed to and could not then complain. It is not open to the courts to rewrite a contract entered into between the parties or to excuse any of them from the consequences of the contract that they have freely and voluntarily accepted, even if they are shown to be onerous or oppressive.

It was clear that the Court was aware of the oppressive nature of the contracts but chose not to interfere. The employer was allowed by the Court to continue to take advantage of the weakness of the workers because of high levels of unemployment.

Another classical interpretation from the Supreme Court in disciplinary matters not properly handled by the employer was the case of Air Zimbabwe (Pvt) Ltd v Chiku Mnesa and another,[55] in which Chief Justice Chidyausiku stated the following:

> A person guilty of misconduct should not escape the consequences of his misdeeds simply because of a failure to conduct disciplinary proceedings properly by another employee. He should escape such consequences because he is innocent.

This judgement, though factual, flew in the face of the developed principle that 'justice delayed is justice denied'.

By contrast, in State v Zimbabwe Congress of Trade Unions,[56] former Justice Chidyausiku granted a permanent stay of prosecution of the ZCTU for violating the Exchange Control Act. There was a delay of four years in prosecuting the ZCTU. The Court did not apply the same principle of innocence to escape the consequences.

The Supreme Court also reviewed judgements made by lower courts. In Mashonaland Turf Club v Mutangadura,[57] the Court castigated and overturned a penalty of final warning granted by an arbitrator and confirmed by the Labour Court. Justice Ziyambi warned that:

> In the exercise of their powers in terms of s 12B (4) of the Labour Act, the Labour Court and arbitrators must be reminded that the section does not confer upon them an unbounded power to alter

55 Case No.SC 89/04.
56 Case No. SC 137/12.
57 Case No. SC 5 of 2012.

a penalty of dismissal imposed by an employer just because they disagree with it. In the absence of a misdirection or unreasonableness on the part of the employer in arriving at the decision to dismiss an employee, an appeal court will generally not interfere with the exercise of the employer's discretion to dismiss an employee found guilty of a misconduct which goes to the root of the contract of employment.

The Court's reasoning was an empowerment to the employer and undermined the power of an arbitrator provided by law. Section 12B (4) of the Labour Act grants an adjudicating authority power to substitute an employer's decision depending on the circumstances of the matter, the mitigating factors, special circumstances of the employee and the length of the employee's service.

Another concern in which the court failed to uphold the rights of employees was in the area of awarding compensation to employees who were unfairly dismissed and where the employer refused to reinstate the employee opting to use its economic power to buy the employee out of employment. In Charles Ambali v Bata Shoe Company Ltd,[58] the Court set the precedent that a dismissed employee was entitled to wages and salaries he would have earned had his contract not been prematurely terminated. He could also be compensated for any loss of benefits he was entitled to but he had to mitigate his loss immediately. He had to look for alternative employment; he was not entitled to sit around and do nothing. The employee would be compensated for the period between his dismissal and the date when he could reasonably have been expected to find alternative employment. The Court placed a burden on the victim rather than on the aggressor that deliberately refused to reinstate the employee.

However, there were other progressive decisions in this respect. In Geoffrey Nyaguse v Mkwasine Estates Pvt Ltd,[59] the employee was awarded two years' net salary as future damages. The Court ordered the payment of past damages from the date of dismissal to the date of the Court order for reinstatement, bonuses, leave pay, medical aid contributions and allowances. The burden of proof was on the employer to show that the employee earned income from other sources. The employee was also awarded interest from the date on which each salary cheque and each bonus was due up to the date on which final payment was made and the

---

58 1999 (1) ZLR 417 (S).
59 Case No. SC 34/2000.

costs of appeal. This progressive reasoning was also applied in Kuda Madyara v Globe and Phoenix Industries,[60] in which the former employee was awarded three years' net salary in addition to back pay and other benefits to which he was contractually entitled.

In a surprise turn, the Supreme Court changed the principle set out in the two progressive cases and put another burden on the dismissed employee. In Olivine Industries (Pvt) Ltd v Caution Nharara,[61] the Court ordered the consideration of earnings made by the employee in selling tomatoes and repairing cell phones. The Court ordered that such earnings be deducted from the employee's damages because he was employed while waiting for the matter to be finalised. This trend of denying employees damages was also applied in First Mutual Life Ltd v Muzivi,[62] in which the Supreme Court refused to award a bonus to the dismissed employee and reasoned as follows:

> Payment of an annual bonus is generally discretionary on the part
> of the employer. It could not be said that the employee would have
> been awarded a bonus under all circumstances. A bonus would have
> depended on a clear record of performance. Having been suspended,
> it could not be said that the employee performed so well that he
> would have been entitled to a bonus.

This kind of reasoning put fault to the employee despite the fact that the same Court found the employee innocent of the charges laid against him. The employer should have been ordered to pay a bonus to the innocent employee.

As the Supreme Court continued its onslaught on labour rights, it went further to hold that back pay from the date of dismissal to the date of decision and damages must not be separated. In Madhatter Mining Company v Marvellous Tapfuma,[63] it was held that:

> What is eminently clear from this analysis is that damages in lieu
> of reinstatement become due and are to be reckoned from the date
> of an employee's wrongful dismissal. Further, that in relation to the
> period from and during which the damages were to be assessed,
> no distinction was made between the salary arrears and benefits
> on the one hand, and damages proper on the other. All had to be

60 Case No. SC 63/02.
61 Case No. SC 65/04.
62 Case No. SC 9/07.
63 Case No. SC 51/14.

assessed within the same period albeit varying time periods and considerations peculiar to the assessment in question may apply.

In simple terms, the Court required back pay, damages and benefits to be bundled as one. As a result of these retrogressive Court decisions, an employer who lost a case no longer wanted to reinstate the dismissed employee, preferring to pay the little damages. The employers were aware that the Courts were on their side in the assessment of damages. It was the workers who were the losers, as the burden to mitigate losses was placed on them.

The responses of labour and other social partners to the judicial and legislative frameworks

The ZCTU continued to oppose all unjust state policies in defence of the workers and society in general, despite the onslaught from both the government and the judiciary. As the government embraced ESAP, and pursued a market driven economy, the ZCTU embarked on mass mobilisation to oppose the ill-conceived policies. In 1992, scores of workers heeded the call for a public demonstration against the Labour Relations Amendment Bill, which was designed to take away workers' rights by weakening centralised bargaining in preference to workplace bargaining, and to accede to the demands of investors who had argued that the labour laws were too rigid. The demonstration was banned by the police under the inherited colonial legislation, the Law and Order Maintenance Act, of 1960. Despite the ban, the ZCTU went ahead with the demonstration, resulting in a clash between the police and the demonstrators. Many workers were arrested. The Supreme Court rescued the workers in the famous case of in re Munhumeso.[64] The Supreme Court ruled that the ban on the protest action violated the demonstrators' constitutional right to freedom of expression.

As demonstrations were no longer tolerated by the state, the ZCTU engaged in job stayaway on 9 December 1997 that closed all businesses in the country; 3.5 million people were reported to have heeded the call to stay away from work. the *Financial Gazette* of 11 December 1997 carried the headline, 'Shocking signs of the changing times, ZCTU bills strike the most successful ever, Collapse of ZANU PF's Authoritarian rule'.

The demonstration followed the government's attempt to compensate the veterans of the armed struggle. They were paid Z$50,000.00 each

64 1994 (1) ZLR 143 (S).

and a pension of Z$2,000.00 per month. The money was unbudgeted for. The government then introduced a 5 per cent levy, as well as increases in sales tax and petrol duty. This led to the crash of the Zimbabwean dollar on 14 November 1997, which became known as 'Black Friday'. The ZCTU successfully mobilised to oppose the levies and the government backtracked. Subsequently the then Secretary General of the ZCTU, Morgan Tsvangirai, was attacked at his offices in Harare by unknown people. Police investigation of the assault did not yield anything.

A further incidence of state brutality occurred in 2006, when the ZCTU organised a protest action demanding the availability of antiretroviral drugs, the protection of the informal economy workers, and salary increases in line with the poverty datum line. The demonstration was disrupted by heavily armed police officers. ZCTU protesters were arrested and tortured by police. The torture had the approval of President Mugabe; addressing journalist in Cairo, he had this to say:

> Police were right in dealing sternly ... because the trade unionists want to become a law unto themselves. We cannot have a situation where people decide to sit in places not allowed, and when the police remove them, they say no. We can't have that, that is a revolt to the system. When the police say move, move. If you don't move, you invite the police to use force.[65]

Establishment of the Tripartite Negotiating Forum

The ZCTU's 'Beyond ESAP' research of 1996 led to a tripartite visit to South Africa to study the country's social dialogue system, the National Economic Development and Labour Council. The tripartite partners then recommended a Zimbabwe Economic Development and Labour Council, and in response the government established the National Economic Consultative Forum (NECF) in July 1997 without the agreement of other social partners.

The labour unions opposed the setting up of the NECF, as it was not tripartite. This led to the formation of the Tripartite Negotiating Forum (TNF) in 1998.

In January 2001, the 'Declaration of Intent towards a Social Contract' was signed, under which the parties agreed to negotiate and conclude the following protocols: Incomes and Pricing; Economic Recovery and

---

65 'President blasts ZCTU Leaders', *The Herald*, 25 September 2006.

Development Policy; Productivity Enhancement; Urban Transport; National Health Insurance Scheme; and Labour Law Reform. Surprisingly, the government responded by unilaterally increasing the cost of fuel by 70 per cent, forcing the ZCTU to pull out of further negotiations for a social contract.

In the same year, the cost of living was increasing for vulnerable agricultural workers, and the parties in the TNF negotiated for minimum wages for agriculture, agroindustry and industry and commerce. The government response was to unilaterally enact Statutory Instruments 307A on minimum wages control and 307B on price controls. The unilateralism of government was not welcomed by the other social partners. In 2001, the Kadoma Declaration was not concluded because of political violence.

In 2007, the following protocols were adopted: Incomes and Pricing Stabilisation; Mobilisation, Pricing and Management of Foreign Currency; and Restoration of Productivity Viability. These protocols were not implemented.

In 2009, the 'Kadoma Declaration: Towards a Shared National Economic and Social Vision' was signed; it was launched by President Mugabe on 26 February 2010. The declaration identified the country's risk factors as including policy inconsistency, non-respect for human rights, corruption and lack of political tolerance.[66] The declaration to address the country's risk factors was not implemented.

From 2010 until 2017, the social partners engaged in a programme to reform the labour laws and legislation of the TNF. This work remained incomplete due to government's lack of political will to reform the labour laws despite agreements in the TNF.

On 24 May 2017 the ZCTU demanded a review of the Kadoma Declaration of 2009 and its implementation. The ZCTU noted that the lack of implementation was a political problem, as identified by the National Peoples Working Convention in 1996, and informed the government that a political settlement was required first before adopting any other social contract.

---

66 Kadoma Declaration Towards a Shared National Economic and Social Vision , Zimbabwe, 4 Sept 2009.

Legislation to impinge freedom of association and expression

In 2002, as the government felt challenged by labour and civil society mass mobilisation strategies, it introduced legislation to control the activities of civil organisations. The Public Order and Security Act Chapter 11:17 was enacted. The Act required anyone organising a public gathering to notify the regulating authority (police) responsible for the area. The regulating authority was empowered to sanction the event or disallow it.[67]

Although the law provided for an exemption to trade union activity, in practice the police demanded the notification and in some instances disrupted the ZCTU activities. In the case of ZCTU v Officer Commanding Police, Harare District and Commissioner of Police,[68] police disrupted a ZCTU General Council meeting in Harare citing that the labour body had not sought permission to hold such a meeting as provided in the Act. The High Court ruled that the police had no right to interfere in the labour body's activities as it was exempted.

Subsequently, the Criminal Law Codification and Reform Act Chapter 9:23 was enacted, to criminalise anyone who criticised the president, the police force, the defence force or the prison force. The Act provides as follows in section 33: 'Any person who publicly, unlawfully and intentionally –

> (*a*) Makes any statement about or concerning the President or an acting President with the knowledge or realising that there is a real risk or possibility that the statement is false and that it may:
>
> > (i) engender feelings of hostility towards; or
> > (ii) cause hatred, contempt or ridicule of;
> > > the President or an acting President,
> > > whether in person or in respect of the President's office;
> >
> > or
>
> (*b*) makes any abusive, indecent or obscene statement about or concerning the President or an acting President, whether in respect of the President personally or the President's office; shall be guilty of undermining the authority of or insulting the President and liable to a fine not exceeding level six or imprisonment for a period not

---

67 Public Order and Security Act section 24-25: 'Organiser to notify regulating authority of intention to hold public gathering and regulating of public gatherings'.
68 Case No. H.H 56/2002.

exceeding one year or both.'

In addition to the above, the Access to Information and Protection of Privacy Act Chapter 10:27 was enacted to stifle media freedom. Scores of journalists were arrested for publishing information regarded as false by government.[69] These laws resulted in many trade unionists being arrested and detained.

International campaign and the effective use of the International Labour Organization (ILO)

Faced with inadequate domestic remedies to the onslaught on labour rights, the ZCTU filed complaints to the ILO against the Government of Zimbabwe for not respecting the Convention on Freedom of Association and Protection of the Right to Organise, and the Right to Organise and Collective Bargaining.[70] The ILO's Committee on Freedom of Association heard 12 cases from the ZCTU from 1996 to 2016, all of which were successful.[71]

Furthermore, the Government of Zimbabwe appeared 13 times at the ILO Conference Committee on the Application of Standards for violating labour rights and civil liberties, and was found guilty in all the cases.[72]

In 2008, the ILO set up a Commission of Inquiry having observed the relentlessness of the Government of Zimbabwean in stifling freedom of association and expression through harassment, torture, arrests, intimidation and detention of trade unionists.[73] The Commission of Inquiry is the ILO's highest supervisory body. The workers group, led by the International Trade Union Confederation, filed the following complaint to the ILO:

> We, Workers' delegates to the 97th Session of the International Labour Conference (Geneva, June 2008), whose names are included hereunder, support the conclusions on Zimbabwe adopted in the Committee on Application of Standards, calling for a complaint under article 26 of the ILO Constitution against the Government of the Republic of Zimbabwe for violations of the Freedom of Association and Protection of the Right to

---

69 'Media Landscape Still a Minefield for Journalists', *Zimbabwe Independent*, 20 June 2003.

70 ILO Conventions 87 and 98 respectively.

71 Mtimtema et al., 2016.

72 Ibid.

73 ILO, 97th Session, June 2008.

Organise Convention, 1948 (No. 87), and the Right to Organise and Collective Bargaining Convention, 1949 (No. 98), ratified by Zimbabwe on 9 April 2003 and 27 August 1998, respectively.[74]

Subsequently, the employer delegates also supported the complaint:

Taking into account the discussion that took place at the Committee on Application of Standards and the conclusions adopted that followed, the undersigned Employers delegates to the 97th Session of the International Labour Conference (Geneva, June 2008), would like to file a complaint under article 26 of the ILO Constitution against the Government of Zimbabwe for non-observance of the Freedom of Association and Protection of the Right to Organise Convention, 1948 (No. 87), ratified by Zimbabwe on 9 April 2003, and which came into force for Zimbabwe on 9 April 2004.[75]

The Commission came to Zimbabwe in 2009; after carrying out investigations, it came to the following conclusions:

The Commission sees a clear pattern of arrests, detentions, violence and torture by the security forces against trade unionists that coincided with ZCTU nationwide events, indicating that there had been some centralised direction to the security forces to take such action. The Commission is of the opinion that there was another clear pattern of control over ZCTU trade union gatherings, be they internal meetings or public demonstrations through the application of the POSA. The Commission believes that the intimidatory nature of the detentions of trade unionists is evident in the fact that they were often for short amounts of time, were accompanied by violence and threats and did not lead to convictions in court.[76]

The Commission recommended the harmonisation of labour laws. A draft labour bill was agreed on at the TNF but there were persistent delays by government in bringing it to the legislative house.

Training of judges by the ILO

The judiciary played an important role in ensuring that legislation was respected and people's constitutional rights guaranteed. As illustrated

---

74 Ibid.
75 Ibid.
76 ILO Report of the Commission of Inquiry in Zimbabwe, 2009.

above, the judiciary was in some respects capable of upholding the rights of workers and in others made controversial decisions some of which resulted in massive loss of jobs. One of the issues identified by the ILO Commission of Inquiry was the security of the independence of the judiciary. In an attempt to address the problem of unfavourable judgements by the judiciary, the ZCTU influenced the training of the judges and law enforcement agencies on freedom of association and civil liberties.

In 2011 the ILO trained 45 magistrates, judges, and law enforcement agencies on freedom of association and collective bargaining and on how to apply international labour law into domestic law. The impact of the training was observed when some judges started to use ILO standards in resolving disputes. The case of Maranatha Ferrochrome v Stephen Kwava and another[77] was testimony to the impact of the training. In deciding whether a worker's representative had the right to speak to the press without permission from the employer, Justice Kachambwa made reference in the Labour Court to the ILO principles of freedom of association:

> The right to express opinions without previous authorisation through the press is one of the essential elements of the rights of occupational organisations.

It followed therefore that the workers' committee member should not be required to clear his communication with any manager/employer. The judgement protected a fundamental right of freedom of expression.

Conclusion

Zimbabwe's labour legislation remains fragmented, and there is no political will to harmonise the labour laws with the constitution and international labour standards. The ZCTU and progressive civil society organisations joined forces to build a mass movement that tackled political, social and economic issues beyond the workplace. The formation of the MDC in 1999 changed the political landscape by providing Zimbabweans with an alternative choice. As a result, labour law reforms of 2002 were spearheaded with great assistance from MDC MPs.

The ZCTU's strategy of campaigning for a new constitution was rewarded in 2013. For the first time in the history of Zimbabwe, the new constitution had a strong bill of rights and its Section 65 is dedicated to labour rights. It recognised the fundamental right to strike, collective

---

77 Case No. LC/H/155/2012.

bargaining and freedom of association and assembly.

The ZCTU's mass mobilisation and protest action from 2000 kept the government on its toes. Although the government responded with brutality to workers' protest actions, that did not deter the workers' quest for justice, good governance and good working conditions.

At an international level, the ZCTU and its international partners, including the International Confederation of Free Trade Unions successfully put Zimbabwe in the spotlight at each International Labour Conference. Zimbabwe became a perennial candidate on the list of errant governments. Other trade unions supported the ZCTU both financially and morally. The struggle for workers' emancipation had its success and failures, but many of the failures could be attributed to the repressive regime that does not recognise labour rights and human rights. A climate of fear, intimidation, harassment, torture and detention was deliberately created by the regime to cow the trade unions. However, although weakened, the trade unions remained resilient under the circumstances.

The judiciary's intervention in cases such Greatermans Stores and anor v Minister of Public Service, Labour and Social Welfare that ordered an employer to pay compensation in retrospect was welcome. On the other hand, the judiciary fell short in its protection of workers' rights against unfair dismissal. The case of Don Nyamande and Kingstone Donga v Zuva Petroleum was such an example, in which the judiciary carried out a miscarriage of justice by allowing an employer to exercise its common law right to terminate a contract without valid reason resulting in mass termination of employment contracts. The judiciary's intervention in critical matters was mainly pro-capital in order to facilitate the government's neoliberal policies.

The government's quest for economic development has been dismantling labour rights despite international calls for labour reforms to protect vulnerable workers.[78] Labour law reforms should be undertaken to comply with both constitutional and international labour standards.

---

78 ILO Commission of Inquiry Report, 2009.

Chapter 10

Conclusion

Brian Raftopoulos, Lloyd Sachikonye and Godfrey Kanyenze

The period between 2000 and 2017 represented the most dramatic and in many ways the most destructive period in Zimbabwe's post-colonial politics. The country witnessed huge convulsions in the political landscape that brought new social forces onto the terrain of politics and set the scene for massive new challenges for the state. In this changed political configuration, the labour movement played a central role in building a national, mass-based opposition force in alliance with other parts of Zimbabwean civil society, that not only provided the most serious challenge to ZANU(PF)'s hegemony but was in 2008 the first party to defeat an incumbent liberation movement in southern Africa and be denied the right to take up state power.

The platform of constitutionalism and democratisation that marked the narratives of both the labour movement and opposition politics in Zimbabwe from the late 1990s set the parameters for ZANU(PF)'s discursive and repressive responses from 2000. Moreover, the dynamics that were operative in this period not only impacted on the opposition and labour movements as well as the broader citizenry of the country, but also contributed to the changes in the ruling party. Following the military coup in November 2017 that removed Robert Mugabe, an outcome of factional battles within the ruling party, ZANU(PF) was forced to cast its language of change in the very terms of constitutionalism, economic reform and international re-engagement that had been central to opposition and labour movement political discourses for nearly two decades.

Tracking this political journey through the history of the labour movement has been instructive. Even though the emphasis of the book has been on the period between 2000 and 2017, the analysis has attempted to rethink the changes in trade unionism throughout the post-colonial era. Drawing on a wide range of source material from both the trade union movement and the state, we have examined the changes from the state attempts to co-opt and dominate the labour movement in the early 1980s to the growing critical autonomy of trade unionism thereafter. For much of this period, the unions faced massive challenges, including state violence and repression, funding limitations, splits, factionalism, and the problems around organising at factory level.

However, perhaps the greatest challenge faced by the labour movement was the massive structural change in the economy since 2000. The rapid deindustrialisation and informalisation of work in all sectors of the economy decimated the potential membership of the unions and redefined the trajectory of the movement. The growing precarity of work and the loss of formal employment, a general problem in the global economy, placed the future of trade unions in great jeopardy. As has been observed elsewhere, the 'intensification and expansion of precariousness, the fragmentation of productive processes, and the disregarding of rights and dignity associated with labour relations'[1] led to demands for new forms of struggle and organisation under conditions of informalisation.

A central feature of this growing informality and loss of employment was the devaluation of labour, a persistent development highlighted in this study. This devaluation took several forms: the loss of employment; structural redeployment of labour from high productivity and income sectors to low productivity and income sectors; the degradation of work processes; wage theft through delay and non-payment; erosion of incomes through hyperinflation, and currency debauchery. The more vulnerable segments of the labour force such as women, youth and the disabled faced particular challenges under these changed conditions which the trade unions were ill equipped to deal with.

In addition, the loss of pension payments during the period of hyperinflation contributed further to the devaluation of labour. As a recent commission of enquiry into pensions observed, the removal of 25 zeros during the period August 2006 to February 2009 resulted in insurance companies and pension funds technically extinguishing their obligations to policyholders and pensioners without actual payments being made. The industry players duly removed zeros on promised sums-assured or pension benefits when the ZW$ was debased; some pensioners received

---

1   Estanque and Costa, 2012, p. 268.

as little as US$0.05, and most received nothing, despite many years of contributions.[2]

At a broader level, this devaluation of labour also affected the accumulation dynamic in the economy. Combined with the loss of linkages between the agricultural, mining and manufacturing sectors, the depletion of internal demand through the shrinkage of the formal sector and income losses deprived the economy of a central accumulation driver. This in turn will have long-term implications for providing a dynamic developmental model for the country's future.

Faced with such a combination of degrading work conditions, several cases of anti-labour legislation, state repression and the loss of some sense of progress attached to formal sector employment, it was not surprising that for many workers trade unionism appeared to have lost its relevance. Notwithstanding these challenges, the importance of the labour movement continued to resonate with workers. Slogans and forms of struggle from the long history of labour activism still found a place in the movement. Two examples follow.

First, a slogan from the 1948 General Strike still reverberates at ZCTU meetings today. One of the many slogans used, is 'Tikatingachitsve ngachitsve', 'When we say it must burn let it burn'.[3] In 1948, striking workers proclaimed 'Kana sora rotsva ngaritsve', 'If the grass burns let it burn'.[4]

Second, in the 1940s and 1950s women played an important role in defining the demands of their striking husbands. As Barnes observed, married workers in this period based their working demands at least in part on the difficulties faced by their wives in coping with their social and economic responsibilities.[5] In October 2013, the wives of struggling workers at Hwange Colliery made their concerns known in public protests over the non-payment of salaries and labour conditions of their husbands. As the Centre for Natural Resource Governance reported:

> Also among the women are spouses of company workers, who believe the company would do well to acknowledge the role they played by taking care of their families ever since 2013 when the

---

2 Kanyenze, 2017.
3 Notes recorded during the Federation of Food and Allied Workers' Union of Zimbabwe meeting, 19 November 2016.
4 Phimister and Raftopoulos, 2000.
5 Barnes, 1995.

company stopped paying their husbands. As they took on the breadwinner role, the women have been engaging in various forms of informal economic activities ranging from cross border trade, buying and selling airtime, farming and vending vegetables to mobile canteens and working other menial jobs that include doing other people's laundry, gardening and cleaning houses. This has ensured that their husbands, on who the company depends for labour, continued reporting for duty even as they were not payed salaries.[6]

Thus, even as the challenges for trade union organisation have grown at an alarming rate, workers have continued to draw on past labour struggles and point to the urgent need to reorganise and revamp the labour movement in order to deal with these challenges. While these protests suggest an encouraging resurgence of trade unionism, they remain disjointed and discrete. Going forward, the labour movement needs to reconnect with its social base at the workplace, rebuild its structures from below and reach out to the new and emerging social bases that include the informal economy, the new forms of production relations in the rural sector, residents associations, and social media movements to form a formidable national labour coalition as happened in the 1990s. This is a critical post-Mugabe agenda that should be seized by the labour movement at all levels, from shop-floor to district, regional and national spaces.

---

6   Centre for Natural Resource Governance, 'CNRG Condemns Labour Minister's Treatment of protesting Hwange Women.' 9 March 2018.

Bibliography

Acemoglu, D., S. Johnson, and J.A. Robinson. 2005. 'Institutions as a Fundamental Cause of Long-Run Growth', in P. Aghion and S. Durlauf [eds], *Handbook of Economic Growth*. New York: Elsevier.

Acemoglu, D., and J. Robinson. 2010. 'The Role of Institutions in Growth and Development', *Review of Economics and Institutions*, 1, 2.

African Development Bank Group. 2013. 'At the Center of Africa's Transformation: Strategy for 2013–2022'. Tunis: African Development Bank.

African Development Bank Group, OECD Development Centre, ECA and UNDP. 2013. 'African Economic Outlook Report 2013: Structural Transformation and Natural Resources'. Tunis: African Development Bank.

Alexander, J. 2006. *The Unsettled Land: State-Making and the Politics of Land in Zimbabwe, 1893-2003*. Oxford: James Currey; Harare: Weaver Press.

———2017. 'Loyalty and Liberation: The Political Life of Zephaniah Moyo', *Journal of East African Studies*, 11,1.

Alexander, J., J. McGregor and B-M. Tendi. 2014. *Politics, Patronage and the State in Zimbabwe*. Harare: Weaver Press.

Alexander, P. 2000. 'Zimbabwean Workers, the MDC and the 2000 Election', *Review of African Political Economy*. 27, 85.

Barchiesi, F. 2011. *Precarious Liberation: Workers, the State, and Contested Social Citizenship in Post-apartheid South Africa*. New York, SUNY Press.

Barchiesi, F. and S. Bellucci. 2014. 'Introduction: African Labor Histories', *International Labor and Working Class-History*, 86, Fall.

Barnes, T, 1995. '"So that a Labourer could live with his family": Overlooked factors in Social and Economic Strife in Urban Colonial Zimbabwe, 1945-1952', *Journal of Southern African Studies*, 21, 1.

———2003. 'Democracy and Historiographies of Labour in Zimbabwe', *International Review of Social History*, 48, 3.

Beckman, B. and L. Sachikonye [eds]. 2001. *Labour Regimes and Liberalisation: The Restructuring of State-Labour Relations in Africa*. Harare: University of Zimbabwe Publications.

———2010. 'Introduction: Trade Unions and Party Politics in Africa', in Beckman, Buhlungu and Sachikonye, 2010.

Beckman, B., S. Buhlungu and L. Sachikonye [eds]. 2010. *Trade Unions and Party Politics: Labour Movements in Africa.* Cape Town: HSRC Press.

Besada, H. [ed.]. 2011. *Zimbabwe: Picking up the Pieces.* New York: Palgrave Macmillan.

Bhebe, Q. and M. Mahapa. 2014. 'The decline in trade union density in the 21st century in Zimbabwe. A case of ZCTU', *Journal of HR Management and Labor Studies*, 2, 1.

Birdsall, N. 2007. 'Do No Harm: Aid, Weak Institutions, and the Missing Middle in Africa'. Center for Global Development, Working Paper Number 113, March 2007.

Bloch, B. (2005) 'The Developmental Potential of Zimbabweans in the Diaspora', *IOM Migration Research Series,* 17.

Bolt, M. 2014. 'The sociality of the wage: money rhythms, wealth circulation, and the problem with cash on the Zimbabwean-South African border', *Journal of the Royal Anthropological Institute,* 20.

———2015. *Zimbabwe's Migrants and South Africa's Border Farms: The Roots of Impermanence.* Johannesburg: Wits University Press.

Bond, P. 2001. 'Radical Rhetoric and the Working Class during Zimbabwean Nationalism's dying days', in Raftopoulos and Sachikonye, 2001.

——— and M. Manyanya. 2002. *Zimbabwe's Plunge: Exhausted Nationalism, Neoliberalism and the Search for Social Justice.* Harare: Weaver Press

——— and R. Saunders. 2005. 'Labour, the State and the Struggle for a Democratic Zimbabwe', *Monthly Review*, 57, 7.

Bonner, P., J. Hyslop and L. van der Walt. 2007. 'Rethinking Worlds of Labour: Southern African Labour History in International Context', *African Studies,* 66, 2-3.

Bracking, S. and L. Sachikonye. 2006. 'Remittances, poverty reduction and the informalisation of household wellbeing in Zimbabwe', Global Poverty Research Group working paper no.45.

——— 2010. 'Remittances, Informalisation and Dispossession in Urban Zimbabwe', in J. Crush and D.S. Tevera, 2010.

Bratton, M. and E. Masunungure. 2010. 'The Anatomy of Political Predation: Leaders, Elites and Coalitions in Zimbabwe, 1980–2010', *Developmental Leadership Programme,* Research Paper 9.

Burchell, G., C. Gordon and M. Miller [eds]. 1991. *The Foucault Effect – Studies in Governmentality.* Chicago: Chicago University Press.

Central Statistical Office (CSO). 1998. *Poverty in Zimbabwe.* Harare: CSO.

Chagonda, T. 2011. 'The Response of the Working Class in Harare, Zimbabwe to Hyper-Inflation and the Political Crisis 1997-2008'. PhD Thesis, University of Johannesburg.

―――― 2016. 'The other face of the Zimbabwe crisis: the black market and dealers during Zimbabwe's decade of economic meltdown 2000-08', *Review of African Political Economy*, 43, 147.

Chakanya, N. 2016. 'Working and Living Conditions of Workers in the Agriculture Sector in Zimbabwe'. Lome: ALREI.

Chakanya, N and T. Siwela. 2011. 'Women in Trade Unions in Zimbabwe', in Shindondola-Mote et al., 2011.

Chambati, W. 2011. 'Restructuring of agrarian labour relations after Fast Track Land Reform in Zimbabwe', *Journal of Peasant Studies, 38*, 5.

―――― 2013 'Changing Agrarian Relations after Land Reform in Zimbabwe', in S. Moyo and W. Chambati [eds], *Land and Agrarian Reform in Zimbabwe.* Dakar: Codesria.

Chamber of Mines. 2015. 'State of the Mining Industry Survey Report'. Harare: Chamber of Mines of Zimbabwe.

―――― 2016. 'State of the Mining Industry Survey Report'. Harare: Chamber of Mines of Zimbabwe.

Chan, S. and J. Gallagher. 2017. *Why Mugabe Won: The 2013 Elections in Zimbabwe and Their Aftermath.* Cambridge: Cambridge University Press.

Chaturvedi, R. 2016. 'Agentive Capacities, Democratic Possibilities, and the Urban Poor: Rethinking Recent Popular Protests in West Africa', *International Journal of Politics and Culture*, 29, 3.

Cheater, A. [ed.]. 1992. *Industrial Sociology in the First Decade of Zimbabwean Independence.* Harare: University of Zimbabwe Publications.

Chenery, H. 1979. *Structural Change and Development Policy.* Oxford: Oxford University Press for the World Bank.

Chenery, H. and M. Syrquin. 1975. *Patterns of Development, 1950-1970.* Oxford: Oxford University Press for the World Bank.

Chetsanga, C. and T. Muchenje. 2003. *An Analysis of the Cause and Effect of the Brain Drain in Zimbabwe.* Harare: SIRDC.

Chikanda, A. 2005. *Medical Leave: The Exodus of Medical Professionals in Zimbabwe.* Cape Town: Idasa.

Chimonyo, G., S. Mungure and P. Scott. 2012. *The Social, Economic and Environmental Implication of Diamond Mining in Chiadzwa.* Mutare: Centre for Research and Development.

Cliffe, L. 2009. 'Remittances and Social Protection in Zimbabwe's Transition'.

Paper prepared for *Wahenga: Regional Hunger and Vulnerability Programme.*

Confederation of Zimbabwe Industries. 2015. 'CZI Manufacturing Sector Survey Report'. Harare: CZI.

—— 2017. 'State of the Manufacturing Industry Survey Report'. Harare: CZI.

Cooper, F. 1996. *Decolonisation and African Society: The Labour Question in French and British Africa.* Cambridge: Cambridge University Press.

Crush, J. and D. Tevera [eds]. 2010. *Zimbabwe's Exodus: Crisis, Migration, Survival.* Ottawa, IDRC.

Cuneo, C.N., R. Sollom and C. Beyrer. 2017. 'The Cholera Epidemic in Zimbabwe, 2008–2009: A Review and Critique of the Evidence', *Health and Human Rights*, 19, 2.

Dansereau, J. 2001a. 'Legacy of Colonialism in Zimbabwe's Labour Utilisation Model: Mineworkers' Wages, Skills and Migration', in Raftopoulos and Sachikonye, 2001.

—— 2001b. 'Zimbabwe: Labour's Options within the Movement for Democratic Change', *Review of African Political Economy*, 28, 89.

Davis, M. 1986. *Prisoners of the American Dream: Politics and Economy in the History of the US Working Class.* London: Verso.

—— 2004. 'Planet of Slums, Urban Involution and the Informal Proletariat', *New Left Review*, 26.

Dorman, S.R. 2016a. *Understanding Zimbabwe: From Liberation to Authoritarianism.* London: Hurst and Co.

—— 2016b. '"We have not made anybody homeless": Regulation and control of urban life in Zimbabwe', *Citizenship Studies,* 20, 1.

Eley, G. 2002. *Forging Democracy: The History of the Left in Europe, 1850-2000.* Oxford: Oxford University Press.

Estanque, E. and H.A. Costa. 2012. 'Labour Relations and Social Movements in the 21st Century', in D. Erasga [ed.], *Sociological Landscapes – Theories, Realities and Trends.* Rijeka, Croatia: In Tech.

Freund, B. 1988. *The African Worker.* Cambridge: Cambridge University Press.

Gono, G. 2008. *Zimbabwe's Casino Economy: Extraordinary Measures for Extraordinary Challenges.* Harare: Zimbabwe Publishing House.

Government of Zimbabwe. 1981. 'Report of the Commission of Inquiry into Incomes, Prices and Conditions of Service', Riddell Commission, Harare.

—— 1984. 'Report of the National Trade Union Survey, Vol. 1', Department of Research and Planning, Ministry of Labour, Manpower Planning and Social Welfare. Harare.

Gramsci, A. 1971. *Selections from Prison Notebooks.* London: Lawrence and Wishart.

Gukurume, S. 2015. 'Livelihood resilience in a hyperinflationary environment: experiences of people in money-burning (kubhena mari) transactions in Harare, Zimbabwe', *Social Dynamics: A Journal of African Studies,* 41, 2.

Gwisai, M. (2006) *Labour and Employment Law in Zimbabwe.* Harare: University of Zimbabwe Publications.

Hammar, A. [ed.]. 2015. *Displacement Economies in Africa: Paradoxes of Crisis and Creativity.* London: Zed Books.

Hammar, A., J. McGregor and L. Landau. 2010. 'Special Issue: The Zimbabwe Crisis through the Lens of Displacement', *Journal of Southern Africa Studies,* 36, 2.

Hammar, A., B. Raftopoulos and S. Jensen [eds]. 2003. *Zimbabwe's Unfinished Business.* Harare: Weaver Press.

Hanke, S.H. and A. Kwok. 2009. 'On the Measurement of Zimbabwe's Hyperinflation', *Cato Journal,* 29, 2.

Hartnack, A. 2005. 'My life got lost: Farm workers and displacement in Zimbabwe', *Journal of Contemporary African Studies,* 23, 2.

———2009. 'Transcending Global and National (Mis)representations through Local Responses to displacement: The case of Zimbabwean (ex-)Farm Workers', *Journal of Refugee Studies,* 22, 3.

——— 2016. *Ordered Estates: Welfare, Power and Maternalism on Zimbabwe's (Once White) Highveld.* Harare: Weaver Press.

Harvey, D. 2011. *The Enigma of Capital and the Crisis of Capitalism.* London: Profile Books.

Hobsbawm, E. 1984. *Worlds of Labour: Further Studies in the History of Labour.* London: Weidenfield and Nicolson.

Human Rights Watch. 2009. 'Diamonds in the Rough: Human Rights Abuses in the Marange Diamond Fields of Zimbabwe'. New York: HRW.

Hussmanns, R. 2004. *Measuring the Informal Economy: From Employment in the Informal Sector to Informal Employment.* Integration Working Paper No. 53. Geneva: International Labour Office.

International Labour Organization (ILO). 2009. *Truth, Reconciliation and Justice in Zimbabwe.* Geneva: ILO.

——— 2015. 'Skills for Youth Employment and Rural Development Programme in Zimbabwe: An Assessment of Firms in Economic Subsectors'. Harare: ILO.

International Monetary Fund. 2016. 'Zimbabwe Staff Report for the 2016 Article IV Consultation and the Third Review of the Staff-Monitored

Program – Press Release; Staff Report; and Statement by the Executive Director for Zimbabwe'. IMF Country Report No. 16/109. Washington, DC: IMF.

—— 2017. 'Zimbabwe 2017 Article IV Consultation Staff Report'. IMF Country Report No. 17/196. Washington, DC: IMF.

International Poverty Centre. 2008. 'Jobs, Jobs, Jobs: The Policy Challenge', *Poverty in Focus*, 16.

IRIN, 2010. 'Mining Industry attracts child labour as economy picks up.' IRIN News, 14 October 2010.

Jauch, H. and R. Traub-Merz. 2006. 'The Future of the Textile and Clothing Industry in Sub-Saharan Africa'. Bonn: Friedrich-Ebert-Stiftung.

Jones, J.L. 2010. '"Nothing is Straight in Zimbabwe": The Rise of the Kukiya-kiya Economy 2000–2008', *Journal of Southern African Studies*, 36, 2.

Kamete, A. 2008. 'Planning versus youth: Stamping out spatial unruliness in Harare', *Geoforum*, 39, 5.

—— 2012. 'Not Exactly like the Phoenix – But Rising all the Same: Reconstructing Displaced Livelihoods in Post-Cleanup Harare', *Society and Space,* 30.

Kamete, A. and I. Lindell. 2010. 'The Politics of "Non-Planning" Interventions in African Cities: Unravelling the International and Local Dimensions in Harare and Maputo', *Journal of Southern African Studies,* 36, 4.

Kanyenze, G. 2000. 'The Implications of Globalisation on the Zimbabwean Economy'. Paper prepared for the Zimbabwe Human Development Report.

—— 2004. 'The Zimbabwe Economy 1980-2003: a ZCTU Perspective', in D. Harold-Barry [ed.], *Zimbabwe: The Past is the Future.* Harare: Weaver Press.

—— 2018. 'Briefing paper to the Parliamentary Portfolio Committee on Finance and Economic Development on the findings of the Commission of Inquiry into the Conversion of Insurance and Pension values from ZW$ to US$', 7 May.

Kanyenze, G. and B. Chiripanhura. 2001. 'The State of Trade Union Organisation in Zimbabwe'. (Unpublished paper.)

Kanyenze, G., T. Kondo, P. Chitambara and J. Martens. 2011. *Beyond the Enclave – Towards a Pro-Poor and Inclusive Development Strategy for Zimbabwe.* Harare: Weaver Press.

Karekwaivanane, G. 2012. 'Legal Encounters: Law, State and Society in Zimbabwe, c.1950-1990'. PhD Thesis, Oxford University.

Keynes, J.M. 1919. *The Economic Consequences of the Peace.* New York: Harcourt, Brace and Howe.

Kriger, N. 2003. 'War veterans: Continuities between the past and the present', *African Studies Quarterly*, 7, 2.

Larmer, M. 2011. *Rethinking African Politics: A History of Opposition in Zambia*. London: Ashgate.

Le Bas, A. 2011. *From Power to Parties: Party Building and Democratisation in Africa*. Oxford: Oxford University Press.

LEDRIZ. 2016. 'Employment Creation Potential Analysis by Sector'. Report prepared for the ILO.

LEDRIZ and Solidarity Center. 2016. *Working Without Pay: Wage Theft in Zimbabwe*. Washington and Harare: Solidarity Center.

Lewanika, M. 2016. 'Zimbabwe and the Future of Work'. theSpace working papers, 2016-01. Harare: theSpace.

Madhuku, L. 2001. 'Trade Unions and the Law', in Raftopoulos and Sachikonye, 2001.

——— 2015. *Labour Law in Zimbabwe*. Harare: Weaver Press

Magaramombe, G. 2010. 'Displaced in place: Agrarian displacements, replacements and resettlement among farm workers in Mazowe District', *Journal of Southern African Studies*, 36, 2.

Magaramombe, G. and W. Chambati (2008) 'An abandoned question: Farm workers', in Moyo et al., 2008.

Magunha, F., A. Bailey and L. Cliffe. 2009. 'Remittance Strategies of Zimbabweans in Northern England', Policy brief, School of Geography, University of Leeds.

Maimbo, S. and D. Ratha [eds]. 2005. *Remittances, Development Impacts and Future Prospects*. Washington: World Bank.

Makina, D. and G. Kanyenze. 2010. *The Potential Contribution of the Zimbabwean Diaspora to Economic Recovery*. Harare: UNDP.

Mamdani, M. 1996. *Citizen and Subject: Contemporary Africa and the Legacy of Late Colonialism*. Princeton: Princeton University Press.

——— 2008. 'Lessons of Zimbabwe', *London Review of Books*, 4 December.

Mandaza, I. 2016. *The Political Economy of the State in Zimbabwe: The Rise and Fall of the Securocrat State*. Harare: SAPES Books.

Maphosa, F. 2007. 'Remittances and Development: The impact of migration to South Africa on livelihoods in southern Zimbabwe', *Development Southern Africa*, 27, 1.

Marcus, R. and M. Gavrilovic. 2010. *The Impacts of the Economic Crisis on Youth: Review of Evidence*. London: Overseas Development Institute.

Marongwe, N. 2003. 'Farm Occupations and Occupiers in the New Politics of

Land in Zimbabwe', in Hammar et al., 2003.

Masunungure, E.V. and J.M. Shumba [eds]. 2012. *Zimbabwe: Mired in Transition*. Harare: Weaver Press.

Matombo, L, and L. Sachikonye. 2010. 'The Labour Movement and Democratisation in Zimbabwe', in Beckman, Buhlungu and Sachikonye, 2010.

Matyanga, D. 2011. 'Mining', in Kanyenze et al., 2011.

Mawowa, S. (2014) 'The Political Economy of Artisanal and Small-scale Gold in Central Zimbabwe', in Alexander et.al., 2014.

McCandless, E. 2011. *Polarization and Transformation in Zimbabwe: Social Movements, Strategy Dilemmas and Change*. Lanham, MD: Lexington Books.

McGregor, J. 2002. 'The Politics of Disruption: War Veterans and the Local State in Zimbabwe', *African Affairs*, 101.

McGregor, J. and R. Primorac. 2010. *Zimbabwe's New Diaspora: Displacement and the Cultural Politics of Survival*. Oxford: Berghahn Books.

McIlroy, J. and R. Croucher. 2013. The turn to transnational labor history and the study of global trade unionism', *Labor History*, 54, 5.

Mezzadra, S. 2011. 'How many histories of labour? Towards a theory of post-colonial capitalism', *Postcolonial Studies*, 14, 2.

Moore, D. 2012. 'Two perspectives on Zimbabwe's National Democratic Revolution: Thabo Mbeki and Wilfred Mhanda', *Journal of Contemporary African Studies*, 10, 1.

Moyo, S. 2001. 'The Land Occupation Movement and Democratisation in Zimbabwe: Contradictions of Neoliberalism', *Millenium*, 30, 2.

––––– 2011. 'Changing agrarian relations after redistributive land reform in Zimbabwe', *The Journal of Peasant Studies*, 38, 5.

Moyo, S. and W. Chambati [eds]. 2013. *Land and Agrarian Reform in Zimbabwe*. Dakar: Codesria.

Moyo, S. and P. Yeros. 2007. 'The Radicalised State: Zimbabwe's Interrupted Revolution', *Review of African Political Economy*, 34, 1.

Moyo, S., K. Helliker and T. Murisa [eds]. 2008. *Contested Terrain: Land reform and civil society in contemporary Zimbabwe*. Pietermaritzburg: Shuter and Shooter.

Mtapuri, O. 2006. 'Social Dialogue Discord: The Views of Key Informants in the Case of Zimbabwe', *Loyola Journal of Social Sciences*, 20, 2.

Mtimtema, Z., M. Chikamba, L. Tarabuku, F. Magaya and N. Muchichwa. 2016. *Compendium of the decisions of the ILO supervisory bodies: Zimbabwe 1987-2016*. Harare: Zimbabwe Congress of Trade Unions.

Mugure, B. 2008. 'The State, Labour and the Politics of Social Dialogue in Zimbabwe 1996-2007: Issues Resolved or Matters Arising?' *African and Asian Studies*, 7, 1.

Munck, R. 2004. 'Reconceptualizing Labour in the Era of Globalization: From Labour and "Developing-area studies" to Globalization and Labour', *Labour, Capital and Society*, 37.

Musiwaro, N. 2017. 'State, Civil Society and the Politics of Economic Indigenisation in Zimbabwe, 1980-2007'. PhD Thesis, University of the Free State.

Mutangi, T. 2016. '3rd Draft Discussion Paper on: The Future of Work for Women in Zimbabwe'. Harare: International Labour Organization.

Muzondidya, J. 2009. 'From Buoyancy to Crisis: 1980-1997', in Raftopoulos and Mlambo, 2009.

Ndlela, D. and G. Kanyenze. 2017. 'Zimbabwe's Economic Structural Issues and Engines for Growth – Opportunities, Challenges and Risks'. Paper prepared for the Zimbabwe Institute and the Centre for Peace Initiatives in Africa and presented at the Inaugural Launch of the Multi-stakeholder Dialogue Platform – Zimbabwe Dialogues, 31 March 2017, Harare.

Ndlovu-Gatsheni, S. 2011. *The Zimbabwean Nation State Project – A Historical Diagnosis of Identity and Power-Based Conflicts in a Postcolonial State*. Uppsala: NAI.

Neocosmos, M. 2016. *Thinking Freedom in Africa: Towards a Theory of Emancipatory Politics*. Johannesburg: Wits University Press.

Nordlund, P. 1996. 'Organising the Agora: Domination and Democratisation in Zambia and Zimbabwe'. PhD Thesis, Uppsala University.

Nyamunda, T. and P. Mukwambo. 2012. 'The State and the Bloody Diamond Rush in Chiadzwa: Unpacking the Contesting Interests in the Development of Illicit Mining and Trading, c.2006–2009', *Journal of Southern African Studies*, 38, 1.

OECD. 2005. *Migration, Remittances and Development*. Paris: OECD.

Phimister, I. and B. Raftopoulos. 2000. '"Kana sora ratswa ngaritswe": African Nationalists and Black Workers – The 1948 General Strike in Colonial Zimbabwe'. *Journal of Historical Sociology*, 13, 3.

Potts, D. 2006. 'Restoring Order? Operation Murambatsvina and the Urban Crisis in Zimbabwe', *Journal of Southern African Studies*, 36, 2.

——— 2007. 'City Life in Zimbabwe at a Time of Fear and Loathing: Urban Planning, Urban Poverty and Operation Murambatsvina', in G. Myers and M. Murray [eds], *Cities in Contemporary Africa*. New York: Palgrave.

—— 2008. 'Displacement and Livelihoods: The Longer-term Impacts of Operation Murambatsvina', in M. Vambe [ed.], *The Hidden Dimensions of Operation Murambatsvina in Zimbabwe*. Harare: Weaver Press.

Raftopoulos, B. 1994. 'The State and the Labour Movement in Zimbabwe', Harare: Zimbabwe Institute of Development Studies. Unpublished paper.

—— 2001. 'The Labour Movement and the Emergence of Opposition Politics in Zimbabwe', in Raftopoulos and Sachikonye, 2001.

—— 2003. 'Labour Internationalism and Problems of Autonomy and Democratisation in the Trade Union Movement in Southern Rhodesia, 1951-1975', in T. Ranger [ed], *The Historical Dimensions of Democracy and Human Rights in Zimbabwe*. Harare: University of Zimbabwe Publications.

—— 2009. 'The Crisis in Zimbabwe, 1998–2008', in Raftopoulos and Mlambo, 2009.

—— 2013. *The Hard Road to Reform*. Harare: Weaver Press.

—— 2018. 'State Politics, Constructions of Labour and Labour Struggles 1980-2000', in this volume.

—— (Forthcoming 2019). 'Trade Unions, Labour and Politics in Zimbabwe since the late 1990s', in: J. Alexander, J. McGregor and B-M. Tendi [eds], *Zimbabwean Politics since the late 1990s*. Oxford: Oxford University Press.

Raftopoulos, B. and I. Phimister. 1997. *Keep on Knocking: A History of the Labour Movement in Zimbabwe 1900-1997*. Harare: Baobab Books.

Raftopoulos, B. and A. Mlambo [eds]. 2009. *Becoming Zimbabwe: A History from the Pre-Colonial Period to 2008*. Harare: Weaver Press.

Raftopoulos, B. and L. Sachikonye, [eds]. 2001. *Striking Back: The Labour Movement and the Post-Colonial State in Zimbabwe 1980-2000*. Harare: Weaver Press.

Raftopoulos, B. and T. Yoshikuni. 1999. *Sites of Struggle: Essays in Zimbabwe's Urban History*. Harare: Weaver Press.

Ranchod-Nilsson, S. 2006. 'Gender Politics and the Pendulum of Political and Social Transformation in Zimbabwe', *Journal of Southern African Studies*, 32, 1.

Ranger, T. 2004. 'Nationalist Historiography, Patriotic History and the History of the Nation: The Struggle over the Past in Zimbabwe', *Journal of Southern African Studies*, 30, 2.

Raymond, K. 2017. 'Zimbabwe's Young People are Keeping the Economy Afloat'. Baltimore, MD: International Youth Foundation.

Research and Avocacy Unit. 2009. *Reckless Tragedy: Irreversible? A survey of human rights violations and losses suffered by commercial farmers and farm workers in Zimbabwe from 2000 to 2008*. Harare: JAG and GAPWUZ.

—— 2016. 'Conflict or Collapse? Zimbabwe in 2016'. Harare: RAU.

Rutherford, B. 2001a. 'Farm Workers and Trade Unions in Hurungwe District in Post-colonial Zimbabwe', in Raftopoulos and Sachikonye, 2001.

—— 2001b. *Working on the Margins: Black Workers, White Farmers in Postcolonial Zimbabwe*. Harare: Weaver Press.

—— 2008. 'Conditional Belonging: Farm Workers and the Cultural Politics of Recognition in Zimbabwe', *Development and Change*, 39, 1.

—— 2009. '"We Wanted Change Yesterday!" The Promise and Perils of *Poritikisi:* Zimbabwean Farm Workers, Party Politics and Critical Social Science', *Anthropologica*, 51, 2.

—— 2010 'Zimbabweans on the Farms of Northern South Africa', in Crush and Tevera, 2010.

—— 2011. 'On the promise and perils of citizenship: heuristic concepts, Zimbabwean example' *Citizenship Studies*, 15, 3-4.

—— 2014. 'Organization and (De)mobilization of Farm Workers in Zimbabwe: Reflections on Trade Unions, NGOs and Political Parties', *Journal of Agrarian Change*, 14, 2.

—— 2017. *Farm Labor Struggles in Zimbabwe: The Ground of Politics*. Bloomington: Indiana University Press.

Sachikonye, L. 1986. 'State, Capital and Trade Unions', in I. Mandaza [ed.], *Zimbabwe: The Political Economy of Transition*. Dakar: CODESRIA.

—— 1993. 'Structural Adjustment, State and Organised Labour,' in P. Gibbon [ed.], *Social Change and Economic Reform*. Uppsala: NAI.

—— 1997. 'Unions, Economic and Political Developments', in Raftopoulos and Phimister, 1997.

—— 1999. *Restructuring or De-industrializing: Zimbabwe's Textile and Metal Industries under Adjustment*. Research Report No. 110. Uppsala: NAI.

—— 2001. 'The Institutional Development of Unions in Zimbabwe', in Raftopoulos and Sachikonye, 2001.

—— 2003. 'The Situation of Commercial Farm Workers after Land Reform'. Report prepared for the Farm Community Trust of Zimbabwe, Harare.

—— 2004. 'Land reform and farm workers', in D. Harold-Barry [ed.], *Zimbabwe: The Past is the Future*. Harare: Weaver Press.

—— 2011. *When a State turns on its Citizens*. Johannesburg: Jacana Media.

—— 2012. *Zimbabwe's Lost Decade: Politics, Development & Society*. Harare: Weaver Press.

———— 2016. 'Old wine in old bottles? Revisiting contract farming after agrarian reform in Zimbabwe', *Review of African Political Economy*, 43.

Sachikonye, L. and L. Matombo. 2010. 'The Labour Movement and Democratization in Zimbabwe', in B. Beckman, S. Buhlungu and L. Sachikonye, 2010.

Saunders, R. 2001. 'Striking Ahead: Industrial Action and Labour Movement Development in Zimbabwe', in Raftopoulos and Sachikonye, 2001.

———— 2008. 'Crisis, Capital and Compromise: Mining and Empowerment in Zimbabwe', *African Sociological Review,* 12, 1.

Saunders, R. and T. Nyamunda [eds]. 2016. *Facets of Power.* Harare: Weaver Press.

Scarnecchia, T. 2008. *The Urban Roots of Democracy and Political Violence in Zimbabwe.* New York: University of Rochester Press.

Schiphorst, F.S. 2001. 'Strength and Weakness: The Rise of the Zimbabwean Congress of Trade Unions and the Department of Labour Relations, 1980-1995'. PhD Thesis, University of Leiden.

Schler, L., L. Bethlehem and G. Sabar. 2011. 'Rethinking Labour in Africa, Past and Present', *African Identities*, 7, 3.

Schmitter, P. and G. Lehmbruch [eds]. 1979. *Trends towards Corporatist Intermediation.* Beverley Hills: Sage Publications.

Scoones, I. 2014. 'What prospects for the next generation of rural Zimbabweans?' Available at: https://zimbabweland.wordpress.com/tag/informal-economy/

Scoones, I., N. Marongwe, B. Mavedzenge, J. Mahenehene, F. Murimbarimba and C. Sukume. 2010. *Zimbabwe's Land Reform: Myths & Realities.* Woodbridge: James Currey.

Scott, J. 1987. 'On Language, Gender, and Working-Class History, *International Labor and Working-Class History,* 31.

Shadur, M. 1994. *Labour Relations in a Developing Country: A Case of Zimbabwe.* Aldershot: Avebury.

Shelton, G. and C. Kabemba. 2012. 'Win Win Partnership? China, Southern Africa and the Extractive Industries'. Johannesburg: SARW.

Shindondola-Mote, H., K.N. Otoo and T. Kalusopa. 2011. *Status of Women in trade unions in Africa: Evidence from 8 Countries.* Accra: African Labour Research Network.

Spiegel, S.J. 2014. 'Legacies of a nationwide crackdown in Zimbabwe: *Operation Chikorokoza Chapera* in gold mining communities', *The Journal of Modern African Studies,* 52, 4.

———— 2015. 'Shifting Formalization Policies and Recentralizing Power: The Case of Zimbabwe's Artisanal Gold Mining Sector', *Society and Natural Resources,* 28, 5.

Sukume, C., B. Mavedzenge and F. Murimbarimba. 2010. 'Space, markets and employment in agricultural development: Zimbabwe'. Policy Brief 37. Cape Town: PLAAS.

Sutcliffe, J. 2013. 'The Labour Movement in Zimbabwe 1980-2012'. http://www.e-ir.info/2013/03/07/the-labour-movement-in-zimbabwe Accessed on 18 November 2017.

Sylvester, C. 2000. *Producing Women and Progress in Zimbabwe: Narratives of Identity and Work from the 1980s.* Portsmouth, NH: Heinemann.

Tandon, Y. 2001. 'Trade Unions and Labour in the Agricultural Sector in Zimbabwe', in Raftopoulos and Sachikonye, 2001.

Tengende, N. 1994. 'Workers, Students and the Struggles for Democracy: State-civil Society Relations in Zimbabwe'. PhD Thesis, Roskilde University.

Tibaijuka, A. 2005. *Operation Murambatsvina. Report of the Fact-Finding Mission to Zimbabwe to Assess the Scope and Impact of Operation Murambatsvina.* By the UN Special Envoy on Human Settlements Issues in Zimbabwe, New York, United Nations.

Transparency International. 2017. 'Corruption Perceptions Index 2016'. Berlin: Transparency International.

Transparency International (Zimbabwe Chapter). 2012. *Annual State of Corruption Report.* Harare: Transparency International.

UNDP. 2008. 'Comprehensive Economic Recovery in Zimbabwe'. Harare: UNDP.

UNICEF. 2013. 'Living Conditions Among Persons with Disability Survey: Key Findings Report'. Harare: UNICEF.

───── 2017. 'Zimbabwe 2017 National Budget Brief: An Overview Analysis'. Harare: UNICEF.

Webb, E.J., D.T. Campbell, R.D. Schwartz and L. Sechrest. [1966]. *Unobtrusive Measures: Nonreactive Research in the Social Sciences.* Chicago: Rand McNally.

Webster, E. 1988. 'The rise of social movement unionism: The two faces of the black trade union movement in South Africa', in P. Frankel, N. Pines and M. Swilling [eds], *State, Resistance and Change in South Africa.* London: Croom Helm.

───── 2004.'South African Labour Studies in a Global Perspective, 1973–2006', *Labour, Capital and Society,* 37.

Wood, B. 1987. 'Roots of Trade Union Weakness in Post-Independence Zimbabwe', *South Africa Labour Bulletin,* 12, 6-7.

World Bank. 2012. 'Zimbabwe – FinScope MSME survey 2012'. Washington, DC: World Bank Group.

261

────── 2018. 'Zimbabwe Jobs (Jobs Jobs) Diagnostic: Initial Findings', Workshop report by Dino Merotto, Reyes Aterido, Jorg Langbein, Adrian Scutaru, Michael Weber and Brian Blankespoor, Harare, 4 April.

World Economic Forum. 2016. 'The Global Gender Gap Report 2016'. Geneva: World Economic Forum.

Yeros, P. 2001. 'The ZCTU's Internationalism in a Global Era', in Raftopoulos and Sachikonye, 2001.

────── 2013a. 'The rise and fall of trade unionism in Zimbabwe, Part 1: 1990–1995', *Review of African Political Economy,* 40, 136.

────── 2013b. 'The rise and fall of trade unionism in Zimbabwe, Part 11: 1995–2000', *Review of African Political Economy*, 40, 137.

Yeros, P. and S. Moyo 2007. 'The Radicalised State: Zimbabwe's Interrupted Revolution', *Review of African Political Economy*, 34, 111.

ZCTU. 2006. 'Minutes of the ZCTU 6th Silver Jubilee Congress', Harare: Celebration Centre.

────── 2016. 'Resolutions passed at the 8th Ordinary Congress of the ZCTU', Harare: Pandari Hotel.

Zimbabwe African National Union (ZANU). 1978. Component of the PF Department of Manpower Planning and Labour, Presentation at an ILO seminar on Labour Matters, Lusaka, Zambia.

ZimStat. 2004, 2011 and 2014. 'Labour Force and Child Labour Survey'. Harare: ZimStat.

────── 2015. 'National Accounts 2009 – 2014 Report'. Harare: ZimStat.

────── 2016. 'Understanding Gender Equality In Zimbabwe: Women and Men Report 2016'. Harare: Zimstat.

Zimbabwe Institute. 2007. 'Progressive Zimbabwe: Sustainable Growth and Transformation'. Cape Town: The Zimbabwe Institute.

www.ingramcontent.com/pod-product-compliance
Lightning Source LLC
Chambersburg PA
CBHW060031030426
42334CB00019B/2271